T0304105

THE EMERGING MIDDLE CLASS IN AFRICA

The emergence of the middle class as a driver of Africa's economic growth stands out as an important milestone in contemporary economic history. This growth, though uneven, is a source of hope for Africa, but also a signal to the rest of the world on the prospects for economic recovery and renewal, particularly because it has been steady despite the global downturn.

The Emerging Middle Class in Africa analyzes specific aspects of the lives of the middle class in Africa. It looks at how people become and remain in the middle class through a series of thematic chapters. It examines how behavior changes in the process, in terms of consumption patterns and spending on health and education. A further dimension taken up in this analysis is how class impacts gender relations and whether women are able to reap the same benefits of social advancement available to men. Africa is a continent of such scale and diversity that experiences across countries vary widely. The book thus captures the common patterns across the continent.

This text is primarily aimed at Africanist researchers, policymakers, development practitioners, and bilateral and multilateral institutions, as well as students of African studies, political science, political economy, development studies, and development economics.

Mthuli Ncube is Chief Economist and Vice-President of the African Development Bank Group. He oversees the process of knowledge generation and management within the bank and its regional member countries. Professor Ncube is a Senior Research Fellow at the Blavatnik School of Government, University of Oxford, UK and a Research Fellow at St Anthony's College, University of Oxford, UK.

Charles Leyeka Lufumpa is Director of the Statistics Department at the African Development Bank Group. He oversees the bank's activities to build statistical capacity as well as the data needs for results measurement in its operations in African countries.

'Since the beginning of this new Millennium Africa has enjoyed an unprecedented growth spell and a significant reduction in poverty. One of the correlates of the present growth spell is the emergence of a middle class. This volume describes clearly the importance of education and health in helping poor households move gradually into a higher and more diversified consumption pattern. Likewise, a successful structural transformation providing workers moving out of agriculture with stable and salaried jobs in non-agricultural sectors is crucial to the creation of a middle class. Another contribution of this book is to show the close interrelationship between the existence of a middle class and improved governance and the appearance of democratic institutions. While many obstacles still need to be overcome before a strong and sustainable middle class dominates the social fabric in Africa, this volume provides the reader with a bright ray of hope.'

—*Erik Thorbecke, Cornell University, USA*

'The global economic sentiment around Sub-Saharan Africa has changed dramatically over the last few years. From being viewed as a continent rife with political and economic uncertainty, together with a tendency toward economic and social collapse, the current dominating view is that Sub-Saharan Africa remains the last of the great untapped markets, ripe for rapid growth and development. These views are supported by the data, which show that six of the world's ten fastest growing economies during 2001–2010 were in Sub-Saharan Africa. In this timely book, we are given a unique and data-rich insight into one of the key manifestations of this great African renaissance – the rise of the African middle class. Through the expert hands of Mthuli Ncube and Charles Lufumpa, the various authors deal carefully and systematically with issues ranging from the size and shape of this new, huge consumer market to the role played by educational institutions in ensuring the sustenance of this class. As a compendium for those interested in understanding one of the key drivers of this continent's economic future this volume will prove indispensable.'

—*Haroon Bhorat, University of Cape Town, South Africa*

'These are exciting times in Africa. The region has witnessed sustained growth for about two decades in proportions that parallel Asian tigers. The Africa growth renaissance is not accidental, but generated by fruits of extensive economic and financial sector reforms, including empowerment of private initiative and human capital development resulting from investment in quality education and technology. The growth dividend has manifested itself in improved access to health, clean water, education, reduction in infant mortality, and reduction in poverty. While the growth syndrome is widely celebrated in the "Africa Rising" story, there are still issues of lack of growth inclusiveness and insufficient sharing of prosperity. However, one dimension that has not yet received sufficient attention, and that needs to be equally celebrated, is the emergence of African middle class which is associated with strong African growth. Ncube and

Lufumpa (Eds.) provide the first comprehensive documentation of the rising African middle class based on a consumption model, and, equally important, they catalogue the drivers of this emerging class, along with its multiplier effect on future growth, improved governance, innovation, and even enhanced global integration of the region. The book makes it clear that the lower end of the middle class is still vulnerable, and on the edge, with the possibility of devolving into subsistence, but they provide a menu of risk management mechanisms to mitigate such vulnerabilities. This book is uplifting, methodologically and intellectually sound, and rich in policy prescriptions. A must read for researchers, educators, policy makers, and global partners. As AERC (www.aercafrica.org) Executive Director, I am heartened by this policy and intellectually rich book, since it is getting widely known that informed policy making is among the key factors of production for Africa growth, and the resulting middle class, with AERC at the center of capacity building for informed policy making over the last 25 years. I salute Mthuli and Lufumpa for putting together such an informative and timely book.'

—Lemma W. Senbet, African Economic Research Consortium, and University of Maryland, USA

'A timely topic, by genuine experts.'

—Paul Collier, University of Oxford, UK

THE EMERGING MIDDLE CLASS IN AFRICA

Edited by Mthuli Ncube and
Charles Leyeka Lufumpa

Routledge
Taylor & Francis Group

LONDON AND NEW YORK

First published 2015
by Routledge
2 Park Square, Milton Park, Abingdon, Oxon OX14 4RN

and by Routledge
711 Third Avenue, New York, NY 10017

Routledge is an imprint of the Taylor & Francis Group, an informa business

© 2015 African Development Bank

British Library Cataloguing in Publication Data
A catalogue record for this book is available from the British Library

Library of Congress Cataloging-in-Publication Data
The emerging middle class in Africa / edited by Mthuli Ncube and Charles Leyeka Lufumpa.
      pages cm
   1. Middle class–Africa. 2. Africa–Economic conditions.
   I. Ncube, Mthuli, 1963- editor of compilation. II.
   Lufumpa, Charles Leyeka.
   HT690.A35E44 2015
   305.5096--dc23   2014016030

ISBN: 978-1-138-79642-3 (hbk)
ISBN: 978-1-138-79643-0 (pbk)
ISBN: 978-1-315-75789-6 (ebk)

Typeset in Bembo
by HWA Text and Data Management, London

CONTENTS

FIGURES

TABLES

CONTRIBUTORS

Oluyele Akinkugbe is a Professor of Economics at the School of Economics and Management Sciences at the University of the Witwatersrand, Johannesburg, South Africa. He specializes in development economics and applied econometrics with research interests in education, health, trade and capital flows, youth skills development and employment, and socio-economic policy analyses. With over 25 years of teaching, research, and consulting experiences, Oluyele Akinkugbe has taught at both undergraduate and graduate levels in different universities across Africa and North America.

Mohamed Ayadi is a Professor of Econometrics and Quantitative Economics at the University of Tunis, Tunisia, with over 25 years of teaching and research experience in consumer behaviour and public economic policies, welfare and poverty analysis, financial international economics and international trade, and econometric and statistical modeling. He is the Director of UAQUAP (Research Unit on Quantitative and Applied Economics), Tunisia. Dr Ayadi holds a PhD in mathematical economics and econometrics from GREMAQ, University of Toulouse, France. He has published extensively on quantitative economics.

Mohamed Safouane Ben Aïssa is a Professor of Economics at the University of Tunis El Manar, Tunisia, and a long-term consultant at the African Development Bank for Statistics and North African Regional Departments. He has published numerous articles on monetary policy and financial stability in North African countries. He holds a PhD in economics from the University of Aix-Marseille II, GREQAM, Marseille, France, and CEDERS, Aix-en-Provence, France.

Oliver J.M. Chinganya is currently a Division Manager responsible for Statistical Capacity Building in the Statistics Department, African Development Bank. He holds an MSc in Statistics from the University of Southampton, UK, an MBA from the Jomo Kenyatta University of Technology, Nairobi, Kenya, and is a Chartered Statistician (CStat), Royal Statistical Society, UK; a Chartered Scientist (CSci), Royal Council of Scientists, UK; and an Elected Member of the International Statistical Institute (ISI). Prior to joining the African Development Bank, he was a Regional Advisor of the GDD at the IMF and a Deputy Director of the Central Statistical Office, Zambia.

Lee Crawfurd is a member of the Cross-Cutting and New Business Development teams at Oxford Policy Management (OPM), UK. Previously he has worked as an economist in the Labour Market Policy Division of the UK Government Department for Work and Pensions and as an economist in the Ministry of Finance in South Sudan. He holds an MSc in economics for development from the University of Oxford, UK, and a BSc in development economics from the School of Oriental and African Studies (SOAS) in London, UK. He has worked in Ghana, South Sudan, the UK, Uganda, and the USA.

Simone Dettling is a member of the Oxford Policy Management Team, UK. She is an economist and political scientist focusing on program and project evaluation. She has extensively worked on survey design and implementation as well as data management and data quality assurance. She holds an MA in international relations from the Johns Hopkins University, School of Advanced International Studies (SAIS), USA. She has worked in Malawi, Bangladesh, Germany, Lebanon, Belgium, Syria, and Guatemala.

Helen Johansen is an Adjunct Professor in the Department of Community Medicine and Epidemiology at the University of Ottawa, Canada. Her main research is in person-oriented health information based on the linkage of registry, health care, survey, and vital statistical data. She has over 30 years' work experience as a Senior Analyst at Statistics Canada and Health Canada in the health field. Dr Johansen has published over 70 peer-reviewed scientific articles on cardiovascular diseases and related health outcomes. She has a PhD in Physical Chemistry from the University of California at Berkeley, USA.

Benedict Kunene is a Principal Education Analyst, Science and Technology Education Division, in the Human Development Department at the African Development Bank. He is responsible for management of higher education, science and technology (HEST) projects in Nigeria, SADC Secretariat, Botswana; Malawi, Kenya, Uganda, Tanzania, and Zambia; and studies on education and skills development in Sierra Leone, Tanzania, Niger, and Zambia. He holds an MA in educational planning and economics from the Institute of

Education, University of London, UK. He also holds an Advanced Diploma in Education from the Institute of Education, London University, UK, and a BA in Accounting and Economics from the University of Swaziland. Prior to joining the African Development Bank, Mr Kunene worked with UNICEF Swaziland as Assistant Project Officer.

Michael Lofchie is Professor of Political Science at the University of California, Los Angeles, USA. He has 50 years of teaching and research experience in political science. Prof. Lofchie holds a PhD from the University of California, Berkeley, USA. He has held positions as Associate Dean, Division of Social Sciences, UCLA, Chair, Inter-Departmental Program in International Development Studies, Chair, Department of Political Science, Chair, Academic Senate Committee on Privilege and Tenure, and Director, James S. Coleman African Studies Center. Dr Lofchie has published five books, monographs, and numerous peer-reviewed journal articles on political economy and democratic governance in Africa.

Charles Leyeka Lufumpa is the Director of Statistics Department at the African Development Bank. He holds a PhD in resource economics and statistics from Iowa State University, USA, an MSc in agricultural economics from the same university, and a BA in economics and statistics from the University of Zambia. Dr Lufumpa also has a certificate in environmental economics and policy analysis from Harvard University, USA. Dr Lufumpa has 30 years of professional work experience in statistics and in formulating and analyzing policies and strategies on poverty, agricultural, and environmental economic issues in Africa. Twenty-one years of this work experience have been with the African Development Bank Group (AfDB), 16 years of which have been at the managerial level.

Marta Moratti is a consultant at OPM (Oxford Policy Management), UK. She has experience in socio-economic data collection and analysis. Her areas of interest focus on survey design and implementation and she is specialised in consumption and poverty measurement and analysis. She holds a PhD from Bocconi University/Sussex University, Italy/UK, and a Masters in Development Economics from Sussex University, UK. She has undertaken research and consultancy work in different countries in Africa and Latin America.

Maurice Mubila is a Chief Statistician in the Statistics Department, African Development Bank. He holds an MSc in social statistics, University of Southampton, UK, a BA in economics from the University of Zambia, and a BSc (Hons) in statistics from the University of Southampton, UK. Mr Mubila has over 20 years of experience at the African Development Bank, developing methodological frameworks and applying statistical methods in such areas as monitoring of Millennium Development Goals (MDGs), civil registration and vital statistics, poverty analysis, analysis of infrastructure statistics (transport, energy, water, ICT), and price statistics in African countries among other things.

Prior to joining the bank, Mr Mubila spent 10 years as a professional and then Head of Price Information and Statistics Unit, of the Zambia Central Statistics Agency.

Alice Nabalamba is Chief Statistician in the Statistics Department at the African Development Bank and currently works on gender and health statistics. She holds a PhD in Planning from University of Waterloo, Canada, and an MA in Urban and Regional Planning from the University of California, Los Angeles, USA. Prior to joining the African Development Bank, Dr Nabalamba spent over 10 years in the Government of Canada as a Research and Health Analyst at Statistics Canada and the Center for Chronic Disease Prevention and Control, Public Health Agency of Canada. She has published widely on health-related matters in peer-reviewed journals.

Mthuli Ncube is Chief Economist and Vice President of the African Development Bank, a Senior Research Fellow at the Blavatnik School of Government and Research Fellow of St Anthony's College, University of Oxford, UK. He holds a PhD in Mathematical Finance from Cambridge University, UK, for which his thesis was titled 'Pricing Options under Stochastic Volatility'. As Chief Economist, he oversees the Economics Complex, which is focused on the process of knowledge management within the bank and with its partners, and the general economic strategic direction of the bank. As a Vice President, he is a member of the senior management of the bank and contributes to its general strategic direction.

Before joining the bank, Prof. Ncube was Dean of the Faculty of Commerce, Law and Management at the University of the Witwatersrand (Wits), Johannesburg, South Africa, and Dean and Professor of Finance at Wits Business School, South Africa. Prof. Ncube was also a regulator, and served as a board member of the South African Financial Services Board (FSB), which regulates non-bank financial institutions in South Africa. He is Chairman of the Board of the African Economic Research Consortium, a network of development economists in Africa, with which he has been associated for the last 20 years. Prof. Ncube is also a Governor of the African Capacity Building Foundation, Zimbabwe.

He has published widely in the area of finance and economics, and some of his papers have won awards. Some of the papers have been published in international journals such as the *Journal of Econometrics, Journal of Banking and Finance, Mathematical Finance, Applied Financial Economics, Journal of African Economies*, among others. He has also published four books, namely: *Mathematical Finance; South African Dictionary of Finance; Financial Systems and Monetary Policy in Africa*; and *Development Dynamics: Theories and Lessons from Zimbabwe*; and a book manuscript on finance and investments in South Africa.

Abena F.D. Oduro is currently Vice Dean, Faculty of Social Studies at the University of Ghana, Legon, and a Senior Lecturer in the Department of Economics at the same university. She holds an MA (Hons) in political economy and geography, an MLitt in political economy from the University of Glasgow, UK. Ms Oduro has published widely in the field of economics, and on gender and related issues.

Felix Schmieding is an economist and statistician with experience in quantitative survey design, implementation, and analysis. His main areas of specialization are the support and analysis of living standards, household surveys, capacity building in national statistical systems, and quantitative impact evaluations. He has worked in these areas in Rwanda, Zambia, Kenya, Lesotho, and Ethiopia. Mr Schmieding holds an MSc in economics for development from the University of Oxford, UK, and a BA in International Relations (1st class), University of Dresden, Germany.

Mary Strode is a Principal Consultant at Oxford Policy Management. Ms Strode is a statistician with over 20 years of experience in developing countries, including Africa, Central Asia, the Pacific, and Central America. She is currently supporting the data quality component of the Millennium Challenge Accounts in Namibia and Vanuatu, the analysis of the most recent Zambian Living Conditions Monitoring Survey, and the development of district statistical capacity in Mozambique. Ms Strode previously worked for DFID and OECD. She holds an MSc in survey methods from City University, London, UK, and a Diploma in urban and regional planning, Polytechnic of Central London (now University of Westminster), UK.

FOREWORD

One of the most inspirational stories of this decade is the steady growth of African economies despite the global downturn. This growth, though uneven, is a source of hope for Africa but also a signal to the rest of the world on the prospects for economic recovery and renewal. The emergence of the African middle class as a driver of this growth stands out as an important milestone in Africa's contemporary economic history.

This book provides detailed testimony of this important feature of Africa's development. It outlines measures that are needed to sustain economic growth. More importantly, the book provides original and first-hand information that will help guide African policymakers and investors on how to leverage the rise of the middle class as a force for prosperity.

Following African countries' independence, the continent has struggled with a seemingly endless array of development challenges, from civil war and political instability to food insecurity, droughts, disease, pervasive poverty, and corruption. But in recent years, Africa has started to see an economic resurgence. Better economic policies, governance, and use of natural resources, coupled with more business-friendly policies and stronger demand for Africa's commodities, have led to consistently high growth levels in Africa, despite the global downturn.

One of the results of this economic growth in recent years has been a significant increase in the size of the African middle class. By 2010 more than a third of the African population was middle class according to the African Development Bank (AfDB). It is not an easy task to define what middle class means or how many people fall in this category across the 47 countries of Sub-Saharan Africa. Falling somewhere between Africa's poor population and the small, rich elite, the middle class of Africa appears to be in large part young, well educated, and business-minded. We can observe that this middle class has disposable income and is demanding an increasing amount of goods and services that contribute to the overall well-being of society.

Technology adoption is an important part of the story of the African middle class. Cell phone use has grown faster in Africa than in any other region of the world since 2003, according to the United Nations Conference on Trade and Development. Sales of refrigerators, television sets, automobiles, and other durable consumer goods have surged in virtually every African country in recent years. Demand for tertiary technical education is also on the rise. In fact, Africa will need to rapidly reform its higher education system to focus on expanding opportunities for training in the technical fields, especially engineering and technology.

Global confidence in the economic impetus we can expect from the African middle class is also strong, as evidenced by major consumer retail chains and large international banks recently deciding to establish a presence in Africa. Across Africa, change is in the air. Many of the old problems remain. But strong economic growth together with the emergence of an African middle class, the rise of a new generation of entrepreneurs, innovators, and consumers, is remarkable and creates new opportunities for ancient lands.

Ultimately, the emergence of the African middle class can only be sustained if the continent puts in place strategies that increase prosperity for all. Without such measures, which include expanding opportunities for technical training and job creation, the growth of the middle class is likely to be undermined by social friction. The same cell phones that are helping to expand demand for consumer products could become handy tools for protest and agitation. The time to capitalize on the rise of the middle class as a force for spreading prosperity is now.

Calestous Juma
Professor of the Practice of International Development
Harvard Kennedy School of Government

PREFACE

In 2011, the African Development Bank (AfDB) published a report assessing the state of the middle class in Africa. This report captured the imagination of the public and the world's media, adding analytical perspective to the growing reality of economic and social transformation in Africa.

Robust economic growth over the past 20 years has led to visible changes across the continent. Visitors to the metropolises of a number of African countries cannot help but notice the emerging African middle class.

This book builds on the analysis contained in the initial report, and delves more deeply into specific aspects of the lives of the middle class. The investigation looks at how people become middle class – be it through education, access to the formal labor market, or entrepreneurship. It also examines how behavior changes in the process, in terms of consumption patterns, spending on education and health. A further dimension taken up in this analysis is how class impacts gender relations and whether women are equally reaping the benefits of social advancement as men. The book analyzes the political economy of the middle class, providing context of its development since independence. Needless to say, Africa is a continent of such scale and diversity that experiences across different countries differ widely, but we hope in this book to have captured some commonalities.

The emergence of the middle class in Africa is driving a growing consumer market for African businesses and a demand for better governance and public services. The African Development Bank will play a key role in the coming years in supporting African governments to provide both the hard and soft infrastructure that African people and businesses will require to connect with each other and generate increased prosperity for all.

Mthuli Ncube and Charles Leyeka Lufumpa

ACKNOWLEDGMENTS

The editors wish to thank the authors of the various chapters for their contribution to the realization of this project. Thanks also go to the anonymous reviewers for their invaluable comments and suggestions that helped to improve the book.

The editors also wish to thank Dr Alice Nabalamba for anchoring *The Emerging Middle Class in Africa* project, including managing the communication with the authors and the publisher. The book could not have been produced without her help.

The editors also would like to thank Sandra Jones, who carried out the copy-editing work so meticulously. Any remaining errors and omissions, however, remain the responsibility of the editors.

INTRODUCTION

Mthuli Ncube

Strong economic growth over the past two decades has helped to reduce poverty in Africa and to increase the size of the middle class. As a result, 323 million Africans now have a consumption expenditure between $2 and $20 a day.

The emerging middle class on the continent will continue to grow: from 323 million (34 percent of Africa's population) in 2010 to 1.1 billion (42 percent of the population) in 2060. The middle class, which is strongest in countries with robust and growing private sectors, is crucial not only for economic growth, but also for the growth of democracy. This middle class will assume the traditional role of the US and European middle classes as major consumers, and will play a key role in rebalancing the African economy. Consumer spending in Africa, primarily by the middle class, proved surprisingly resilient during the global recession of 2008/2009. In 2009, it reached an estimated $1.2 trillion in 2009 PPP US dollars, rising to $1.6 trillion in 2011. Given the continent's consumption expenditure growth over the past 20 years, it is estimated that by 2020 Africa will likely reach $2.6 trillion in PPP annual household consumption expenditure and comprise a sizable proportion of global household consumption.

The emergence of this new middle class has strong positive potential for the region. It has the capacity to increase domestic consumption; contribute to private sector growth and entrepreneurialism; boost demand for better governance and public services; improve gender equality; and raise standards of living, allowing many people to exit from poverty.

The middle class is defined here primarily according to income or consumption. Although some researchers adopt a relative definition, we use an absolute definition of per capita daily consumption of $2 to $20 in 2005 purchasing power parity (PPP) US dollars, disaggregated into three subcategories. The first and largest of these is the 'floating class,' with per capita consumption levels of $2 to $4 per day. The second subcategory is the 'lower-middle class,' with per capita consumption levels of $4 to $10 per day. This group lives above the subsistence level and is able to save and consume non-essential goods. The third subcategory is the 'upper-middle class,' with per capita consumption levels of $10 to $20 per day.

About 63 percent of Africa's middle class – approximately 204 million people – remain barely out of the poor category. They constitute the 'floating class,' earning between $2 and $4 a day. They are in a vulnerable position, constantly at risk of dropping back into the poor category in the event of any unexpected shocks, such as the loss of income.

A study by Ncube and Shimeles (2013), using asset ownership, corroborated the size of the middle class when consumer expenditure was used. The asset-based measure is highly correlated with the consumption-based measure, thus confirming that Africa has a credible middle class.

What is the middle class doing?

Technology adoption is an important part of the story of the African middle class. Cellphone use has grown faster in Africa than in any other region of the world since 2003, according to the United Nations Conference on Trade and Development. Sales of refrigerators, television sets, automobiles, and other durable consumer goods have surged in virtually every African country in recent years. Vehicle ownership is also associated with a middle-class lifestyle, and many countries are showing an upward trend.

Demand for tertiary technical education is also on the rise. In fact, Africa will need to rapidly reform its higher education system to focus on expanding opportunities for training in technical fields, especially engineering and technology. A growing middle class in Africa requires housing, but political and economic instability often contributes to shortages. Financing home purchases is difficult in a number of countries. In recent times, mortgage markets have been on the rise across Africa, and this is a reflection of middle-class opportunity. The middle class is also more likely to seek better health care, and they are more likely to pay for private health care.

Global confidence in the economic impetus we can expect from the African middle class is also strong, as evidenced by major consumer retail chains and large international banks recently establishing a presence in Africa. As well, the growing middle class are travelling and are discovering domestic tourism.

Empirical evidence shows that the growth of the middle class is associated with better governance, economic advancement, and poverty reduction. As people gain middle-class status, they use their greater economic clout to demand more accountability and transparency from their governments. This includes pressing for the rule of law, clearer property rights, and a higher quality of public service provision.

Education and spatial mobility are often key factors in procuring a middle-class job. They allow people to move into a new sector or industry with higher wage rates, or to relocate to an urban agglomeration where job opportunities are greater.

The region has witnessed strong expansion in manufacturing and service industries such as telecommunications and finance in recent years. This is expected to translate into sustained growth of middle-class jobs in the future. African cities will continue to expand at a rapid pace, creating the dynamic environments conducive to innovation and higher labor productivity. Nevertheless, despite these positive trajectories, the informal sector will continue to dominate the African labor market in the medium term, as the growth of steady, well-paid employment is starting from a low level.

What needs to be done to increase the middle class?

The emergence of the middle class in Africa is driving a consumer market for African businesses and a demand for better governance and public services. Faster growth of the middle class requires investment in human development – education and health, with national savings efficiently mobilized and appropriate economic policies and good governance adopted. Overall, economic growth determines the rise of the middle class, but economic growth is, in turn, driven by social and economic factors.

Africa's middle class is strongest in countries that have a robust and growing private sector, as many members of the middle class tend to be local entrepreneurs. In a number of countries, a new middle class has emerged as a result of opportunities offered by the private sector. Other determining factors include the establishment of stable, secure, well-paid jobs and improved access to jobs, as well as skills, employability, and higher levels of tertiary education. The size of the middle class is rising in most African countries. The probability of maintaining middle-class status is also fairly high, with real possibilities to move up, but also to slip back into poverty. From a policy perspective, it is evident that improving governance conditions and investing in education and health can take countries a long way toward expanding the size of the middle class.

Organization of the book

This book is divided into eight chapters. Chapter 1 on the dynamics of the middle class provides the context for the emerging middle class in Africa and addresses definitional issues, data sources, and the methodology used in computation of middle-class categories. The middle class can be defined in relative or absolute terms. Chapter 1 uses an absolute definition of per capita daily consumption of $2 to $20 in 2005 PPP US dollars. It identifies three categories: the 'floating class,' with per capita consumption of $2 to $4 per day; the 'lower-middle class,' with per capita consumption of $4 to $10 per day; and the 'upper-middle class,' with per capita consumption of $10 to $20 per day.

Chapter 2 on the political economy of Africa's middle class provides both a historical and a contemporary context for the emergence of the middle class in Africa. The chapter discusses the structure of the middle class in the post-independence period and how it has evolved. It analyzes some of the strategic decisions taken by post-colonial governments and their effect on middle-class growth. The post-colonial middle class consisted overwhelmingly of government employees and employees in parastatal corporations that were government entities. The contemporary middle class is larger in numerical terms, and it has a solid basis in private sector growth and diversification. It is composed of both government employees and the entrepreneurial class – business owners in activities that include banking, finance, information technology, retail, and industrial processing.

Chapter 3 discusses consumption habits of Africa's emerging middle class. Consumption patterns reflect households' material living conditions and shed light on changes in their tastes and habits, and on increases in discretionary income. Investigating consumption patterns and how they change over time helps policymakers, as well as producers of goods and services, to assess current and future household needs. Furthermore, consumption better reflects long-term welfare than does income, as 'consumption is smoother and less variable than income' (Deaton and Zaidi, 2002).

Chapter 4 on jobs and employment discusses the key factors driving the growth of the contemporary middle class in Africa. This requires an understanding of how people earn their income. The chapter analyzes the characteristics that distinguish someone who earns more than $2 a day from someone who earns less. First, those in the middle class have moved away from agricultural self-employment toward non-agricultural wage employment. Second, the terms of employment for middle-class workers and poor workers differ. Among wage workers, the difference between casual laborers paid on a daily basis and salaried workers typically paid a regular monthly wage is profound. Casual workers lack job security; their hours are unpredictable, and their benefits are few. Salaried employees, on the other hand, enjoy steady and predictable working hours and pay, which enable them to better plan for the future (Banerjee and Duflo, 2008). Education and geographic mobility are also key factors in procuring a middle-class job. They allow people to move into a new sector or industry with higher wage rates, or to relocate to an urban agglomeration where job opportunities are more abundant.

Chapter 5 on entrepreneurship delves into the expansion of manufacturing and service industries such as telecommunications and finance, and how this contributed to the emergence of the middle class. This expansion is expected to translate into sustained growth of middle-class jobs in the future. As African cities continue to grow, they will create an environment conducive to innovation and higher labor productivity. Nevertheless, despite these positive trajectories, the informal sector will continue to dominate the African labor market in the medium term, as the growth of steady, well-paid employment is starting from such a low level (IMF, 2011). Today, around 80 percent of the non-agricultural workforce in Sub-Saharan Africa is informal (IMF, 2011). Many enterprises operate informally because the cost, time, and effort of formal registration are too high. Similarly, credit costs are prohibitive for many, because interest rates tend to be too high. In most Sub-Saharan African countries, people find remuneration in activities that provide minimal subsistence support (Charman and Peterson, 2009). This reflects a weakness of African economies in fostering entrepreneurship and creating more productive jobs.

Chapter 6 discusses the role of education in increasing the middle class. The emergence of the middle class must be set against the expansion of educational opportunities over the past four decades. Between 1970 and 2010, enrollment in primary education rose from 23 million to 129 million.[1] Many African countries have already achieved the Millennium Development Goal (MDG) of universal primary enrollment. Advances are being made in secondary school enrollment, which grew from 4 million to 42 million during the same period. Enrollment at the tertiary level is lower than at primary and secondary levels, but although considerably smaller in absolute terms, it increased 22-fold, from 0.2 million in 1970 to 4.5 million in 2008. Education is a key driver of the growth of the middle class. Education opens up new avenues for upward mobility. In turn, growth of the middle class helps to bolster education and economic progress.

Chapter 7 on gender highlights some of the methodological challenges in analyzing middle-class characteristics. Recent studies that 'counted' the middle class in Africa were unable to disaggregate the middle class by sex. Identifying the middle class solely on the basis of household consumption precludes the possibility of conducting gender analysis. Adults in the same household may not benefit equally from middle-class status. A gender analysis of the middle class is especially necessary because women and men do not participate equally in the labor market. Women's average earnings in paid employment are typically lower than those of men, even after accounting for human capital differences (Agesa, Agesa, and Dabalen, 2008; Kolev and Robles 2010; Siphambe and Thokweng-Bakwena, 2001). Female labor force participation rates remain below 50 percent in a number of countries, compared with 80 percent for males.

While the gender gap in primary education has narrowed during the last two decades and is virtually non-existent in several African countries, it remains wide at the secondary and tertiary levels, despite an increase in the enrollment rates of both sexes. Inequality in educational attainment between the sexes has repercussions later in life; for example, girls are more likely to undertake low-paid domestic work than are boys, and even fewer end up in professional or managerial jobs.

Property rights are a cornerstone of gender equality, especially since they often provide the basis for self-subsistence. In Africa, gender relations determine access to and ownership and control of property. These dimensions define incentives to increase productivity, engage in other productive non-farm activities, and improve access to financial resources. Women have less access to formal financial services that would allow them to transition to self-sufficiency and start a business. The World Bank Global Findex (Global Financial Inclusion Database) shows that in 2011, the percentage of females with an account in a formal financial institution such as a commercial bank, credit union, co-operative, or microfinance institution is very low, ranging from less than 5 percent in Niger, Democratic Republic of Congo, Guinea, Central African Republic, Sudan, and Madagascar to nearly 40 percent in Zimbabwe, Angola, and Kenya. The exceptions are South Africa and Mauritius, where female financial inclusion is 51 percent and 75 percent, respectively. The implications of financial exclusion of females include limited access to financing for start-up businesses in the formal sector. It also means that more than half of Africa's population never gets to use bank products such as savings and checking accounts, loans, or credit cards, or other services.

Our analysis shows that attainment of middle-class status is not sufficient in itself to bring about gender equality. What is required in addition are changes in cultural practices, norms that treat women as equal, and regulations and laws that aim at correcting social biases.

Chapter 8 discusses the relationship between health and wellbeing of the population and the emergence of the middle class. Health is a key challenge for improving the wellbeing of populations across the continent. Good health is a precondition for development and individual ability to earn a living and contribute to the economic growth of a nation. It is becoming clear that achievement of this goal is not reliant on the health sector alone; rather, it is mediated by environmental, social, infrastructural, and regulatory systems.

The health landscape in Africa has transformed dramatically since the independence of many countries more than 50 years ago, and this is expected to continue over the next several decades as the middle class grows and the continent progresses. Africa has made considerable headway in improving the health outcomes of its populations, despite the challenges posed by persistent poverty, epidemic diseases, and food insecurity. Communicable diseases of HIV/AIDS, malaria, and tuberculosis remain the main drivers of mortality. Maternal and infant mortality also remain challenging in the most fragile countries. But as the middle-class share of the population increases, mortality rates decline and life expectancy rises. However, this brings a number of challenges including an aging population, and a concomitant rise in physical and mental disability and long-term non-communicable conditions such as cardiovascular diseases, diabetes, and cancer – all associated with a middle-class lifestyle. This creates a double disease burden that underfunded, overstretched African health care systems are ill-equipped to handle. However, an expanding middle class means that more families have more to spend on health care and health insurance. This also presents an opportunity for private sector engagement in health service delivery, particularly specialized health care. An expanding middle class also provides a bigger tax base to fund much-needed social programs.

Conclusions

This book presents a multifaceted picture of the emerging middle class in Africa and its driving forces. Statistics on the political economy, consumption patterns, jobs, education, entrepreneurship, gender, and health of the middle class all tell a story about how the middle class is growing, and the implications for policymakers. We analyze how people become middle class – be it through education, access to the formal labor market, or entrepreneurship. We also examine how behavior changes in terms of consumption patterns, by looking at middle-class spending on material goods, health, and education. We also review the impact of class on gender relations and how to ensure greater equity in this area as populations grow richer.

Policies that foster sustained and shared growth, enhanced human resources, private sector participation, and improved accountability and governance also spur the growth of the middle class. Governments will need to focus on bolstering the incomes of those already in the middle class, as well as assisting the mass of the population seeking to escape the cycle of poverty. Social policies can accelerate this emerging trend, for example, through increased spending on higher education, science and technology, and health. Over the next 20 years, with the appropriate policies focused on human capital development and job generation, and increased democratic space, Africa can transform its social fabric, as more and more of its population exit poverty to join the ranks of the middle class.

Note

1 UNESCO-UIS online; AfDB Data Portal 2013.

References

AfDB (2014). *The International Comparison Program, Results from 2005 Round of ICP-Africa*. Tunis: AfDB.

Agesa, R.U., J. Agesa, and A. Dabalen (2008), 'Changes in Wage Distributions, Wage Gaps and Wage Inequality by Gender in Kenya,' *Journal of African Economies*, vol. 18, no. 3, pp. 431–460.

Banerjee, A.V., and E. Duflo (2008). 'What is Middle Class about the Middle Classes around the World?' *Journal of Economic Perspectives*, vol. 22, pp. 3–28.

Charman, A.J., and L.M. Peterson (2009), 'An Investigation of Characteristics Distinguishing Entrepreneurs from the Self-employed in South Africa'. Paper presented at the Second Annual International Conference on Entrepreneurship. Johannesburg: WITS Business School.

Deaton, A., and S. Zaidi (2002), *Guidelines for Constructing Consumption Aggregates for Welfare Analysis*. Washington DC: World Bank.

IMF (2011), *Regional Economic Outlook: Sub-Saharan Africa*. Washington DC: International Monetary Fund.

Kolev, A., and P.S. Robles (2010). 'Exploring the Gender Pay Gap through different Age Cohorts: the Case of Ethiopia.' In J.S. Arbache, A. Kolev, and E. Filipiak (eds), *Gender Disparities in Africa's Labor Market*. Washington DC: Agence française de développement and World Bank.

Ncube, M. and A. Shimeles (2013). The Making of Middle Class in Africa: Evidence from DHS Data. IZA DP no. 7352. Bonn, Germany: Institute for the Study of Labor.

Siphambe, H.K., and M. Thokweng-Bakwena (2001). 'The Wage Gap between Men and Women in Botswana's Formal Labour Market,' *Journal of African Economies*, vol. 10, no. 2, pp. 127–142.

1

THE DYNAMICS OF THE MIDDLE CLASS IN AFRICA

Charles Leyeka Lufumpa, Maurice Mubila, and Mohamed Safouane Ben Aïssa

Introduction

Empirical evidence shows that the growth of the middle class is associated with better governance, economic advancement, and poverty reduction. As people gain middle-class status, they are more likely to use their greater economic clout to demand more accountability and transparency from their governments (Lipset, 1969; Asian Development Bank, 2010). This includes pressing for the rule of law, clearer property rights, and a higher quality of public service provision.

Robust economic growth in Africa over the past two decades has been accompanied by the emergence of a sizable middle class and a significant reduction in poverty. There has also been a concomitant increase in consumption spending. Indeed, consumption in the continent now stands close to one-third that of developing EU countries.

Fostering the growth of the middle class should be of primary interest to policymakers. It represents a strong medium- and long-term development indicator, partly because of its close association with accelerated poverty reduction. This provides an opportunity for African governments to leverage middle-class growth to accelerate poverty reduction by harnessing appropriate policies.

This chapter argues that the middle class holds the key to a rebalancing of African economies toward greater dependency on domestic demand rather than an over-reliance on export markets. The evidence presented here is based on research and studies undertaken in 45 African countries.

Definitional issues, data sources, and methodology

Who are 'the middle class'?

The middle class can be defined in relative or absolute terms. In relative terms, the middle class refers to households falling between the 20th and 80th percentile of the consumption distribution, or individuals falling between 0.75 and 1.25 times median per capita income (Birdsall, Graham, and Pettinato, 2000). Using the absolute definition, the middle class usually refers to individuals with an annual income exceeding $3,900 in PPP terms (Bhalla, 2009). Banerjee and Duflo (2008) consider two separate groups: (i) those with a daily per capita expenditure between $2 and $4 and (ii) those with a daily per capita expenditure between $6 and $10.

The middle class is widely acknowledged to represent Africa's future, as the group crucial to the continent's economic and social development (McConnell, 2010). But it is difficult to define exactly who falls into this category and harder still to establish how many middle-class people there are in Africa. Recent estimates put the size of the African middle class in the region of 300 to 500 million people, representing the segment of population that lies between the vast number of the poor and the continent's few elite. Africa's emerging middle class is thus roughly the size of the middle class in India or China (Mahajan, 2009). It is also argued that this segment of the population is strongest in countries that have robust and growing private sectors (Ramachandran, Gelb, and Shah, 2009). The middle class is crucial not only for the growth of Africa's economy but also for the growth of democracy.

Definition used in this chapter

This chapter uses an absolute definition of per capita daily consumption of $2–$20 in 2005 PPP US dollars to characterize the middle class in Africa. The study provides three subcategories of the middle class. The first is that of the 'floating class,' with per capita consumption levels of $2–$4 per day. Individuals with this level of consumption are only slightly above the developing-world poverty threshold of $2 per day, which is used in some studies (Ravallion, Chen, and Sangraula, 2008). Such people are at risk of relapsing into poverty in the event of exogenous shocks such as a rise in the price of foodstuffs or loss of income. This 'floating class' subcategory is the demarcation between the poor and lower-middle class. This class is vulnerable and unstable, but it reflects the direction of change in population structure over time.

The second subcategory is that of the 'lower-middle class,' with per capita consumption levels of $4–$10 per day. This group lives above the subsistence level and is able to save and consume non-essential goods. The third subcategory is the 'upper-middle class,' with per capita consumption levels of $10–$20 per day.

Data sources

A variety of data sources were used in our study to create the population distributions and determine the size of the African middle class. The primary source for the distribution data is the World Bank's PovcalNet database, updated for 2012, which provides detailed distributions of either income or household consumption expenditures by percentile, based on household survey data. In addition, PovcalNet provides information on mean household per capita income or consumption levels in 2005 PPP US dollars.

This database primarily provides sample distributions based on consumption, except in instances where only income measures exist. At lower income levels, the difference between consumption and income is small. However, this difference increases with wealth and thus should be considered a potential measurement error in the analysis. Nevertheless, we expect these differences to be relatively minor, as there is generally a high correlation between income and consumption and thus they should have little effect on overall computations. We also focus on consumption, as it better captures individual welfare and is less prone to fluctuations caused by negative and positive shocks.

The data used in the identification of the characteristics of the middle class were obtained mainly from the AfDB Data Portal and other international sources (Penn World Table, 2009; UNU-WIDER World Income Inequality Database, Version 2.0c 2008; also see Appendix 1.4).

Methodological approach[1]

The tabulated distributions and their means are used to generate a Lorenz curve for each country to show the share of income for each subclass of the population. The line of equality depicts a situation of perfect equality in a society where a given proportion of the society would have an equal proportion of the income. The extreme opposite would be where an individual has all the income while everyone else has none. The Lorenz curve is normally used to represent inequality in the distribution of income among the population. The further the curve is away from the line of equality, the more unequal is the income distribution in a given society. The Gini coefficient also measures levels of inequality and is derived from the Lorenz curve. It represents the proportion of the area between the line of equality and the Lorenz curve and the total area above and below the Lorenz curve.

The literature on the estimation of Lorenz curves provides a number of different functional forms. Two of the best performers are the general quadratic (GQ) Lorenz curve (Villasenor and Arnold, 1984, 1989) and what may be called the Beta Lorenz curve (Kakwani, 1980). There is some evidence from Indonesia that the Beta model yields more accurate predictions of the Lorenz ordinates at the lower end of the distribution, though the same study found that the GQ model is more accurate over the whole distribution (Ravallion and Huppi,

1990). The GQ model, however, does have one comparative advantage over the Beta model, in that it is computationally simpler (Datt, 1998).

This chapter therefore uses the Beta approach for estimating the various points of the Lorenz curve, showing the proportion of the population and their share of national income (see Appendices 1.1 and 1.2). Using a system of six equations, each representing a trapezoid-shaped area under the Lorenz curve for a series of coordinates, we obtain three unique values representing the proportions of the population associated with the per capita daily income levels of $4, $10, and $20 (see Appendices 1.1 and 1.2). These represent the floating class, the lower-middle class, and the upper-middle class subclasses defined by this chapter.

Africa's emerging middle class

The results of our study reveal that Africa's middle class has increased in size and purchasing power as strong economic growth over the past two decades has helped to reduce poverty. By 2010, the middle class (including the floating class) had risen to 34 percent of the population (373 million people) (see Table 1.1 and Figure 1.1). This shows a progressive increase over the previous 30 years, from 147 million in 1980, to 196 million in 1990, to 261 million in 2000.

In the 1980s and early 1990s, the slow growth of the middle class meant that only a small percentage of poor households were becoming better off. This trend accelerated slightly during 2000–2010, when a greater number of poor households transitioned into the middle class. At the same time, the decade of the 2000s witnessed an opposite movement – from the rich into the middle

TABLE 1.1   Distribution of Africa's population by subclass, 1980–2010

Year	Floating class*	Lower-middle**	Upper-middle***	Middle class without floating class		Middle class with floating class	
	(000s)	(000s)	(000s)	(000s)	%	(000s)	(%)
1980	81,629	55,309	10,290	65,599	14%	147,228	31%
1990	128,612	65,545	1,938	67,482	11%	196,095	31%
2000	164,880	82,935	13,659	96,594	12%	261,474	32%
2010	236,608	115,933	20,629	136,562	13%	373,170	36%

Source: AfDB Statistics Department.

Notes: *Floating class ($2–$4), ** Lower-middle class ($4–$10), *** Upper-middle class ($10–$20), 2010 figures revised based on updated data in PovcalNet in 2012.

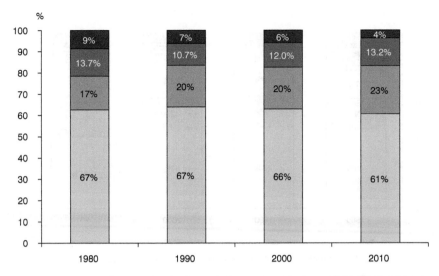

FIGURE 1.1 Distribution of Africa's population by subclass, 1980–2010 (source: authors' calculations based on AfDB Data Portal and World Bank PovcalNet database (updated in 2012))

class, implying a slight rebalancing toward greater income equality. However, income inequality in Africa remains very high. About 100,000 Africans recorded a net worth of $800 billion in 2008, which equates to about 60 percent of Africa's GDP or 80 percent of SSA's GDP (Merrill Lynch, 2010).

Africa's middle class is characterized by a high concentration in the 'floating class', i.e. with per capita consumption levels between $2 and $4 per day (Ravallion, 2012). Many of these households remain in a vulnerable position and at high risk of relapsing into poverty in the event of any exogenous shocks. The results of our study show that about 23 percent (or 237 million) of Africa's population fell into this category in 2012, and barely above the poverty line (see Figure 1.2, Appendices 1.3 and 1.5).

A stricter definition of the middle class that excludes the floating class (i.e., using a minimum threshold of per capita consumption of $4 per day), yields a middle-class population of about 137 million people in Africa.[2] According to this definition, the middle class is further removed from the poverty lines of $1.25 and $2 and is therefore more stable and resilient to shocks. The results of the 2011 International Comparison Program show that per capita expenditure among Africa's middle class has almost doubled, compared with more marginal increases in developed countries.

It is worth noting that in 2010 some 61 percent of Africa's population fell below the $2 poverty line, while 41 percent fell below the $1.25 poverty line, based on updated data (see Figures 1.1 and 1.2). Access to employment and income-generating opportunities could help such households to transition into the lower-middle-class level.

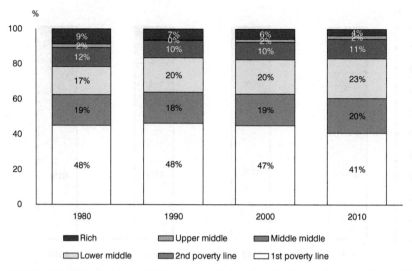

FIGURE 1.2 Distribution of Africa's population by subclass and poverty line, 1980–2010 (source: authors' calculations based on AfDB Data Portal and World Bank PovcalNet database (updated 2012))

Figure 1.3 shows the asymmetric distribution of the middle class by subclass. As mentioned previously, the floating class represents the largest concentration of the middle-class population in almost all African countries. Although there is evidence of noticeable movement from the poor to the floating class, there has been little transition of this class into the more stable middle-class subcategories with consumption levels of $4–$20 per day. This presents policymakers with the challenge of not only stabilizing this floating class but also ensuring its transition to a higher-income subcategory.

North African countries have a much higher concentration of the middle class among their population, with Tunisia leading (91 percent), followed by Morocco (84 percent), and Egypt (84 percent) (see Figure 1.3). However, a significant number of this middle class belong to the vulnerable floating subclass, living on less than $4 per day. This is most evident in Egypt, where more than half of the middle class falls into this category. The case of Mauritania is similar; although nearly 49 percent of the population is classified as middle class, only 15 percent have income levels above $4 per day. Apart from the North African countries, Botswana, Gabon, and South Africa all have a larger middle class with consumption expenditure of $4/day or more compared with their floating middle class of $2–4/day.

Characteristics of the middle class

Consumption or income levels capture only one dimension of the middle class. Other variables such as housing, education, employment, aspirations, lifestyle

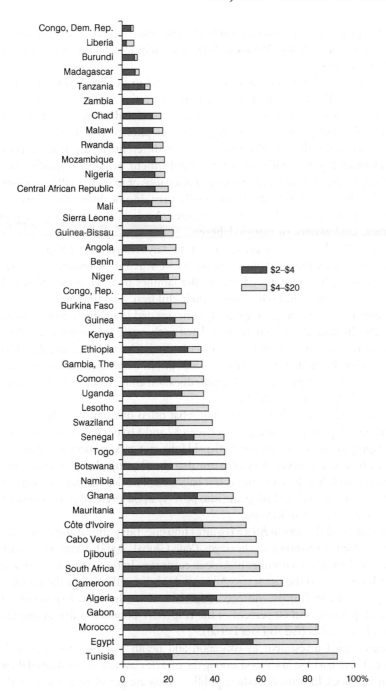

FIGURE 1.3 Percentage of floating class ($2–$4) and middle class ($4–$20) in selected African countries, 2010 (source: authors' calculations based on AfDB Data Portal and World Bank PovcalNet database (data updated in 2012))

and other physical and financial assets (Ncube and Shimeles, 2013; Oduro, Baah-Boateng, and Boakye-Yiadom, 2011) also help to establish who belongs to the middle class.

In terms of residence, middle-class people tend to live in bigger and more permanent dwellings equipped with modern amenities. With respect to asset accumulation, the middle class is typically associated with ownership of household durable goods such as refrigerators, telephones, and automobiles.

There are a number of characteristics that differentiate the middle class in developing regions with regard to employment patterns. Middle-class individuals are much more likely to have salaried jobs or to own small businesses (Asian Development Bank, 2010). Generally they do not derive their income from agricultural and rural economic activities. As such, they are less likely to be farmers, landowners, or manual laborers.

The middle-class population tend not to rely entirely on public health services but to seek more expensive medical care when ill, sometimes drawing on their savings. As a rule, they have smaller families than the poor and spend more on the nutrition and schooling of their children. The middle class is also better educated and more geographically concentrated in urban or coastal areas.

The rise in class status may be correlated with a rise in progressive values conducive to economic growth. In particular, it is claimed that middle-class values are closely aligned with market competition, better governance, gender equality, and greater investment in higher education and science and technology (Asian Development Bank, 2010).

Banerjee and Duflo (2008) argue that what often distinguishes the middle class (whom they define as living on between $2 and $10 per day) from the poor in developing countries are steady, well-paid jobs, not greater success at running small businesses. However, they confirm that the floating class dominates the middle class and that the structure is not balanced. This leaves this subcategory with the ever-present risk of relapsing into poverty in the event of any exogenous shocks, such as loss of an income.

A growing middle class in Africa requires housing, but political and economic instability often contributes to shortages (Yale Global, 2007). Financing home purchases is difficult in a number of African countries. In recent times, mortgage markets have been on the rise across Africa and this is a reflection of the middle-class opportunity. In Tunisia, Morocco, Algeria, and South Africa, 76 percent, 72 percent, 66 percent, and 60 percent of the respective population live in owner-occupied households (AfDB Data Portal).

Human capital investment in education and health also rises together with affluence. There is a high likelihood among the middle class that they will send their children to school. In countries where public schools are perceived not to provide a good education, private schools offer an alternative option for those willing and able to pay. Enrollment rates in private schools at pre-primary, primary, and secondary levels have been augmented in a number of countries. This may provide an indication of a strong middle class (see Figures 1.4 and 1.5 and Chapter 6).

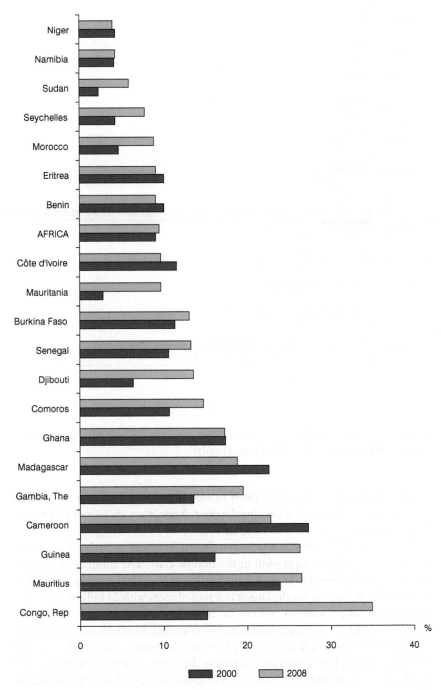

FIGURE 1.4   Private enrollments in primary schools in selected African countries, 2000 and 2008 (%) (source: AfDB Data Portal)

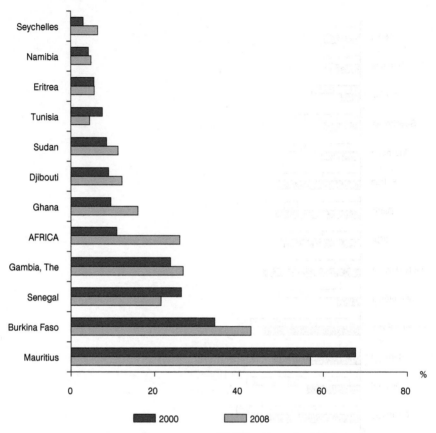

FIGURE 1.5 Private enrollments in secondary schools in selected African countries, 2000 and 2008 (%) (source: AfDB Data Portal)

The middle class is also more likely to seek better health care for themselves and their families than is the case for the poor. Again, they are more likely to pay for private health care (see also Chapter 8).

Turning to ICT, we can see a correlation between growth in access to improved technology and growth in the middle class. The number of internet users increased massively from 4.5 million people in 2000 to over 80 million people in 2008. Nigeria has the largest number of users with 24 million accounts, followed by Egypt with 14 million in 2008. The countries with the lowest number of internet users are Equatorial Guinea and Sierra Leone, with about 12,000 and 13,900 people respectively. Generally countries with predominantly poor populations have fewer internet users. In terms of internet users per 100 people, this rose from 0.6 in 2000 to 8.8 in 2008, with Seychelles the highest at 39 people and Sierra Leone the lowest at 0.3.

Subscription to fixed broadband internet is another indicator that may be attributed to the growth of the middle class. At the continental level, numbers

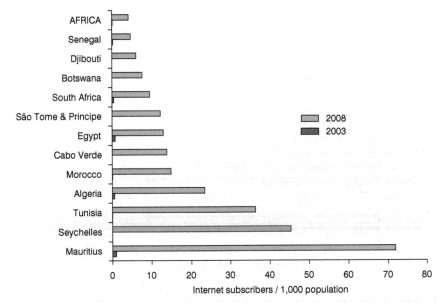

FIGURE 1.6 Fixed broadband internet subscribers per 1,000 population in selected African countries, 2003 and 2008 (source: AfDB Data Portal (accessed 2014))

rose from 0.1 subscribers per 1,000 persons in 2003 to 4.1 subscribers in 2009. A number of countries (Algeria, Cabo Verde, Mauritius, Morocco, São Tomé and Príncipe, Seychelles, and Tunisia) recorded substantial growth in subscriber numbers between 2003 and 2008 (see Figure 1.6).

Vehicle ownership is also associated with a middle-class lifestyle and many countries are showing an upward trend for this indicator (see Figure 1.7). Similarly, consumption of petroleum products has increased. Total petroleum consumption in Africa increased from 1.5 million barrels per day in 1980 to 3.2 million barrels per day in 2009 (AfDB Data Portal, accessed April 2014).

Access to electricity for household use is also closely associated with middle-class status. There was a noticeable increase in total electricity consumption from 170 million kilowatt-hours (kWh) in 1980 to 514 million kWh in 2007. Electricity consumption per household increased by 15 percent from 1980 to 2007, from 2,386 kWh to 2,740 kWh. The increase in total electricity net consumption over the period 1985–2007 is illustrated at the national level in Figure 1.8 and at the household level in Figure 1.9, for selected African countries.

Factors driving the growth of the middle class

Economic growth is critical to both poverty reduction and the growth of the middle class. However, policies aimed at reducing income inequality also play a key role. Africa's middle class is strongest in countries that have a robust and growing private sector, as many middle-class individuals tend to be local

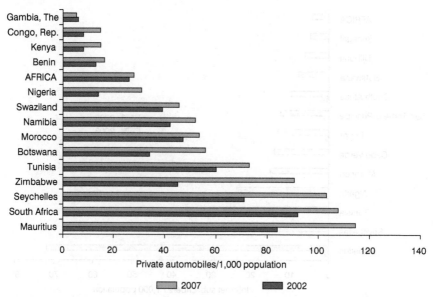

FIGURE 1.7   Private automobiles per 1,000 population in selected African countries, 2002 and 2007 (source: AfDB Data Portal)

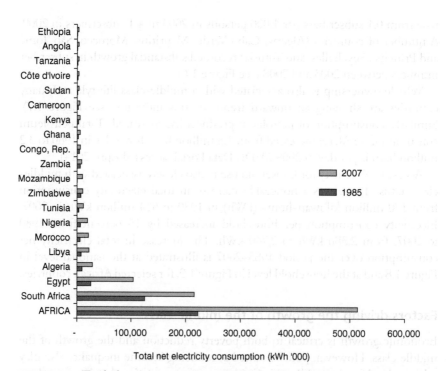

FIGURE 1.8   Total electricity net consumption in selected African countries, 1985 and 2007 (kWh 000s) (source: AfDB Data Portal)

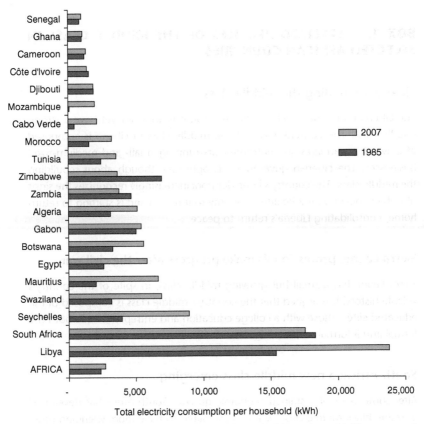

FIGURE 1.9 Electricity net consumption per household in selected African countries, 1985 and 2007 (kWh) (source: AfDB Data Portal)

entrepreneurs. In a number of countries, a new middle class has emerged due to opportunities offered by the private sector (see Box 1.1).

Research has highlighted two other factors that are central to the creation and sustenance of the middle class: (i) stable, secure, well-paid jobs with good benefits; and (ii) a higher incidence of tertiary education. A large portion of the middle class holds a job that provides a stable income in comparison to the largely self-employed poor. Evidence from other countries, such as the US, also points to the importance of education to the growth of the middle class. Countries that have higher levels of educational attainment, with improved health and overall human development, tend to have larger middle-class populations than those with lower human development indicators. In particular, access to tertiary education displays a strong positive correlation with the growth of the middle class (see Figure 1.10). (Also see Chapter 6 for more on the linkage between the middle class and higher levels of education.)

Similarly, countries with more developed infrastructure tend to have larger middle-class populations. This is partly due to the fact that such countries enjoy

BOX 1.1   STYLIZED PROFILES OF THE MIDDLE CLASS IN SELECTED AFRICAN COUNTRIES

Liberia: rebuilding the middle class

The Liberian authorities believe that the country does not yet have a strong middle class. The consensus is that the middle class in Liberia is composed of university graduates and entrepreneurs running small- and medium-sized businesses. The Liberian government is optimistic though about rebuilding the middle class. The country's large diaspora increasingly recognizes the signs of stability needed for a healthy economy to function and is starting to return home, consolidating Liberia's return to peace.

Sierra Leone: professionals make progress after the civil war

Sierra Leone has a small but growing middle class, in spite of the country's volatile history. It is argued that the country's middle class is composed of the educated elite – those with a college education and entrepreneurs in both the formal and informal sectors.

South Africa: a new middle class emerging

After some years of sustained economic growth, South Africa has developed a sizable black middle class, which is estimated to have more spending power than the country's white population. The black middle class has mainly emerged through a government program called Black Economic Empowerment (BEE), which was initiated after the first democratic elections of 1994.

A study carried out by Statistics South Africa, profiling the South African middle-class households and based on a set of aspects of material standard of living, found a modest increase in this segment of the population from 23% to 26% between 1998–2000 and 2004–2006. The material middle-class standards of living include residing in formal housing with the following facilities: water tap in the residence, flush toilet, electricity or gas as a main cooking source, and a telephone landline or cellphone.

Tunisia: companies turning more to the middle class

A number of companies across Africa recognize that their future growth depends on the middle class. The Arab Tunisian Bank (ATB) acknowledges that competition is very tough for the 4% to 10% of the population in the upper class (the rich), so it is focusing more attention on the middle class. ATB is consequently targeting the youth and designing products that suit this group of customers, including expanding the network of banking services.

Nigeria: middle class on the rise

Nigeria's new middle class has emerged alongside an expansion of the private sector in industries such as banking, telecommunications, and services. It is centered in urban areas, particularly Lagos. The purchasing power of the new middle class can be observed at a number of new shopping malls that have recently opened in the country. A study carried out by the National Bureau of Statistics in 2007 estimates that Nigeria's middle class accounts for 30% of the population.

Sources: Meldrum (2010); Estey (2010); Statistics South Africa (2009); Johnson (2010); Brulliard (2010).

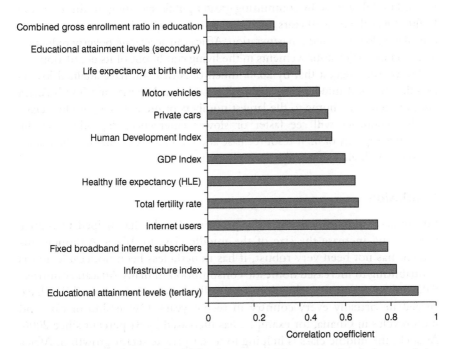

FIGURE 1.10 Correlation of middle-class size with country-level characteristics (sources: AfDB Data Portal and World Bank PovcalNet Database (updated in 2012))

a more competitive economic environment that attracts both foreign direct investment (FDI) and private domestic investment. This helps to create more stable employment and income-generating opportunities, which are taken up by the middle class. As was the case in the US and in Europe, Africa's emerging middle class is likely to assume the traditional role of global consumers. In this respect, they should contribute to a rebalancing of the African economy.

Consumer spending in Africa, primarily by the middle class, proved surprisingly resilient during the global recession of 2008/2009. In 2009, it reached an estimated $1.2 trillion in 2009 PPP US dollars, rising to $1.6 trillion in 2011. Given the continent's consumption expenditure growth over the past 20 years, it is estimated that by 2020 Africa will likely reach $2.6 trillion in PPP annual household consumption expenditure and comprise a sizable proportion of global household consumption.

North Africa exhibits greater spending power because of its larger middle-class population. This provides an opportunity for the subregion to accelerate its shift from export-oriented and investment-led growth to domestic, demand-led growth.

The continued rise of Africa's middle class will require governments to introduce policies that bolster the incomes of those in the floating class, to prevent them from relapsing into poverty. Policymakers can consolidate the upward mobility trend by committing greater public spending to education and health. Over the next 20 years, with the appropriate policies focused on human capital development and job generation, Africa can accelerate poverty reduction and leverage major improvements in the living conditions of its population.

Projections suggest that by 2030, much of Africa will have attained lower-middle-class and middle-class majorities. Ethiopia, Nigeria, and South Africa are expected to be home to the largest numbers of the emerging middle class. Smaller countries will see faster or slower emergence, depending on the absorptive capacity of their resource base and their ability to channel their labor markets into higher value-added supply chains.

Conclusion

Strong economic growth over the past two decades has helped to reduce poverty and increase the size of the middle class in Africa. Although this growth has not been very robust, it has nonetheless been noticeable and is contributing to increased domestic consumption in many African countries. Sales of refrigerators, television sets, cell phones, and automobiles have surged in virtually every country in recent years. Ownership of cars and motorcycles in Ghana, for example, has increased by 81 percent since 2006. As such, the middle class is helping to foster private sector growth in Africa by boosting demand for goods and services supplied by private sector entities.

The middle class is better educated, better informed, and has greater awareness of human rights. It is the main source of the leadership and activism that create and operate many of the non-governmental organizations that call for greater accountability, better governance, and improved public services. This augurs well for the creation of a sociopolitical environment conducive to sustainable future growth and development.

Policies that foster strong, sustained, and shared growth, improved infrastructure, enhanced human resource development, promotion of private sector growth, and increased accountability in public affairs, also promote middle-class growth. Broad policies such as these tend to be more cost-effective and efficient in generating long-term poverty-reducing benefits than those that focus solely on addressing the immediate physical needs of the poor.

Notes

1 See Appendices 1.1 and 1.2 for more details on the methodological approach.
2 On the basis of extrapolation across Africa (44 countries or 91 percent of Africa's population) in 2012.

References

Asian Development Bank (2010). *The Rise of Asia's Middle Class: Key Indicators for Asia and Pacific*. Manila: AsDB.

Banerjee, A., and E. Duflo (2008). 'What is Middle Class about the Middle Classes around the World?' *Journal of Economic Perspectives*, vol. 22, no. 2, pp. 3–28.

Bhalla, S. (2009). *The Middle Class Kingdoms of India and China*. Washington DC: Peterson Institute for International Economics.

Birdsall, N., C. Graham, and S. Pettinato (2000). 'Stuck in the Tunnel: Is Globalization Muddling the Middle?' Working Paper no. 14. Washington DC: Brookings Institute.

Brulliard, N. (2010). 'South Africa's "Black Diamonds" Overtake Whites,' *GlobalPost* (online), May 19.

Datt, G. (1998). 'Computational Tools for Poverty Measurement and Analysis.' Discussion Paper no. 50, Food Consumption and Nutrition Division. Washington DC: IFPRI.

Estey, M. (2010). 'Rebuilding Liberia's Middle Class,' *GlobalPost* (online), May 19.

Johnson, K.S. (2010). 'Sierra Leone's Middle Class Gains Traction,' *Global Post* (online), May 19.

Kakwani, N. (1980). 'On a Class of Poverty Measures,' *Econometrica*, vol. 48, no. 2, pp. 437–446.

Lipset, S.M. (1969). *Political Man*. London: Heinemann.

Mahajan, V. (2009). *Africa Rising: How 900 Million African Consumers Offer More Than You Think*. New Jersey: Pearson Prentice Hall.

McConnell, T. (2010). 'Kenya's Middle Class Challenges Political System,' *GlobalPost* (online), May 19.

Meldrum, A. (2010). 'Africa's Middle Class: Striving to Develop a Continent,' *GlobalPost* (online), May 19.

Merrill Lynch (2010). *World Wealth Report 2009*, Capgemini and Merrill Lynch Global Wealth Management (Bank of America Corp.)

Ncube, M., and A. Shimeles (2013). 'The Making of the Middle Class in Africa: Evidence from DHS Data.' IZA DP no. 7352. Bonn, Germany: Institute for the Study of Labor.

Oduro, A.D., W. Baah-Boateng, and L. Boakye-Yiadom (2011). *Measuring the Gender Asset Gap in Ghana*. Accra: Woeli Publishing Services and University of Ghana.

PENN World Table (2009). Center for International Comparisons at the University of Pennsylvania.

PovcalNet (2010, updated 2012). Online Poverty Analysis Tool. Washington DC: World Bank.

Ramachandran, V., A. Gelb, and M.K. Shah (2009). *Africa's Private Sector: What's Wrong With the Business Environment and What to Do About It.* Washington DC: Center for Global Development.

Ravallion, M. (2009). 'The Developing World's Bulging (but Vulnerable) "Middle Class".' Policy Research Working Paper no. 4816. Washington DC: World Bank.

Ravallion, M., and M. Huppi (1990). 'Poverty and Undernutrition in Indonesia during the 1980s' PPR Working Paper Series no. 286. Washington DC: World Bank.

Ravallion, M., S. Chen, and P. Sangraula (2008). 'Dollar a Day Revisited'. Policy Research Working Paper no. 4620. Washington DC: World Bank.

Statistics South Africa (2009). 'Profiling South African Middle-class Households, 1998–2006.' Report no. 03-03-01. Pretoria: Statistics South Africa.

UNU-WIDER World Income Inequality Database, Version 2.0c (2008). World Institute for Development Economics Research of the United Nations University (UNU-WIDER).

Villasenor, J., and B.C. Arnold (1984). 'The General Quadratic Lorenz Curve.' Technical Report, Mexico City: Colegio de Postgraduados.

Villasenor, J., and B.C. Arnold (1989). 'Elliptical Lorenz Curves,' *Journal of Econometrics*, vol. 40, no. 2, pp. 327–338.

Yale Global Online (2007). A Publication of the Yale Center for the Study of Globalization.

Appendix 1.1: Methodological approach – the Lorenz curve

Step 1: Gini coefficients for many African countries are provided covering a number of years, For some years where they are not available, we estimate them assuming a linear trend between two observations. The Gini coefficient can be written according to the Lorenz curve as follows:

$$Gini = 1 - 2\sum_{i=1}^{6} S_i \tag{1}$$

where S_i is the area of the trapezoid under the Lorenz curve. AC and AE represent the proportions of the population associated with the first and the second poverty lines. Similarly, BC and DE represent the shares of income associated with people at and below the first and the second poverty lines,

Step 2: For each African country and each year, we estimate points F, H, and J corresponding respectively to the income levels of $4/day, $10/day and $20/day, which satisfy the Gini coefficient for a given country and year. This is done by solving for the three points from the constrained optimization system of equations represented by equation (1). Using the trapezoidal method, this corresponds to estimating the area below the Lorenz curve. This system allows us to identify the position of the three points so that the desired equation (1) is satisfied. The system is presented as follows:

$$\begin{cases} S_1 = \int\limits_C^A f(x)\,dx \\ S_2 = \int\limits_E^C f(x)\,dx \\ S_3 = \int\limits_G^E f(x)\,dx \\ S_4 = \int\limits_I^G f(x)\,dx \\ S_5 = \int\limits_K^I f(x)\,dx \\ S_6 = \int\limits_M^K f(x)\,dx \end{cases} \xrightarrow[\text{Trapezoidal method}]{} \begin{cases} S_1 = \dfrac{AC \star BC}{2}; S_1 \text{ is given} \\ S_2 = CE \star \dfrac{(BC + DE)}{2}; S_2 \text{ is given} \\ S_3 = EG \star \dfrac{(DE + FG)}{2} \\ S_4 = GI \star \dfrac{(FG + HI)}{2} \\ S_5 = IK \star \dfrac{(HI + JK)}{2} \\ S_6 = KM \star \dfrac{(JK + LM)}{2} \end{cases}$$

where $f(x)$ is the Lorenz curve,

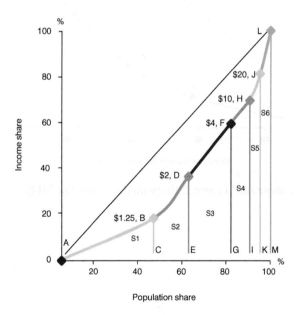

FIGURE A1.1   The Lorenz curve

After identifying the three points for each sample country, the results are aggregated at the Africa level using a double weighting approach – the share of the country population in the total population sample and the share of the country income in the total income sample.

This allows us to generate an Africa Lorenz curve (see Appendix 1.2), which also provides information on the proportion and size of the population falling under certain income levels as well as their income shares.

Appendix 1.2

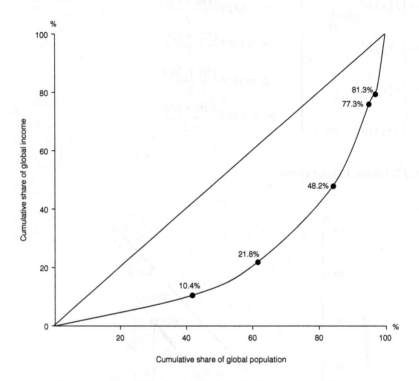

FIGURE A1.2 Lorenz Africa curve, 2010 (with data revised in 2012)

Appendix 1.3

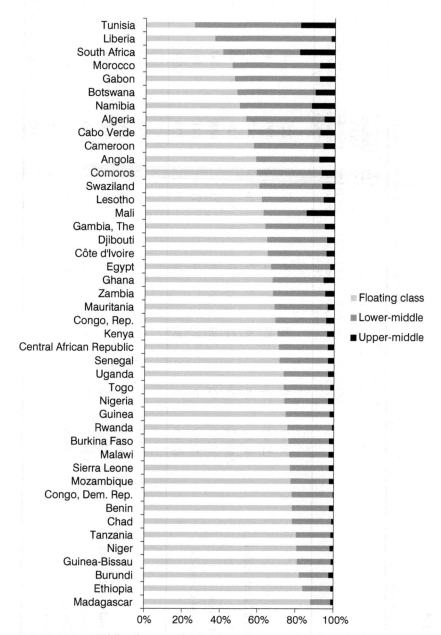

FIGURE A1.3   Middle-class distribution by subcategory in selected African countries (sources: AfDB Data Portal and World Bank PovcalNet Database (updated in 2012))

Appendix 1.4

TABLE A1.1 Summary of population and class size, by global region (1990 and 2008, based on household survey means)

Region	Total pop (million)	Population (%)			Aggregate annual income/expenditures (2005 PPP $ billion)			
		Poor (<$2 per person per day)	Middle ($2–$20 per person per day)	High (>$20 per person per day)	Poor (<$2 per person per day)	Middle ($2–$20 per person per day)	High (>$20 per person per day)	Total
1990								
Africa*	584.0	69	27	4	77	225	64	366
SSA	274.8	75	24	1	70	109	44	224
Middle East and North Africa	162.3	18	80	2	16	247	39	303
Developing Asia	2,692.2	79	21	0	843	721	42	1,605
Developing Europe	352.3	12	84	4	23	638	141	802
Latin America and Caribbean	352.5	20	71	9	31	641	480	1,153
OECD	639.0	0	24	76	0	735	9,636	10,371
2008								
Africa*	910	62	33	5	110	449	121	680
SSA	393.5	66	33	1	100	206	69	376
Middle East and North Africa	212.8	12	86	3	14	365	66	445
Developing Asia	3,383.7	43	56	1	696	3,285	350	4,331
Developing Europe	356.6	2	87	11	4	974	425	1,403
Latin America and Caribbean	454.2	10	77	13	22	1,008	924	1,953
OECD	685.4	0	16	84	0	542	12,617	13,159

Sources: PovcalNet Database, AfDB Statistics Department estimates for Africa; Asian Development Bank for Asia statistics.

Notes (regional definitions):

Africa = All countries without Eritrea, Libya, Mauritius, São Tomé and Príncipe, Seychelles, Somalia, Sudan, Zimbabwe.

SSA = Botswana, Burkina Faso, Burundi, Cameroon, Central African Republic, Ethiopia, Gambia, Ghana, Guinea-Bissau, Kenya, Lesotho, Madagascar, Malawi, Mali, Mauritania, Mozambique, Niger, Rwanda, Senegal, Sierra Leone, South Africa, Swaziland, Tanzania, Uganda.

Middle East and North Africa = Algeria, Djibouti, Egypt, Iran, Jordan, Morocco, Tunisia, Yemen.

Developing Asia = Armenia, Azerbaijan, Bangladesh, Cambodia, People's Republic of China, Georgia, India, Indonesia, Kazakhstan, Kyrgyz Republic, Lao People's Democratic Republic, Malaysia, Mongolia, Nepal, Pakistan, Philippines, Sri Lanka, Tajikistan, Thailand, Turkmenistan, Uzbekistan, Viet Nam.

Developing Europe = Albania, Belarus, Bosnia and Herzegovina, Bulgaria, Latvia, Lithuania, Macedonia, Moldova, Poland, Romania, Russian Federation, Turkey, Ukraine.

Latin America and Caribbean = Argentina, Brazil, Chile, Colombia, Costa Rica, Dominican Republic, Ecuador, El Salvador, Guatemala, Honduras, Jamaica, Mexico, Nicaragua, Peru, Uruguay, Venezuela.

OECD = Austria, Belgium, Denmark, Finland, France, Germany, Greece, Ireland, Italy, Korea, Luxembourg, Netherlands, Norway, Portugal, Slovak Republic, Spain, Sweden, United Kingdom, United States.

Appendix 1.5

TABLE A1.2 Middle–class subcategories as proportion of total population, 2008 (% and millions)

Countries	Floating class		Lower-middle class		Upper-middle class		Total	
	% of pop	Pop (million)	% of pop	Pop (million)	% of pop	Pop (million)	% of pop	Pop (million)
Algeria	40.5	14.5	31.5	11.3	4.2	1.5	76.2	27.3
Angola	18.2	3.3	10.3	1.9	2.5	0.5	31.1	5.7
Benin	19.2	1.7	4.8	0.4	0.6	0.1	24.6	2.2
Botswana	21.5	0.4	18.5	0.4	4.5	0.1	44.5	0.9
Burkina Faso	20.0	2.9	5.6	0.8	0.6	0.1	26.2	3.8
Burundi	5.4	0.5	1.0	0.1	0.2	0.0	6.6	0.6
Cameroon	39.6	7.8	25.3	5.0	4.1	0.8	68.9	13.5
Cabo Verde	31.3	0.2	21.9	0.1	4.4	0.0	57.6	0.3
Central African Rep.	14.1	0.6	5.1	0.2	0.6	0.0	19.9	0.8
Chad	13.1	1.4	3.4	0.4	0.2	0.0	16.7	1.8
Comoros	20.6	0.1	12.0	0.1	2.4	0.0	35.0	0.2
Congo, Dem. Rep.	3.8	2.2	1.0	0.6	0.0	0.0	4.8	2.9
Congo, Rep.	17.6	0.7	6.8	0.3	1.1	0.0	25.4	1.0
Côte d'Ivoire	34.6	6.4	16.5	3.0	2.2	0.4	53.3	9.8
Djibouti	37.7	0.3	18.3	0.1	2.3	0.0	58.4	0.5
Egypt	56.2	42.4	26.1	19.7	1.9	1.4	84.2	63.6
Ethiopia	24.6	20.2	4.3	3.5	0.4	0.3	29.3	24.0
Gabon	37.0	0.5	35.4	0.5	6.3	0.1	78.6	1.2
Gambia, The	27.7	0.4	13.6	0.2	2.2	0.0	43.4	0.7
Ghana	32.3	7.5	12.8	3.0	2.7	0.6	47.8	11.0
Guinea	22.7	2.4	7.0	0.7	0.7	0.1	30.4	3.1
Guinea-Bissau	17.8	0.3	3.9	0.1	0.3	0.0	22.0	0.3
Kenya	22.8	8.9	8.5	3.3	1.2	0.5	32.5	12.6

Lesotho	22.9	0.5	12.1	0.2	2.2	0.0	37.2	0.7
Liberia	1.9	0.1	3.1	0.1	0.1	0.0	5.1	0.2
Madagascar	7.5	1.5	0.9	0.2	0.1	0.0	8.6	1.7
Malawi	11.4	1.6	3.1	0.4	0.4	0.1	14.9	2.1
Mali	13.6	1.8	4.9	0.7	3.2	0.4	21.7	2.9
Mauritania	35.6	1.2	14.5	0.5	1.8	0.1	51.9	1.8
Morocco	38.6	12.0	39.0	12.1	6.6	2.1	84.2	26.1
Mozambique	14.1	3.2	3.7	0.8	0.4	0.1	18.2	4.2
Namibia	22.9	0.5	17.5	0.4	5.6	0.1	46.0	1.0
Niger	20.0	3.0	4.3	0.6	0.5	0.1	24.7	3.7
Nigeria	11.6	17.5	3.6	5.4	0.5	0.7	15.6	23.7
Rwanda	11.8	1.2	3.6	0.4	0.1	0.0	15.6	1.6
Senegal	30.1	3.7	10.7	1.3	1.3	0.2	42.2	5.2
Sierra Leone	16.8	0.9	4.4	0.2	0.5	0.0	21.7	1.2
South Africa	24.2	12.1	24.0	12.0	11.0	5.5	59.1	29.6
Swaziland	22.1	0.3	12.1	0.1	2.4	0.0	36.6	0.4
Tanzania	9.8	4.1	2.2	0.9	0.2	0.1	12.1	5.2
Togo	27.5	1.7	9.1	0.5	0.7	0.0	37.4	2.2
Tunisia	23.4	2.4	50.9	5.3	16.4	1.7	90.7	9.4
Uganda	23.8	7.6	7.6	2.4	1.0	0.3	32.3	10.3
Zambia	10.3	1.3	4.2	0.5	0.7	0.1	15.2	1.9
TOTAL	63.1	203.8	31.3	101.0	5.6	18.2	100.0	323.0

Source: Authors' estimates based on updated data in the World Bank's PovCal Database.

Notes: Floating class = $2–$4; lower-middle = $4–$10 and upper-middle = $10–$20.

2

THE POLITICAL ECONOMY OF THE AFRICAN MIDDLE CLASS

Michael Lofchie

Introduction

Beginning with Aristotle's *Politics*, written in the fourth century before the Common Era, and extending through Seymour M. Lipset's post-World War II classic, *Political Man*, political theorists have viewed the middle class as an indispensable basis for democratic politics and the social anchor for democratic institutions (Aristotle, 1943; Lipset, 1969). The reasons for this conviction are apparent. Middle classes tended to have an interest in political moderation; because they have a material stake in a stable society, they are the ultimate rational actors. Their policy preferences support a political process that represents their interests while maintaining civil peace. They situate themselves midway between the conservatism of the well-to-do and the redistributive motivations of the poor. They withhold support from those who would maintain the existing order at all costs, just as they reject parties and movements that pursue socio-economic transformations at the expense of social peace. As a result, middle-class political involvement helps institutionalize democratic norms and procedures.

Economists are no less emphatic about the contribution of the middle class. Although a society may experience economic growth without a middle class, questions arise about its sustainability. Middle classes are the wellspring of entrepreneurship, innovation and accumulation for investment. Middle-class consumerism is a principal component of the demand side of the supply–demand equation, and middle-class businesses are important in providing the goods and services that satisfy consumer demand. Members of the middle class buying from and selling to one another form the heart of a buoyant market economy. This is why the early development economists believed that sustainable growth could not be based on a single sector and insisted on the importance of demand complementarities across multiple sectors (Chenery,

1979). They were referring to the demand reciprocities created when people in different sectors of an economy buy from and sell to each other. This pattern also provides collateral political benefits such as a greater sense of social cohesion. If diverse social groups occupying different positions in an economy share the gains of economic growth, this helps to dispel the notion that one group can gain only if others lose.

Experience from elsewhere suggests that growth of the middle class is the key to Africa's future. The vital question is whether Africa has a middle class large enough and affluent enough to support democratic institutions and sustain growth of the market economy and share the growth with other segments of society. If Africa develops a strong middle class, whose expansion pulls people out of poverty and into a life of greater security and comfort, this will vastly improve the continent's prospects for democratic politics. If the middle class does not develop or develops in ways that accentuate differences between economic winners and losers, the political processes of African countries could be susceptible to turbulence.

Two narratives

There are no easy answers. The World Bank economists, Shantayan Devarajan and Wolfgang Fengler (2013), have shown that current economic trends have given rise to two narratives about the continent's long-term prospects. The first is the development narrative, or 'Africa Rising.' The second is the poverty narrative, sometimes labelled Afro-pessimism. According to the former, a decade or more of economic growth has begun to yield benefits in reducing poverty and alleviating inequality. 'Since 1996, the average poverty rate in Sub-Saharan African countries has fallen by about one percentage point a year, and between 2005 and 2008, the portion of Africans in the region living on less than $1.25 a day fell for the first time, from 52% to 48%' (Devarajan and Fengler, 2013: 69). This figure is expected to drop further to 36 percent by 2015 (ECA, AU, AfDB, and UNDP, 2013). The Africa Rising narrative also calls attention to other trends such as the rapid increase in foreign investment, which is an indicator of growing international confidence in Africa's economic future. This narrative also directs attention to social trends including increased secondary school enrollment, declining fertility rates and longer life-expectancy. These trends have raised the ratio of working adults to dependants, and the greater overall security of life has encouraged more domestic investment in farms and businesses. The result is that numerous African countries are experiencing a rapid increase in per capita income; by 2025, many will enjoy an average per capita income of $1,000 per year, which will classify them as middle income.

The Afro-pessimist narrative presents a more discouraging scenario. The core of this narrative is that Africa's recent economic growth is largely the product of a commodities boom, whose sustainability and potential to transform society remain in question. This narrative points out that the recent improvement in growth enjoyed by many African countries is attributable to soaring exports of high-value primary commodities such as oil, natural gas, coal and metal ores that are scarce in global markets. The concern is that the wealth generated by these exports has not been re-invested in sectors, such as manufacturing and agriculture, which have a potential to generate employment opportunities and rising incomes. For most African countries, the manufacturing sector still accounts for the same small share of GDP as it did in the 1970s (World Bank, 1981). Consequently, poverty rates have remained high even in countries that have registered improvements in economic growth. According to this scenario, Africa's failure to use its new-found wealth to promote economic diversification has contributed to social inequality, because it has widened the economic disparity between growing sectors and stagnant sectors of national economies. If this pattern predominates, economic growth may not provide a solid basis for democratic politics.

The structure of an economy is of pivotal importance. An influential recent study of the relationship between economic growth and democracy provides a further warning about the effects of a narrow dependence on the strong performance of a single sector such as commodity exports. In *Why Nations Fail*, Acemoglu and Robinson (2012) distinguish between 'extractive' institutions and 'inclusive' institutions. These authors believe that in economies where wealth is narrowly based on a single sector such as the extraction of high-value commodities, governing elites will create political institutions whose purpose is to perpetuate their control of that sector. In such countries, political institutions will tend toward the oligarchic and authoritarian, because political leaders will seek ways to limit opposition to their rule by those who want to share the benefits of that sector more widely. The Acemoglu–Robinson research shows that the evolutionary pattern of the middle class is as important as its size and purchasing power. If an economy is evolving toward greater diversification, a larger portion of the middle class will have its economic basis outside the state, thereby affording a better opportunity for independent organizations to pressure governing elites for inclusive institutions.

The old middle class: 1960s–1980s

The presence of a middle class is nothing new in African societies. However, when African countries first attained independence, the middle class was limited in size and even more limited in its ability to influence the political process. It was neither large enough nor sufficiently autonomous to foster and sustain democratic political environments. Under colonial rule, Africans experienced difficulty in rising to middle-class positions within and outside government. Limited educational opportunities and deliberate discrimination prevented Africans from gaining entry into the higher levels of colonial bureaucracies. As a result, the bureaucracies of the post-colonial governments were still heavily populated with expatriate civil servants from the colonizing countries. What existed in the way of an entrepreneurial middle class outside government was often composed of individuals from non-indigenous communities such as Asians in eastern Africa, Lebanese in western Africa, and Europeans in southern Africa.

Hourglass structure

The social structures of post-colonial societies resembled an hourglass. The top of the hourglass consisted of the leadership of the nationalist movements, generally led by a small stratum of individuals who had managed to obtain university degrees and risen to professional positions, principally teachers, academics, journalists and attorneys. There was a narrow middle stratum of African professionals and entrepreneurs. The bottom of the hourglass consisted of the rank-and-file membership of Africa's nationalist movements, mostly workers and farmers who comprised the overwhelming majority of African societies. Although this pattern began to change from the moment of independence, the hourglass image has persisted in both popular and academic depictions of African societies.

First steps

After independence, social expectations were high. The first step in the process of creating an African middle class began almost immediately, as governments took steps to Africanize their civil bureaucracies. The white-collar bureaucratic positions of departing colonial administrators were filled by Africans, who quickly rose to become the accountants, office managers and principal secretaries in government offices. Independent Africa's early middle class consisted of the tens of thousands of local people recruited to occupy those positions and to become the teachers, policemen, clerks and payroll administrators in new governments. Expanding educational opportunities also created pathways to professional careers for African doctors, attorneys, professors and engineers, all of whom joined the middle class, expanding its size and increasing its occupational diversity.

Import-substituting industrialization

The second source of growth in the post-independence middle class was widespread adoption by many African countries of an economic strategy of centrally planned and state-sponsored industrialization. Many governments implemented some variant of this strategy, which was known globally as import-substituting industrialization (ISI). The idea was to attain economic growth by investing in the creation of domestic industries that would produce a range of goods that had mostly been imported. The ISI strategy expanded the post-independence middle class to the state-based industrial sector, which had its own needs for managerial and technical personnel. In addition to the industrial workers recruited to work on assembly lines, the new industries required legions of accountants, personnel managers and technicians, as well as financial administrators who could interact with the government ministries that were coordinating the process and providing the necessary resources such as investment capital and protection from imports.

The ISI strategy also provided an impetus for the further expansion of government bureaucracy. Centrally planned industrialization meant that government ministries involved in the industrial process had to expand to play an enhanced economic role. Among the many ministries that grew as a direct result of the ISI strategy were ministries of planning, which were responsible for creating the detailed blueprint of a planned economy, and ministries of finance, which expanded to take on the burden of imposing new taxes and transferring tax revenues to the planned industries. Ministries of trade also grew exponentially, because they were responsible for devising and implementing the policy of protectionism; ministries of industry implemented the construction of the new factories and supervised their operation. Other ministries also grew in proportion to their added functions in a planned economy. To finance the expansion of government and to raise the capital for state investment in the new industries, African governments imposed heavy taxes on the agricultural sector, principally agricultural exports. The ISI strategy was not multi-sectoral: it favored large-scale industry over small-holder agriculture.

Political weakness

Both the state-based and industry-based middle classes were politically weak. Employment in government or in government-sponsored industries made political activism difficult. Many civil servants had obtained their appointments through some form of political favoritism, and even those who had risen through the ranks meritoriously were deterred by fear of losing their government positions. The managerial and technical strata in state-sponsored industries had similar constraints. The industrial firms that employed them depended on the government for capital, trade protection and a host of other subsidies, including preferred access to the banking system. Because the government had a major voice in who was hired and who was not, those who rose to middle-class positions had a disincentive to oppose the government in power. Sources of vulnerability were numerous. During the post-colonial era, many civil servants, especially those in the upper ranks, received substantial benefits including government housing. Loss of one's position, therefore, could mean loss of housing and other benefits for oneself and one's family. The decline of democracy during the first decades of independence did not reflect the absence of a middle class; it rather reflected the limited room for maneuver of middle classes based in government institutions.

The principal political characteristic of Africa's post-independence middle classes was their inability to sustain the democratic project that accompanied the transition to independence. The middle class was a hapless bystander as government after government transitioned to one form or another of autocratic rule. Some governments were overthrown in military coups; others resorted to authoritarian measures to maintain power. For much of independent Africa, this pattern lasted for more than a generation. During that period, many governments maintained their stability by restricting political opposition and stifling dissent. Some exploited ethnic identification to divide their opponents, thereby giving Africa its reputation as a continent where ethnic rivalries are paramount, because they provide a basis of political identity and partisan affiliation.

Turning point

The economic turning point was the failure of the ISI strategy, which was brought to an end during the economic liberalization that began in the early 1980s. The reasons for this failure and its effects have been explored elsewhere, particularly in the World Bank's classic study, *Accelerated Development in Sub-Saharan Africa* (World Bank, 1981), widely known as the Berg Report after its principal author, Elliot Berg of the University of Michigan. The Berg Report identified two economic facts. The first was the high cost of the failed experiment in centrally planned industrialization. By the end of the 1970s, most of the planned industries had all but ceased to function, producing goods of inferior quality at a small fraction of their installed capacity. The second was that the costs of industrial failure had largely been borne by the agricultural sectors of African countries, which bore a heavy tax burden to finance industrial growth. The effects of excessive agricultural taxes were readily apparent in Africa's declining share of world markets for exportable agricultural commodities and in the faltering performance of the food-producing sector. Africa was on its way to becoming an aid-dependent and food-dependent continent. The social effect of the failed industrial policy was the impoverishment of Africa's small-holder farmers, who had been subject to the heaviest tax burden.

By the end of the 1970s, when the industrial experiment was brought to an end, Africa's manufacturing and agricultural sectors were in poor condition. Each needed re-capitalization and reforms that would promote economic recovery. The difficult economic conditions that prevailed during that period provide the historical underpinning of the Afro-pessimist narrative. Many of the free-market reform policies set in place since the mid-1980s were aimed at undoing the effects of the ISI strategy, which had absorbed and dissipated untold resources in a vain effort to build large-scale industries. One of the after-effects of the ISI era is a lingering bias against trade restrictions as a policy means of stimulating economic growth.

Maintaining political stability

Referring to the socio-economic consequences of centrally planned industrialization, Robert Bates famously asked, 'Why should reasonable men adopt policies that had harmful [economic] consequences for the societies they governed?' (Bates, 1981). Whatever its deficiencies as a strategy for economic growth, ISI had been kept in place because it conferred advantages as a political strategy – it provided a basis for maintaining urban peace. Confronted with a choice between rural and urban political dissent, governments invariably choose the former. Rural populations face inherent difficulties in mobilizing for political action. They are spread over vast areas and are located at a distance from capital cities. Urban populations do not suffer these constraints. As a result, they pose a greater threat to political stability. The political benefit of the ISI strategy was that it made it easier for governments to stabilize themselves by reducing the economic hardships of their urban middle classes, even if this was obtained by imposing heavy costs on the rural population.

This was one reason for the political quiescence of urban civil servants; they benefited from the income transfers financed by taxes on agricultural producers. The governments that pursued the ISI strategy – the overwhelming majority of the newly independent countries – had done so by taxing agriculture to raise the financial wherewithal for industrial investment. This constituted a transfer of wealth from small-holder farmers to urban residents, especially the middle-class employees of the new industrial firms and expanding ministries. Members of the urban middle class were hardly economic winners because they suffered many of the economic hardships that affected everyone. But owing to the transfer of wealth from agriculture to government and industry, they did not suffer as badly as farmers.

Independent Africa governments, in other words, had increased their middle classes largely through the expansion of government bureaucracy and, therefore, in a manner that encouraged political acquiescence. Corruption provided an additional means of ensuring compliance. Government leaders were aware of their vulnerability if public sector officials turned against them and they were unable to control the situation, thereby facilitating a pattern of civil service corruption that persists to this day. Middle-class civil servants hunkered down, did their jobs and used a variety of economic strategies to maintain their position as a better-off social stratum.

Hidden from view

For several reasons, the relative well-being of the post-colonial middle class did not appear to evoke political discontent among poorer Africans. One was that many members of the middle class seemed to be suffering the effects of economic decline alongside everyone else. Scarcities of imported goods and price inflation made it difficult for members of the middle class to engage in the conspicuous consumption that has become a prominent feature of middle-class life today. Another reason was that the relative well-being of the middle class was hidden from view by the spatial configuration of capital cities. This limited the opportunity for poorer members of society to become aware of how well off the middle and upper strata of their societies really were. Nairobi offers an illustration of this pattern. The most affluent suburbs – Muthaiga, Westlands and Karen – were not only at some distance from the central city, but at an even greater distance from the slum areas such as Mathari Valley, Eastleigh and Kibera where the city's poorest residents lived. Government ministers commuted to work from Muthaiga and Westlands. The custodial personnel who serviced the office buildings and the bus drivers who transported them there commuted from Eastleigh and Mathari Valley. Numerous other African cities replicated that pattern. In Lagos, the wealth of the residents of Ikoyi Island was geographically insulated from the vast majority of urban residents who lived in the densely populated communities north of Lagos Lagoon. Because different social classes lived in physically separate neighborhoods, exposure to middle-class affluence was not a part of the daily experience of poorer Africans.

Effects of economic reform: post-1980

On the eve of economic reform, in the mid-1980s, Africa's white-collar middle class was mostly confined to public sector employees and was barely a middle class at all, owing to the effects of the continent's economic decline. Mid-level employees in private sector institutions such as banks, accounting firms and small service companies were also in a weak position because the government was frequently the largest client of the firms that employed them. Moreover the government was often the largest depositor in the banks, the principal client of companies that provided accounting and audit services, and the major source of contracts for the firms that provided office equipment and furniture, and laundering and catering services.

Entrepreneurs

The post-independence strategy of planned industrialization had at least brought about an increase in the size of the managerial middle class. It had the opposite effect, however, on the entrepreneurial section of the middle class. *Accelerated Development* (World Bank, 1981) and similar studies paid less attention to this outcome than to the effects of ISI on agriculture. This omission is regrettable because the backstory of Africa's entrepreneurial class was a generation of arrested development. The continent has always had entrepreneurs who engaged in the production and marketing of goods. The entrepreneurial stratum consisted of the countless firms that converted used tires into shoes, fabric into garments, sugar cane and flavoring into soft drinks, millet and sorghum into beer and other alcoholic beverages, local tobacco into crude cigarettes, and small workshops that produced furniture, stoves and cooking utensils. There were firms that converted oil drums into charcoal braziers, storage containers and agricultural implements. Many Africans earned their income through retail entrepreneurship, setting up roadside stands to sell food items, watches, kerosene, batteries, soap and medications and whatever other goods could find an on-going demand even under difficult economic circumstances.

Africa's small-scale entrepreneurs always had the skills and motivation to become large-scale entrepreneurs. However, the strategy of planned industrialization suppressed much of this activity. Small, under-capitalized local firms had difficulty competing against heavily capitalized state industries that enjoyed a host of subsidies including monopoly status, overvalued exchange rates, and protection from foreign competition. The state-sponsored firms also enjoyed preferred access to government-guaranteed bank loans as well as requirements that compelled the banks to privilege industries that had government sponsorship. The willingness of African governments to subsidize industrial firms by funding their deficits out of general tax revenues further tilted the economic playing field against small-scale private firms. Local entrepreneurs were caught between two economic forces, each of which enjoyed powerful advantages. They had difficulty competing against the state industrial enterprises that benefited from taxpayer-provided subsidies and protections, and they had equal difficulty competing against the flow of smuggled goods brought into the country to satisfy local demand that could not be satisfied by the failing, state-based industrial firms. Sheer survival under adverse conditions was the great achievement of the African entrepreneurial class during the post-independence era.

All of this changed during the economic and political reforms. The emphasis on market-based development, which began with the structural adjustment programs of the mid-1980s, cleared the path for the formation and rapid expansion of a private-sector-based middle class. This class is not constrained by dependence on government for employment or job security. The political reforms of the 1990s that restored multi-party systems and open elections in the vast majority of countries gave the new private sector middle class unprecedented opportunity to use its economic freedom as a basis of political leverage. When economic liberalization moved the state industrial monopolies out of the way, this cleared the path for Africa's entrepreneurial tradition to reassert itself.

The new African middle class

The foundation document for an understanding of Africa's new middle class is the 2011 report of the African Development Bank, *The Middle of the Pyramid: Dynamics of the Middle Class in Africa* (hereafter, *Pyramid*) (AfDB, 2011). This study offers compelling evidence of a rapidly growing middle class across the continent. Although the size and purchasing power of this class might vary greatly from one country to the next, the middle class has become a substantial portion of the continent's population. 'By 2010, the middle class had risen to 34% of Africa's population – or nearly 350 million people – up from about 126 million or 27% in 1980, 27% in 1990 and about 220 million people or 27% in 2000.'[1] Because the AfDB (2011) definition of middle class included individuals with a daily per capita expenditure that ranged from $2 to $20, the disposable wealth of the lowest and highest strata of the middle class varied correspondingly.

Social heterogeneity

The social heterogeneity of the new African middle class makes precise measurement difficult. In the most general terms, the African middle class can be subdivided into two broad social categories: those who hold salaried positions, i.e. the 'white-collar' portion, and small-scale business entrepreneurs. The salaried segment further subdivides into public sector and private sector employees. The income range in all these categories is large. The white-collar portion, for example, ranges from low-paid receptionists and clerks in government offices to a rapidly growing and increasingly affluent stratum of private sector professionals, including accountants, personnel managers and information technicians in large private firms such as banks, insurance companies and brokerage houses. In Africa, as everywhere, higher education offers access to monetary rewards. Africans who attain degrees in business, education or public administration, for example, can expect significantly higher salaries and levels of disposable income than those who do not.

Middle-class strata

The AfDB (2011) study fueled a debate about the most appropriate imagery to portray the changes taking place in African social structures. To describe the pyramidal image, the AfDB defined the middle class in broad terms, dividing it into three strata: the *upper* middle class (disposable income of $10 to $20 per day); the *lower* middle class ($4 to $10); and a third or *'floating'* stratum ($2 to $4). The authors of the AfDB study noted that the floating tier represented perhaps as much as 60 percent of the total middle-class population – about 180 million people. These individuals and their families were close to the poverty level. Their vulnerability to events such as the death of a family member, climate shocks, and economic recession might cause them to drop back into the poor category. The *Pyramid* study showed that if the floating class were included, the middle class would constitute more than a third of the population of African countries; without this social stratum, the middle class would constitute only about 13 percent. It was to be expected that this analytical approach would stimulate debate, especially in a region where the persistence of the Afro-pessimist metaphor, which presents a more binary imagery of elite wealth and mass poverty, obscured important social changes that were taking place.

Some of this controversy is misplaced. The AfDB's income definition of the middle class is consistent with an established scholarly tradition that defined the middle classes of developing countries in a similar manner. The economists, Abhijit Banerjee and Esther Duflo, who conducted an income-based survey of middle-class families in 13 developing countries, employed a similar definition. They defined the lower middle class as families with a disposable income of $2 to $4 per day, and upper middle-class families as those with a disposable income of $6 to $10 per day (Banerjee and Duflo, 2008). Their key finding was that disposable income of $2 per day is a threshold above which a family's lifestyle begins to improve significantly. Compared with the poor (less than $2 per day), families above that level spend a smaller share of family income on food and a larger share on health care. They also enjoy better housing with more rooms even though family size may be smaller. In addition, their houses have amenities such as tap water, electricity and an indoor latrine. Upper middle-income families also begin spending a portion of their income on entertainment items such as a television set. Perhaps most important, the economic security afforded by middle-class income levels gives them a greater sense of control over their economic future. This frame of mind encourages them to build their own careers and provide opportunities for their children. The three African countries included in the Banerjee and Duflo research (Côte d'Ivoire, South Africa, and Tanzania) conformed closely to these patterns.

Changing image

The *Pyramid* study has had several important effects. The first was that it began to change the imagery of binary social structures and economic stagnation. From having been seen as a region of irremediable poverty and seemingly unending economic dependency, where foreign public assistance provided the margin of difference between starvation and survival, Africa's new image is a continent where rapid economic growth and middle-class purchasing power have created profitable opportunities for international investors. The change of approach in the international media is striking. In its long-remembered January 16, 1984 issue, *Time* magazine proclaimed 'Africa's Woes: Coups, Conflict and Corruption.' Mindful of the disastrous effects of 1970s drought, some observers added a fourth 'c,' climate, to the list. As recently as the spring of 2000, *The Economist*'s writers had spoken of 'Hopeless Africa,' a place where 'brutality, despotism and corruption exist everywhere' (*The Economist*, 2000).

Only 11 years later, *The Economist* described Africa as 'the hopeful continent.' It observed that 'some fundamental numbers are moving in the right direction... Africa now has a fast-growing middle class: according to Standard Bank, around 60 million Africans have an income of $3,000 a year, and 100 million will in 2015' (*The Economist*, 2011).

Over the past decade, six of the world's ten fastest-growing countries were African. In eight of the past ten years, Africa has grown faster than East Asia including Japan. Even allowing for the knock-on effect of the northern hemisphere's slowdown, the IMF expects Africa to grow by 6% this year and nearly 6% in 2012.

(*The Economist*, 2011)

Although failed states and civil strife remain all too common, a new Africa has emerged in the world's field of vision. The new political reality consists of multi-party elections and successful democratic transitions. By drawing attention to the new middle class, the *Pyramid* study demonstrated Africa's normalcy, helping to dispel the negative imagery that has cloaked the continent since the era of slavery and colonialism. The thriving economic conditions that sustain this class have induced the world to see Africa as a region of lucrative investment opportunities, skilled professionals, dynamic entrepreneurs and globally connected businesses.

New dynamic

The AfDB's three-tier approach has been endorsed by several influential groups. These include economists, who are principally concerned with the trajectory of consumer demand; international investment firms seeking opportunities for their clients; and globally oriented businesses motivated to find new markets for their goods. All agree that a powerful new dynamic is underway – growth of the marketplace and the rise of African entrepreneurship within that marketplace. Even the most casual visitors to Africa can corroborate this trend. The Oshodi market along the road to Lagos airport is legendary for the vibrant entrepreneurialism that thrives there. In African cities as dispersed as Dakar, Accra, Johannesburg, Dar es Salaam and Nairobi, markets have expanded at a rapid pace. The international accounting firm Deloitte, whose clientele includes numerous firms that offer goods and services in developing countries, has taken the position that contrary to widespread perceptions, two-thirds of Africa's GDP growth results from increasing consumption of goods and services.

In the markets from Senegal to Swaziland, new traders are setting up mini 'supermarket' stalls selling everything from mobile-phone Sim cards and phone credit vouchers to microscopic 30g sachets of Sunlight and Omo washing powder that appeal to consumers with cramped homes and cramped budgets.[2]

In many African countries, the purchase of relatively expensive consumer goods such as electronic items, home appliances and automobiles has increased dramatically during the past decade. Internet access in Africa is rising at a faster pace than on any other continent.

Long-term implications

The difficulty in assessing the long-term implications of these trends is that seemingly contradictory economic tendencies can coexist. When an economy is expanding, a rising and prosperous middle class may be taking its place in the sun, even as the share of wealth accruing to the wealthiest increases and poverty deepens in absolute and relative terms. Although the emergent middle class attests to the spreading benefits of Africa's economic boom, the percentage of Africans considered poor remains large. Theoreticians who attach importance to the stabilizing value of a growing middle class tend to insist that it must not only grow in absolute numbers, but also become a larger proportion of the population, to the point of altering a country's social structure. Urgent questions arise. The first is whether middle-class growth is drawing people out of poverty in ways that lower the prevalence of poverty and reduce the income gap between social strata. The second is whether the new middle class has its economic base in the productive sectors of an economy, as well as its consumption side. Does the new middle class derive its income principally from the proceeds of the commodities boom, or is it a reflection of more widely diversified economic growth?

Private sector growth

Much more research will be required to provide authoritative answers to these questions. However, it is possible to begin creating a broad profile of Africa's new middle class. Its major characteristics differ substantially from those of the post-colonial era. The principal difference may be its sheer size. Today's middle class is larger in numerical terms, and depending on which definition is chosen, it may also be larger as a percentage of the population. The second difference is that today's middle class has a solid basis in private sector growth. Whereas the post-colonial middle class consisted overwhelmingly of government employees and the employees of parastatal corporations that were governmental entities, the recent expansion of the middle class has a solid base in private sector diversification. This applies to both the white-collar middle class, who derive their incomes from salaried positions, and to the entrepreneurial middle class – business owners in a host of activities including farming and other productive enterprises, service industries such as banking, finance and information technology, and retail sales. In addition, the upper portion of the new middle class enjoys a level of prosperity and purchasing power on a par with its counterparts in Europe and Asia.

The example of Ghana

Ghana is an example of continent-wide trends. Private ownership of cars and motorcycles increased more than 80 percent during the past five years, and in many rural communities the motorcycle has begun to replace the bicycle as the primary means of transport. More than 95 percent of households have at least one mobile phone, and the mean number of phones per household is three. Several private airlines now provide service between various parts of the country; domestic air travel has increased more than fivefold in the last few years (*Financial Times*, 2012). Opportunities for higher education have been expanded by the establishment of a number of private colleges that offer undergraduate and graduate training. There are several indicators of growing confidence in the sustainability of Ghana's middle class. One is the return of skilled Ghanaians who had been pursuing their professions abroad, including medical doctors, designers and engineers, many of whom have capital to invest in private ventures. Another is the willingness of banks to offer long-term mortgage loans for home purchases, a signal of confidence in the security of middle-class incomes (Asunka, 2013). Perhaps most important, the expansion of middle-class opportunity does not appear to be confined to a single sector or subsector of the economy; it encompasses several important sectors including banking, financial services, telecommunications and construction. Ghana has also begun to develop a plan for setting aside a portion of its oil export revenues for development after the oil reserves decline.[3]

Informal sector

Africa's new middle class has a solid footing in the proliferation of private sector enterprises that are diverse in size and in the nature of the goods or services they provide. Many operate in the informal sector. This segment of African economies has long eluded precise definition, exact measurement and government efforts at monitoring, regulation and taxation. If a broadly inclusive definition is employed – any business that operates without fixed walls – the concept of informal sector entrepreneur may well describe the economic behavior of a majority of Africans. Farmers who sell a portion of their goods by the roadside are not only agriculturists, but also retail entrepreneurs. A typical informal sector enterprise may be as small as an improvised kiosk selling food items, batteries or cigarettes, or as large as a proto-manufacturing enterprise producing farm implements, kitchen utensils, furniture or apparel. Many provide valuable services such as vehicle or computer repair and home maintenance. There are countless examples. If those engaged in illegal activities such as smuggling, poaching, petty theft, corruption, drug sales and sex workers were included, the number of informal entrepreneurs would increase still further. Many Africans use the proceeds of their informal sector activities as a source of capital to enter the formal economy.

Economists have found it difficult to assess the magnitude of Africa's informal sector and, therefore, its exact contribution to the GDP of individual countries. If informal sector GDP were added to formal sector GDP, the real size of African economies would be much larger, GDP per capita would be considerably higher, and it would be less difficult to explain the thriving commercial activity that has sprung up everywhere. Estimates of the informal sector contribution to GDP vary greatly because so much of the economic activity in this sector is unrecorded. The inescapable conclusion, however, is that the informal sector provides employment opportunity for countless Africans, many of whom derive levels of disposable income that qualify them as middle class. To the extent that this is so, Africa's informal sector economies provide solid if imprecise validation of the AfDB's view that as many as one in three Africans may now enjoy middle-class levels of disposable income.

Resilience

Increasing numbers of Africa's private sector enterprises are the local affiliates or branches of large global corporations such as banks, insurance firms, brokerage houses, automobile dealerships, hotels and retail chain stores. Visual evidence alone attests to the opportunities they provide for Africans to enjoy middle-income levels of disposable income.[4] Africa's private sector has also expanded into areas that were traditionally the preserve of governments. Many African countries have seen a proliferation of private telephone services and educational institutions including universities as well as primary and secondary schools. There are now numerous private airlines and private medical clinics and hospitals. The Africans who constitute the managerial, professional, technical and clerical personnel in these firms provide the demand for Africa's real-estate boom, the proliferation of shopping malls, the spread of affluent neighborhoods, and the traffic that clogs major urban arteries.

An unfailing constant is the resilience of African entrepreneurialism – the ability to identify economic opportunity and respond to it. Countless Africans earn their incomes from multiple sources that span diverse sectors. The economic geographer, Jacques Enaudeau, has called attention to this pattern.

Local NGO staffers in Dakar have sheep on the terrace of their houses to fatten and sell. Shop owners in Conakry and Ouagadougou own small plots of land outside the city that they farm in their spare time. Private school teachers in Nairobi give as many private lessons outside school as they teach inside the classroom. (Enaudeau, 2013)

Middle-class families

When the unit of analysis is raised to the family, the boundary between the salaried middle class and the entrepreneurial, profit-seeking middle class is even more blurred. Many families engage in economic straddling, which means that individual members engage in different economic activities. One family member may be part of the white-collar middle class, with a lucrative professional career in a government ministry, financial institution, or other large-scale private enterprise. The spouse may earn income in the entrepreneurial realm, operating a small shop, restaurant, or farm. It would be rare to find an urban family with only one income source.

Urban African families frequently combine the nuclear family with a variety of near relatives including parents, cousins, in-laws, and nephews or nieces. Extended family members often pool their incomes, treating the flow of cash from all their activities as a common resource so that when one source of livelihood diminishes, others absorb the slack. Middle-class families who can provide access to education often assume responsibility for raising the children of less well-off relatives. Family ties further extend the pattern of straddling, as when a brother or cousin joins the family unit to attend school, seek urban employment, or simply relieve the economic pressure on a poorer segment of the family. Sometimes, a family's income includes remittances from members working overseas. Remittances also occur internally. Most commonly, an urban family sends cash to rural relatives to supplement meager farm income. However, the flow can be in the opposite direction, when rural families send cash or gifts to economically needy urban relatives. The direction of the flow may vary depending upon the season of the year. All these practices enable African families to maximize their income, reduce economic insecurity by diversifying risk, and lower their exposure to political uncertainty.

Political pressure

Unlike the earlier middle class, which was weakened by dependence on government employment, the new private sector middle class is in a stronger position to demand improvements in government conduct. The members of this class are a potent force for greater transparency and accountability in government operations, including impartiality in the judiciary and improved delivery of essential services such as health, education and infrastructure. Because private sector wages are often higher than public sector wages, the new middle class places pressure on the government to improve the remuneration of civil servants, a major step in the effort to reduce corruption. The greater economic independence of the new middle class also affords a stronger opportunity to demand greater representation by political parties. The freedom to shift between political parties has brought about closely balanced party systems in several countries, including Ghana, Zambia and Kenya.

Source of instability?

The rise of the new middle class, however, could become a source of instability. The income gap between the middle class and the urban poor is a particular concern. Whereas Africa's post-colonial middle class was somewhat hidden from view in residential and commercial areas distant from impoverished neighborhoods, the socio-economic inequalities of Africa's major cities are now on full display. Contemporary urban inequality has the potential to trigger political volatility. Economic growth and population growth, together with the real-estate boom that has spread high-rise construction throughout large portions of major cities, has created an urban environment in which the poor and the well-to-do are in close proximity. As African cities have become more compacted, the spatial separation of affluence and poverty, which helped to alleviate social tensions in the post-colonial era, has all but disappeared. The crowded conditions that now prevail in Africa's major cities make poorer urban strata more aware of the disparity in lifestyle. Perceptions of relative deprivation are accentuated when the poorer elements in a society witness affluence on a daily basis.

The confounding reality of modern Africa, then, is that the development narrative and the poverty narrative are both correct. Africa is experiencing the rise of a middle class that is economically strong, politically independent, and sufficiently influential to have had a significant impact on governmental accountability. Its presence and multi-dimensional influence reflect the resilience and optimism of a continent coming into its own as a region of rapid growth, sound investment opportunity and unprecedented individual political and economic freedom. At the same time, Africa continues to be a region of deep poverty and severe inequality. The African Development Bank has documented this duality. A separate study, *Briefing Note 5: Income Inequality in Africa* (AfDB, 2012) called attention to the scale of Africa's poverty problem.

> Nearly 50% of the population in Sub-Saharan Africa lives on less than US$1 a day today: the world's highest rate of extreme poverty … The number of impoverished people has doubled since 1981. Since the late 1980s, the number of people living on less than US$1 per day in Sub-Saharan Africa rose by 70 million, reaching 290 million in 1998, which is over 46% of the total population. In Liberia, nearly 60% of the population lives on less than US$2 a day. In the Central African Republic, the figure is 50%.
>
> (AfDB, 2012)

Income distribution

The number of poor people in Africa is increasing rapidly. Because the poor constitute a large proportion of the population, population increase alone adds large numbers of people to the category of the very poor. *Briefing Note 5* further attested to Africa's status as one of the world's most unequal continents, a trend also noted in the *Pyramid* study. Africa is the world's second most inequitable region after Latin America. A number of African countries, especially those in its southern tier, have levels of inequality similar to those in Latin America.[5] In most African countries, as in so many others, the trend in income distribution is toward widening differences between the richest and poorest income groups.

The disproportionate income shares going to different social strata are evidence of the need for research that will provide a nuanced profile of African social structures and how they compare with those in other world regions. The Cambridge University economist, José Gabriel Palma, sought to do so by measuring the income share of the middle class in 135 countries. Palma's research estimates the percentages of national income captured by the top decile of the population (decile 10), the middle-income deciles (5 through 9), and the bottom deciles (1 through 4) (Palma, 2011). He showed that, on a global basis, the middle-class deciles capture about 50 percent of national wealth; the greatest disparities are the shares received by the rich versus the poor.

The countries in Sub-Saharan Africa display this pattern, with middle-income deciles (5 through 9) obtaining about half of national income. Although all African countries exhibit considerable inequality, the countries of southern Africa (South Africa, Namibia, Botswana and Zambia) are more unequal than most. The top tier of the population receives about 40 percent of national wealth, and the bottom tier, 10 percent or less. In the rest of Africa, inequality is less extreme, with the top 10 percent receiving, on average, about 30 percent of national income, and the poorest 40 percent, about 20 percent.[6]

The surprising discovery in Palma's data is that the percentage of national income going to the middle class is remarkably uniform, regardless of a country's level of wealth or regime type. In all 135 countries, the middle class captured about 50 percent of national income, a figure so constant that Palma describes middle classes as having attained a kind of property right in a 50 percent share of their national wealth. The reasons are not difficult to understand. Owing to a combination of factors that includes entrepreneurial skills, private ownership of valuable economic assets, and educational qualifications that offer entry into lucrative professional careers, the middle class has been able to stabilize its share of national income at about 50 percent across countries that vary greatly in wealth, GDP per capita, and regime type. This pattern has profound implications. It suggests that the top decile of the population will not be able to increase its share of national wealth at the expense of the middle class. In the future, the wealthy will be able to increase their wealth only by reducing the share of national income going to the poor.

Poverty persists

Briefing Note 5 corroborates that conclusion by showing that the emergence of the new middle class may not have improved the economic position of the majority of Africans, who continue to be rural, agricultural, and desperately poor. The overwhelming majority of the African poor are small-scale farmers who combine subsistence production with modest participation in the cash economy. The conditions of life for these farmers, who may still comprise as much as 70 percent of the population of Sub-Saharan Africa, have changed little, if at all, during the past 20 years. Many continue to live in the perilous margin between bare survival and the near-famine conditions caused by periodic crop failures. For the majority of rural Africans, weather instability, not the trickle-down effects of economic growth, remains the single most important determinant of income fluctuations. Most of these farmers have limited access to arable land, insufficient cash income to acquire purchased inputs, and limited or no opportunities for education beyond the primary level. Moreover, rural population increase, urban encroachment, and land concessions to foreign investors have reduced the amount of arable land per capita. Global climate change may have played a greater role in worsening their circumstances than the economic benefits of an improved policy framework.

World Bank economists use the concept 'growth elasticity of poverty' to measure the extent to which economic growth reduces poverty. By this criterion, Africa performs less well than other developing regions.[7] East Asia and South Asia, which are sometimes combined as the Asia Pacific region, have been more successful in translating economic growth into expansion of the middle class, and, hence, into reduction in the percentage of the population living in poverty. When poverty is defined as an income of $1.25/day or less, East Asia has reduced poverty to 12.5 percent of the population; South Asia, to 31 percent. Based on that measure, Africa's poverty rate remains close to 50 percent.[8] Using a more stringent definition of middle class, Homi Kharas (2010) has shown that Africa's share of the global middle class lags behind that of South and East Asia. According to Kharas' estimates, Africa's middle class is about 32 million people and accounts for about 2 percent of the global middle class. The middle class in the Asia Pacific region totals more than 500 million people and accounts for 28 percent of the global middle class. In addition, the African middle class generates about 1 percent of the purchasing power of the global middle class, compared with 23 percent for the Asia Pacific region (Kharas, 2010). If these measures are even close to correct, they suggest that Africa faces the great risk of a polarized income distribution.

Social inequality

The important question is why such large differences exist between regions. Part of the answer may lie in population growth, which remains higher in Africa than in other developing regions. A high rate reduces economic growth per capita, leaving less additional wealth per person. Africa has lagged behind other developing regions in experiencing a demographic transition toward smaller family size. Large family size means, for example, fewer resources per child, including those that enable children to remain in school longer. This, however, is only a partial answer. A more important reason is the persistence of deep social inequalities, which remain larger than in many other developing regions. In Africa, a large portion of the benefits of economic growth continues to go to the very top income strata. The net result is that the absolute number of the poor is increasing, which results in a growing underclass of impoverished people. If

Africa continues to underperform in using economic growth to alleviate poverty, it will soon house a majority of the world's poor.

As yet, no theory persuasively explains the wide regional variations in the impact of economic growth on poverty alleviation or the impact of poverty on growth. The most promising hypothesis focuses on the investment-to-income ratio among upper income strata. A low ratio can be an important indicator of under-investment in industry and agriculture. The upper classes' preference to use their wealth to engage in consumption rather than investment is not confined to any historical period, world region, or economic type. The landed aristocracies of 18th-century Britain and France come to mind, as do the aristocracies of Tsarist Russia and Ancient China, and the elites of oil-exporting Middle East countries. Those classes have sometimes been described as 'rentier,' because they derive their income principally from ownership of fixed economic assets and because they use their income to finance a high level of personal consumption. A low investment-to-income ratio contributes to slow poverty alleviation and, for that reason, figures prominently in the persistent income disparity between upper and lower income strata.

Poverty does not translate directly into support for or opposition to democratic government. According to the Afrobarometer survey data, people who feel poor mostly want improvement in their lives. Governments that invest in infrastructure to provide water and electricity and in services to improve access to healthcare and education find that perceptions of lived poverty decline significantly. Whatever the cause, Africa's poverty in the midst of plenty is troublesome. The rise of the middle class, which is a strong indicator of socio-economic progress, and which has the potential to provide a lasting basis for social peace and stable democratic politics, could become a source of political unrest. While growth may foster a sense of well-being among those who have enjoyed upward mobility, it also fosters a sense of having been left behind among those who have not.

Afrobarometer has provided survey evidence that many Africans continue to experience their lives as impoverished, despite high levels of recorded economic growth in their countries. Employing a subjective measurement of poverty called the 'Lived Poverty Index' (LPI), which is based on how frequently survey respondents report that they go without clean water, medical care or cash to purchase food, Afrobarometer notes that 'across 16 countries where data are available over the past decade, the average experience of lived poverty has hardly changed' (Dulani, Mattes, and Logan, 2013). There is a clear conclusion to be drawn from these data. Macro-economic data, which show robust rates of growth at the national level, must be considered in conjunction with data from household income surveys that show continuing poverty and a lack of improvement in the economic conditions of poorer families. Much of this can be traced to Africa's investment-to-income ratio, which tends to be low in countries where a large proportion of the income of the upper strata derives from the extraction and export of high-value commodities. Where this is the case, the productive sectors of an economy – manufacturing and agriculture – may experience capital starvation and sluggish growth, even as consumption sectors such as housing and retail sales show great prosperity.

Trade freedom or trade management?

Development economists of the postwar generation identified trade policy as the central issue facing countries seeking economic growth. They were pessimistic about the possibility that trade-openness would promote industrialization, and they insisted that trade management would be necessary to achieve balanced growth that would include the manufacturing sector. Ragnar Nurkse, a leading exponent of that school, argued that developing countries should assign a lower priority to comparative advantage, which emphasizes the benefits of specialization for export, than to policies that regulate trade in ways that promote a country's industrial sector.[9] A number of contemporary economists have embraced this view, echoing the development economists' insistence that late industrializers face disadvantages against countries that have already industrialized. A prominent economic historian has pointed to historical precedents; the successful early industrializing nations often resorted to managed trade practices to promote the growth of their industrial sectors (Chang, 2002). The danger for Africa is that it will become an economic battleground for industrial countries seeking to consolidate their control over valuable and increasingly scarce primary commodities (Moyo, 2012).

Free versus managed trade

Some leading economists believe that the benefits of free trade must be weighed against the possibility that a managed approach to trade may do more to stimulate industrialization (Stiglitz and Charlton, 2005). The decision to follow this advice hinges on the question of whether the growth boom of the past decade reflected improved economic performance in a variety of sectors that complement each other, or whether it consisted principally of increases in the volume and value of primary commodity exports. There is insufficient evidence to answer this question conclusively. Not only is the era of economic growth relatively young, but, as seems inevitable in the early phase of an economic era, the evidence is mixed.

The McKinsey Global Institute, the business and economics research arm of the consulting firm McKinsey & Company, has shown that Africa's impressive growth derives from improved performance in a variety of sectors. Its study, *Lions on the Move: The Progress and Potential of African Economies* (hereafter, *Lions*) documents rapid growth in such diverse sectors as banking, telecommunications, construction and retail (McKinsey, 2010). The study showed that although commodity exports were the fastest-growing sector and accounted for a significant part of Africa's growth, other sectors also exhibited strong growth. Agriculture and manufacturing grew at rates of 5.5 percent and 4.6 percent, respectively, during the five years from 2002 to 2007. During that period, agriculture and manufacturing accounted for 21 percent of total growth, close behind commodity resources, which accounted for 24 percent.[10]

Diversified economic growth

The *Lions* study attributes Africa's economic success to political and policy factors that set the stage for diversified growth. A number of countries have successfully resolved long-standing internal hostilities, thereby creating more stable political environments, which are the precondition for middle-class accumulation of wealth, external private investment, and longer-term government investments in economic rehabilitation. African governments have also implemented more business-friendly fiscal and monetary policies; they have reduced inflation, lowered government indebtedness as a percentage of GDP, and brought their budgets closer to fiscal balance.[11] Perhaps most important, by privatizing state industries and shifting their orientation toward greater approval of entrepreneurship, African governments have made progress in creating a political climate more conducive to private sector activity. The McKinsey study might also have assigned importance to Africa's democratic transitions of the 1990s, which, though still imperfectly implemented in a number of countries, have increased popular pressure on African governments to behave in a socially accountable and economically responsible manner.

Africa's economic diversification has not been uniform – some countries are further ahead than others in the degree to which sectors other than resources contribute to GDP. The McKinsey Institute considers four economies to have made substantial progress: Tunisia, Morocco, Egypt and South Africa. A number of others are well along in this direction, including Ghana, Kenya and Senegal; others, especially countries that have experienced considerable political instability, including the Democratic Republic of Congo and Mali, are not. Today, the Central African Republic, Chad and the newly created South Sudan would join this list. Although all African nations seeking to industrialize face major challenges in attaining and maintaining global competitiveness, the McKinsey study concludes that two decades of economic liberalization have improved economic conditions, and these, in turn, provide a synergistic basis for political stability. As a result, many countries now offer investment opportunities in areas as wide-ranging as agriculture, retail sales, banking and financial services, telecommunications and real estate, as well as further exploitation of natural resources.

Commodity-driven growth

The Economic Commission for Africa (ECA) has a different point of view. Its most recent comprehensive study of African economies, *Making the Most of Africa's Commodities* (hereafter, *Making the Most*), offers a more cautionary assessment and expresses concerns about the limitations and socio-economic effects of commodity-driven growth.

> [R]ecent economic performance has not generated enough economic diversification, job growth or social development to create wealth and lift millions of Africans out of poverty…the deindustrialization of many African economies over the last three decades, resulting in their increasing marginalization in the global economy, was mainly the result of inadequate policies…
>
> (ECA, 2013)

The ECA report notes that 'most African economies still depend heavily on commodity production and exports, with too little value addition and few forward and backward linkages to other sectors…'.[12] The report compares Africa with East Asia, where the ratio of manufacturing to aggregate output is nearly three times as high, and where labor-intensive industrialization has lifted hundreds of millions of citizens out of poverty. It concludes that liberalizing policies, which include specialization for export, have produced commodity-based trade that has had only limited effects in altering the socio-economic structures of African countries.

Making the Most directs attention to weaknesses in Africa's trade relationships with the global community. The first is asymmetry in trade policy. The economic liberalization policies that began in the 1980s call for the closest possible approximation to free trade, which, it is widely assumed, is a superior mechanism for attaining rapid economic growth. The economic reforms implemented since then shifted the trade regimes of many African countries away from the industrial protectionism of the ISI era toward a high degree of trade openness. Africa's trade openness, however, is not consistently reciprocated by its principal trading partners, many of whom have devised subtle mechanisms to protect their manufacturing base. As a result of this policy asymmetry, Africa's trade pattern remains one in which African countries export primary commodities and use some portion of their export earnings to purchase consumer goods, which then compete with domestic products. The major share of value added arises outside Africa. The third asymmetry has to do with power relationships; individual African countries often find themselves dealing with larger, more powerful trading partners, often countries whose aid programs make it difficult to negotiate more advantageous trade terms.

The question confronting Africa's policymakers is what to do. The ECA advocates a policy of managed trade that would enable African countries to use their natural resources as a basis for constructing diversified economies. Unlike the trade management policies of the past, which limited the importation of manufactured goods, commodity-based trade management would limit the export of raw materials that could be used to manufacture exportable commodities. ECA economists offer three examples to illustrate how such a policy might work. In the first, the government of Ethiopia would constrain the export of raw leather and hides to make them more readily available for domestic industries that manufacture shoes and other leather goods. In the second, the government of Botswana would constrain the export of raw diamonds to encourage the creation of a domestic diamond-cutting and diamond-polishing industry. And, in the third, the government of Zambia would constrain the export of copper ingots to facilitate the creation of industries producing end-user products such as copper pipe and wiring.[13]

The policy of commodity-based industrialization faces several challenges. The first is the practical matter of how many African countries export primary commodities that offer this possibility. The international marketplace for Africa's commodities varies greatly from one country to the next. A policy that might work well for a country exporting raw hides or uncut diamonds might not work as well for a country exporting cotton, for which there are many competing suppliers. The main challenge, however, has to do with the after-effects of the ISI era. Early efforts to use trade policy to induce industrialization, as in the ISI experiments of the 1960s and 1970s, failed so dismally that there continues to be a strong intellectual bias against a managed trade approach. Even a modest return to trade management runs counter to the free trade orthodoxy of international organizations such as the World Trade Organization (WTO), the World Bank and the International Monetary Fund, which can bring great pressure to bear on countries that explicitly engage in managed trade. Any attempt to implement a trade management policy will also evoke criticism from free trade theorists, who will attempt to show that industries that enjoy trade protections have a 'crowding out' effect on those that do not, thereby having a net negative outcome on a country's overall economic performance.

Economists concerned with the well-being of the developing world have begun to advocate a heterodox trade policy that combines elements of free trade with elements of trade management. If this approach can be shown to improve the diversity of African economies, the benefits would be considerable. Because of the strong correlation between economic diversity and improved social equality, measures to promote economic diversity would also help African nations to address the inequality problem (Asunka, 2013). At the very least, a proactive policy of economic diversification could provide additional support for the emergent middle class by increasing the bases for employment and incomes.

Notes

1 *Pyramid*, p. 1.
2 Deloitte, *The Rise and Rise of the African Middle Class*. www.deloitte.com/assets/Dcom-SouthAfrica/Local%20Assets/Documents/rise_and_rise.pdf
3 However, we should not overlook the fact that in spite of these gains, macro-economic management remains weak where Ghana performs notably worse compared with other similar countries.

4 The popular website YouTube has numerous videos showing the lifestyle of Africa's new middle class. See for example, www.youtube.com/watch?v=NBaZnl-AaIk&noredirect=1, www.youtube.com/watch?v=fs-q-mdi_yw and www.youtube.com/watch?v=GLrP-gHAGG8. All three of these videos depict the lifestyle of Nigeria's new middle class. Nairobi's new middle class can be seen at www.youtube.com/watch?v=HyNztfyen7Q. The South African middle class can be viewed at www.youtube.com/watch?v=OqkBEv58wzs. The Palms Mall in Lagos can be viewed at www.youtube.com/watch?v=KqIuma1uUlI.
5 *Briefing Note 5*, Figure 1, p. 3.
6 Ibid, Figure 15, p. 109.
7 Francisco Ferreira, 'Relaunching Africa Can and Sharing Africa's Growth,' *Africa Can End Poverty: A Blog about the Challenges and Opportunities Facing Africa,*' http://blogs.worldbank.org/africacan/relaunching-africa-can-and-sharing-africa-s-growth.
8 The World Bank, *Poverty*. http://data.worldbank.org/topic/poverty
9 Ragnar Nurkse, 'Balanced and Unbalanced Growth.' This essay is published as Chapter 10 of his edited volume *Equilibrium and Growth in the World Economy: Economic Essays* (Cambridge: Harvard University Press, 1961).
10 *Lions*, p. 2 and Exhibit 2, p. 11.
11 *Lions*, Exhibit 3, p. 12.
12 *Making the Most*, p. 6.
13 Emmanuel Nnadozie, Economic Commission for Africa, presentation at African Studies Association, November 22, 2013.

References

Acemoglu, D., and J.A. Robinson (2012). *Why Nations Fail: The Origins of Power, Prosperity and Poverty*. New York: Crown Publishers.

AfDB, African Development Bank (2011). *The Middle of the Pyramid: Dynamics of the Middle Class in Africa*. Available online at: http://www.afdb.org/fileadmin/uploads/afdb/Documents/Publications/The%20Middle%20of%20the%20Pyramid_The%20Middle%20of%20the%20Pyramid.pdf (accessed 18 September 2014)

AfDB, African Development Bank (2012). *Briefing Note 5: Income Inequality in Africa*. Tunis: African Development Bank (March).

Aristotle (1943). *Politics*. New York: Random House Modern Library.

Asunka, J. (2013). 'A Short Reflection on Ghana's Middle Class'. Unpublished paper.

Banerjee, A.V., and E. Duflo (2008). 'What is Middle Class about the Middle Class Around the World?' *Journal of Economic Perspectives*, vol. 22, no. 2, pp. 3–28.

Bates, R. (1981). *Markets and States in Tropical Africa*. Berkeley & Los Angeles: University of California Press, p. 3.

Chang, H.-J. (2002). *Kicking Away the Ladder: Development Strategy in Historical Perspective*. London: Anthem Press.

Chenery, H. (1979). 'Comparative Advantage and Development Policy.' Chapter 7 in *Structural Change and Development Policy*. Washington DC: World Bank.

Devarajan, S., and W. Fengler (2013). 'Africa's Economic Boom: Why the Pessimists and the Optimists are both Right.' *Foreign Affairs*. May/June, p. 68.

Dulani B., R. Mattes, and D. Logan (2013). *After a Decade of Growth in Africa, Little Change at the Grassroots* (Afrobarometer, October 2013). Available online at: http://allafrica.com/download/resource/main/main/idatcs/00071205:95b4e60154d6f2157a06a6d60f9 64a1d.pdf (accessed 18 September 2014).

Economic Commission for Africa (2013). *Making the Most of Africa's Commodities: Industrializing for Growth, Jobs and Economic Transformation.* Addis Ababa: United Nations Economic Commission for Africa, p. 4.

Economic Commission for Africa, African Union, African Development Bank, and United Nations Development Programme (2013). *Assessing Progress in Africa Toward the Millennium Development Goals: Emerging Perspectives from Africa on the Post-2015 Development Goals.* Addis Ababa: Economic Commission for Africa, African Union, African Development Bank, and United Nations Development Programme.

Enaudeau, J. (2013). 'In Search of the African Middle Class,' *Guardian Africa Network*, May 3.

Financial Times (2012). December 28.

Kharas, H. (2010). *The Emerging Middle Class in Developing Countries.* OECD Development Center, Working Paper no. 285. OECD Development Center, Table 1, p. 16.

Lipset, S.M. (1969). *Political Man.* London: Heinemann.

McKinsey Institute (2010). *Lions on the Move: The Progress and Potential of African Economies.* Washington DC: McKinsey & Company, p. 1. www.adlevocapital.com/images/Lions_on_the_Move.pdf (accessed 18 September 2014).

Moyo, D. (2012). *Winner Take All: China's Race for Resources and What it Means for the World.* New York: Basic Books.

Nurkse, R. (1961). 'Balanced and Unbalanced Growth.' Chapter 10 in *Equilibrium and Growth in the World Economy: Economic Essays.* Cambridge, MA: Harvard University Press.

Palma, J.G. (2011). 'Homogenous Middles vs. Heterogeneous Tails, and the End of the "Inverted U": It's all About the Share of the Rich,' *Development and Change*, vol. 42, no. 1, pp. 87–153.

Stiglitz, J., and A. Charlton (2005). *Fair Trade for All: How Trade Can Promote Development.* Oxford: Oxford University Press.

The Economist (2000). May 11, p. 1.

The Economist (2011). December 12, pp. 1–2.

Weber, Max (1905). *The Protestant Ethic and the Spirit of Capitalism.* Translated by Talcott Parsons. London and New York: Routledge Classics.

World Bank (1981). *Accelerated Development in Sub-Saharan Africa: An Agenda for Action.* Washington DC: World Bank.

3

CONSUMPTION PATTERNS

Oliver J.M. Chinganya, Mary Strode,
Lee Crawfurd, Marta Moratti, and
Felix Schmieding

Introduction

This chapter delves into the consumption patterns of middle-class households in Africa. Consumption patterns reflect households' material living conditions and shed light on changes in their tastes and habits, as well as increases in discretionary income. Investigating consumption patterns and how they change over time helps policymakers, as well as producers of goods and services, to assess current and future household needs.

The relative strengths and weaknesses of different welfare indicators have been the subject of intense debate, but a clear consensus exists in favor of consumption as a general indicator. This is because families and individuals derive material wellbeing from the consumption of goods and services. Furthermore, consumption better reflects long-term welfare than does income, as 'consumption is smoother and less variable than income' (Deaton and Zaidi, 2002; Deaton and Grosh, 1998).

Various definitions of who constitute the middle class abound, but a key characteristic is having discretionary income. The 2010 McKinsey report used household income to define class distinctions. It found that in 2008, roughly 85 million African households had an annual income of $5,000 or more in 2005 PPP US dollars. This is 'the level above which people start spending roughly half their income on items other than food.' The report also projected that the number of these households would increase by about 50 percent, 'reaching 128 million by 2020.' It concluded that the majority of this growth in the middle class derives from the urban population's growing consumption (McKinsey, 2010).

The next two sections of this chapter explore how middle-class consumption in Africa has changed over time. The analysis focuses on the average consumption level of middle-class households, as well as the total level of consumption attributable to middle-class households in a country.

We then present data from household survey reports of various African countries to explore middle-class consumption patterns. Whenever possible, the analysis disaggregates consumption by its subcomponents (for instance, food, education, health, housing, and leisure) to discern how households' spending strategies vary across the distribution.

The chapter then moves on to examine a less tangible characteristic, namely middle-class self-perceptions. Here we explore middle-class aspirations and levels of life satisfaction. The final section draws some conclusions based on the literature reviewed and the analysis conducted in the present work.

Defining the middle class

Differing definitions have been used in various studies of the middle class in Africa. In its broadest sense, the middle class is defined as those earning more than the poor (i.e. more than $2 a day) but less than the small group of rich elite (i.e. less than $20 per day). Relative methods look at the middle of the income distribution, either as a fixed percentage of the population (e.g. the middle 80 percent) or the group within a certain distance of the median income. A key feature of the middle class is holding a steady job, and so it can be useful to look simply at those with full-time permanent jobs as another proxy for the middle class.

The Organization for Economic Cooperation and Development (OECD) uses a definition of the 'global middle class' as those households with a daily per capita expenditure of $10–$100 per person in 2005 PPP US dollars. It further suggests that there are 1.8 billion people that fall into this category. Sub-Saharan Africa (SSA) and North Africa are considered discrete regions in the OECD categorization. According to this definition, there are only 32 million middle-class people in SSA and they constituted only 2 percent of the world's middle class in 2009. Although the absolute size of the SSA middle class is expected to grow, it will remain constant as a percentage of the world's middle-class population through 2020 and 2030. According to this estimate, the Middle East and North Africa constituency will also stay relatively stable, representing 5–6 percent of the world's middle class during these periods (Kharas, 2010).

The McKinsey report is more positive in terms of trends, defining the 'consuming middle class,' a subsection of discretionary income earners, as households with an annual income of at least $10,000–$20,000 (2005 PPP US dollars). It suggests that such households constituted 11 percent of the African population in 2000, 14 percent of the population in 2008, and will make up 17 percent of total African households in 2020. In absolute numbers, that is the equivalent of 18 million households in 2000, 27 million households in 2008, and 41 million households in 2020.

This chapter adopts an absolute definition of the middle class, as described earlier. An absolute definition has clear advantages when comparisons are drawn across different African countries.[1] The middle class is thus defined in this chapter by per capita daily consumption of $2–$20 in 2005 PPP US$. This includes a floating class with a per capita daily consumption of $2–$4, just above the $2 per day second poverty line (AfDB, 2011).

Middle-class consumption growth

This section presents our estimates of the changes in per capita consumption of middle-class households. However, as the size of the middle class is likely to change, it also presents the overall consumption of the entire middle class. Changes in overall consumption demand can therefore be attributed either to a change in the average consumption level or to changes in the size of the middle class (or to a combination of the two effects).

Data used in this section emanate from PovcalNet, an online tool for poverty measurement developed by the Development Research Group of the World Bank, which presents data on consumption, poverty, and inequality. The database draws on socioeconomic surveys from 125 countries conducted between the 1970s and 2009. The present section uses African countries' consumption data between 1993 and 2004 to compute how middle-class consumption has changed over that time period.[2]

Data on mean consumption are expressed in monthly 2005 PPP US$ and most of the consumption data used are available only at the decile level. Consumption figures are thus averages of the deciles, which can conceal important intra-decile distribution patterns. For example, an average consumption of $2 per day for the first decile of consumption distribution does not mean that every household within that decile consumes exactly $2 worth of goods and services. Households at the bottom of the distribution have a lower consumption level than the average and are likely to fall below the poverty line. The same problem occurs at the top end of the distribution, where households are likely to have a higher level of consumption than the average.[3]

To reduce the degree of approximation as much as possible, a linear function is assumed to apply within deciles. This allows a more precise identification of the cut-off points between the poor and the middle class. Once the position and size of the middle class have been obtained, the average per capita consumption level for the entire class between 1993 and 2004 is computed. By comparing the change over time, we can assess how consumption has changed for the middle class overall.

Household consumption expenditures generally comprise food, non-food (clothing and footwear, medical care and health expenses, transportation, recreation, personal care, miscellaneous goods and services, etc.), education (tuition fees, transportation, books, uniforms), and housing (actual rent or rental equivalence value, expenses – gas, water, electricity, house repairs, etc.).[4]

Table 3.1 presents the countries included in our calculations, the time period for each country, and the average monthly consumption level (in 2005 PPP US$) of middle-class individuals over the time period. 'Total growth' computes the percentage growth during this period, while 'Average annual growth' accounts for slightly different time spans considered for each country. Côte d'Ivoire, Ghana, and Madagascar show the highest annual growth rates, followed by Mali, Niger, and Zambia. Burkina Faso, Ethiopia, and Guinea-Bissau lag behind with negative growth and a reduction in consumption over the period.

TABLE 3.1 Average monthly consumption of middle-class individuals in selected African countries (2005 PPP US$)

Country	Time 1	Time 2	Average monthly consumption T1	Average monthly consumption T2	Total growth %	Average annual growth %
Burkina Faso	1994	2003	130	110	−15.2	−1.7
Burundi	1992	2006	72	71	−1.8	−0.1
Central African Republic	1992	2003	94	103	9.7	0.9
Côte d'Ivoire	1993	2002	118	146	23.0	2.6
Egypt	1995	2004	110	120	8.7	1.0
Ethiopia	1995	2004	109	88	−19.3	−2.1
Ghana	1991	2005	94	121	28.8	2.1
Guinea	1994	2003	111	101	−8.7	−1.0
Guinea-Bissau	1993	2002	121	90	−25.1	−2.8
Kenya	1992	2005	159	162	1.8	0.1
Lesotho	1993	2002	153	140	−8.4	−0.9
Madagascar	1993	2005	105	138	30.7	2.6
Mali	1994	2006	80	96	19.9	1.7
Niger	1992	2005	84	106	25.2	1.9
Nigeria	1992	2003	98	97	−1.8	−0.2
Senegal	1994	2005	101	102	1.8	0.2
South Africa	1993	2005	155	167	7.7	0.6
Uganda	1992	2005	104	107	3.3	0.3
Zambia	1993	2004	99	119	19.4	1.8

Source: Authors' calculations based on World Bank PovcalNet data.

It is important to note that this analysis is based on an absolute monetary definition of the middle class (individuals with consumption expenditure of $2 to $20 per day). For this reason, the average consumption expenditure of the middle class will always lie within the bands of this definition. A main concern is therefore to approximate whether the middle class defined in this way is heavily concentrated at the lower end of the band width and how this might change over time.

The changes in average monthly consumption presented in Table 3.1 can be combined with information on the change in the size of the middle class. Table 3.2 combines average consumption per month with estimates for the size of the middle class. This allows us to estimate the overall monthly consumption demand of the entire middle class in a country. Table 3.2 shows

TABLE 3.2 Total monthly consumption of the entire middle class in selected African countries (2005 PPP $ 000s)

Country	Total consumption T1	Total consumption T2	% Growth total consumption
Burkina Faso	189,892	285,924	50.6
Burundi	33,414	55,680	66.6
Central African Rep.	36,873	79,680	116.1
Côte d'Ivoire	940,817	1,405,344	49.4
Egypt	5,230,406	7,457,377	42.6
Ethiopia	1,029,532	1,495,237	45.2
Ghana	328,332	1,249,064	280.4
Guinea	289,306	130,608	−54.9
Guinea-Bissau	32,481	29,101	−10.4
Kenya	1,640,395	3,491,884	112.9
Lesotho	78,056	101,703	30.3
Madagascar	179,845	359,676	100.0
Mali	83,605	273,560	227.2
Niger	91,709	206,188	124.8
Nigeria	3,057,348	2,135,717	−30.1
Senegal	185,307	453,248	144.6
South Africa	3,414,013	5,063,574	48.3
Uganda	280,554	766,033	173.0
Zambia	174,796	257,658	47.4

Source: Authors' calculation based on AfDB Data Portal and World Bank PovcalNet database.

total monthly private consumption in PPP 2005 US dollars for the time period under analysis, as well as growth of this total consumption over time. Most countries exhibit a positive and large increase in total consumption by the middle class. This can be attributed to both an increase in the size of the middle class and to households moving upward within the bands defined as middle class. For example, the overall middle classes in Ghana, Mali, Uganda, Senegal, Niger, Central African Republic, and Kenya more than doubled their total consumption over ten years.

Breakdown of middle-class household expenditure

We have seen in the previous section that the middle class's total consumption demand increases over time, albeit to different degrees across countries. This section investigates how different expenditure categories within household consumption budgets change over time, along with the overall rise in consumption demand.

The existing literature reveals a number of trends, a principal one being that middle-class households spend less proportionately on food. This is a negative correlation; the share of a household's budget spent on food falls as its standard of living rises. At the same time, there is 'a shift toward better tasting, more expensive foods, so that the number of calories consumed grows more slowly than spending on food' (Deaton, 1997).

Entertainment expenditures as a share of household budget rise with income levels. Moreover, 'despite its reputation for thrift, some "frivolous" consumption is as middle class as a commitment to education or healthcare' (Banerjee and Duflo, 2008).

The McKinsey report encounters the same trend among different income brackets in Africa. Households earning less than $2,000 a year spend 82 percent of their total consumption budget on food, while those earning between $2,000 and $5,000 allocate 65 percent to nutritional needs. The correlation is progressive: those earning $5,000–$10,000 spend 52 percent of their consumption budget on food; households earning $10,000–$20,000 spend 42 percent; and those earning over $20,000 spend just 28 percent of their budget on food (McKinsey, 2010).

The research undertaken by Burger, van der Berg, and Nieftagodien (2004), focusing on the consumption patterns of the emerging black middle class in South Africa, supports this finding. They show that each quintile spends a lower proportion of their overall consumption budget on food (42 percent, 32 percent, and 17 percent in the third, fourth, and fifth quintiles, respectively) and a higher proportion on housing (4 percent, 6 percent, and 11 percent in the third, fourth, and fifth quintiles, respectively). The share of household budgets spent on clothing reveals inconsistent trends, peaking in the third and fourth quintiles at almost 5 percent (Burger et al., 2004).

In order to reach a deeper understanding of consumption patterns and how the middle class differs from the rest of the population, one needs to narrow the level of analysis and look at country-specific experiences. Unfortunately, information on consumption patterns with a high level of disaggregation is rare in the public domain. This section uses data at the highest level of disaggregation available (quintile/decile) to discern how budget shares vary across consumption quintile and over time.

Given the total consumption level that each class can afford, which is obviously higher as one moves up the distribution, budget shares tell us how households vary their resource allocation strategies. It is only to be expected that as households improve their living standards, more resources can be devoted to categories other than food. Households are therefore likely to spend more on education, health, cultural and leisure activities, or on durable assets.

Ghana

The middle class in Ghana significantly expanded during the decade of the 1990s and by 2005 this segment represented almost half of the population. The growth in size was accompanied by an increase in the average consumption level, so that the overall consumption demand increased substantially over time.

Tables 3.3 and 3.4 show the spending patterns across the consumption distribution and identify the budget shares of the different quintiles of the population. The results from PovcalNet analysis suggest that the middle class in Ghana was positioned within the top quintile of the population in 1991 and within the fourth and highest quintiles in 2005. The quintiles that best identify where the middle class is situated within the distribution are shaded in the tables.[5] Table 3.3 shows 1991 figures, while Table 3.4 presents 2005 figures.

It is apparent that the food component significantly decreases between the poor and the middle class. While the poor devote 65 percent of their consumption to food, the middle class spends just above 50 percent, which is significantly below the average. While there seems to be no significant difference with regard

TABLE 3.3 Budget shares by income quintile in Ghana, 1991 (%)

	Q1	Q2	Q3	Q4	Q5	All
Food (actual)	38.0	39.5	40.5	42.3	39.2	40.1
Food (imputed)	27.8	23.5	20.4	17.6	11.9	18.8
Housing	2.1	1.8	1.6	1.6	2.0	1.8
Other non-food (actual)	28.7	31.3	32.9	33.3	40.1	34.3
Other non-food (imputed)	3.3	3.8	4.6	5.2	6.9	5.1
Total	100.0	100.0	100.0	100.0	100.0	100.0
Food as % of total	65.8	63.0	61.0	59.9	51.0	58.8

Source: Ghana Living Standards Survey (GLSS) 3 Report.

TABLE 3.4   Budget shares by income quintile in Ghana, 2005 (%)

	Q1	Q2	Q3	Q4	Q5	All
Food and non-alcoholic beverages	37.2	37.5	37.9	36.4	29.1	30.1
Alcoholic beverages & tobacco	7.5	6.5	6.6	6.3	5.7	4.8
Clothing & footwear	6.6	6.8	6.5	6.5	5.3	5.2
Housing, water, electricity & gas	7.2	7.9	8.2	9.1	8	7.7
Furnishings, household equipment & maintenance	6.8	5.9	5.6	4.8	3.7	4.0
Health	4.6	4.4	4.4	4.3	3.3	3.4
Transport	6.7	7.0	6.4	7.8	27.5	15.4
Communication	1.6	2.9	2.7	3.3	4.9	5.6
Recreation & culture	4.7	3.0	3.0	2.9	5.0	5.2
Education	4.6	5.3	5.5	4.8	3.0	3.4
Restaurants & hotels	5.1	6.1	7.0	7.6	7.5	7.0
Miscellaneous goods	7.4	6.9	6.2	6.3	7.1	8.2
Total	100.0	100.0	100.0	100.0	100.0	100.0

Source: Ghana Living Standards Survey (GLSS) 5 Report.

to housing expenditure, the middle class allocates a higher share to non-food expenditure, which includes education, health, culture, and leisure.

The 2005 data allow further disaggregation of consumption subcomponents. By comparison to 1991, the 2005 food budget share decreases for the entire population. On average, 30 percent of the consumption is spent on food, and the proportion decreases as one moves toward richer households, from the poorest (37 percent) to the fourth (36 percent) and highest quintiles (29 percent), where the middle class is situated. The middle class, in comparison to the poor, spends a proportionately higher share of its consumption on transportation, communication, restaurants, and hotels.[6] Housing consumption slightly increased for all households, but it is proportionately higher for the middle class. The most significant indicator for the upper-middle class is the proportion spent on transportation, namely private automobiles and motorcycles.

South Africa

The South African middle class (defined as the proportion of the population with daily per capita consumption between $2 and $20) expanded during the period 1993–2005 with more than 8 million people transiting out of poverty. The average consumption level for the middle class grew by more than 7 percent during this period, which translates into an overall increase of almost 50 percent in total middle-class consumption expenditure.

The PovcalNet analysis shows that middle-class households are approximately located between the third and ninth deciles. Table 3.5 shows the consumption patterns of the South African population in 2005 by expenditure deciles (the shading indicates the deciles that best approximate the middle classes). As expected, the proportion of total expenditure on food decreases substantially from the poorest segment of the population to the upper deciles. Food accounts for 36 percent of the consumption of the poorest, compared with 31 percent for the 5th decile, 20 percent for the 8th decile, and 7 percent for the top decile of the population. As has already been observed in Ghana, the share of consumption

TABLE 3.5   Budget shares by expenditure decile in South Africa, 2005 (%)

	Lower	2	3	4	5	6	7	8	9	Upper
Food and non-alcoholic beverages	36.1	35.7	34.1	32.6	30.8	28.1	24.5	19.6	13.1	7.0
Alcoholic beverages & tobacco	3.4	2.6	2.0	2.1	2.0	1.9	2.0	1.5	1.3	0.6
Clothing & footwear	9.5	9.3	8.9	9.3	8.7	8.4	7.9	7.0	5.1	2.9
Housing, water, electricity & gas	21.1	19.4	18.7	18.4	18.7	18.1	19.4	22.6	27.4	24.6
Furnishings, household equipment & maintenance	4.9	5.7	6.9	7.3	7.8	8.5	8.9	8.2	6.8	6.3
Health	1.7	1.7	1.6	1.8	1.5	1.5	1.5	1.8	1.5	1.7
Transport	8.2	8.5	9.1	9.9	9.7	10.1	11.0	12.5	14.9	27.6
Communication	2.8	3.2	3.5	3.5	3.7	3.7	3.8	3.9	4.1	3.2
Recreation & culture	1.5	2.0	2.6	2.8	3.2	2.8	4.1	4.2	4.3	5.4
Education	0.9	1.1	1.0	1.4	1.3	1.9	1.9	2.5	3.2	2.5
Restaurants & hotels	3.5	2.8	3.2	2.2	2.3	2.7	2.8	2.0	2.1	2.0
Miscellaneous goods	6.3	7.9	8.1	8.6	10.0	11.1	11.9	14.1	16.0	15.9
Other	0.2	0.2	0.2	0.2	0.2	0.3	0.3	0.3	0.3	0.4

Source: Income and Expenditure Survey (IES) 2005, Statistics South Africa.

BOX 3.1 CHARACTERISTICS OF NIGERIA'S EXPANDING MIDDLE CLASS

With around 4.2 million or 23% of its population classified as middle class, Nigeria is witnessing significant shifts in consumption patterns and demands of this rapidly emerging market. In September 2011, the investment bank Renaissance Capital published the results of their survey into Nigeria's expanding middle class. The survey sampled 1,004 middle-class Nigerians, residing in the cities of Lagos, Abuja, and Port Harcourt, 70% of whom were aged 40 or younger.

The picture of Nigeria's middle-class to emerge from the survey is as follows:

- Average monthly income is in the range N75,000 to 100,000 ($480–$645).
- The middle class is well educated; 92% have obtained post-secondary education or have studied at an institution of higher learning. Educating their children is a top priority, and over half send their children abroad to complete their education.
- A sizable 76% of those sampled work in the public sector. Of those working in the private sector, 38% run their own business.
- The majority live in leased/rented accommodation (68%) with an average household size of 3.7 people. The average number of children is 1.6 (excluding those away at school) vs. a national average of 3 (or larger in rural areas).
- Most do not have mortgages or credit cards. The report considers the consumer lending sector to be 'woefully underdeveloped'.
- The Nigerian middle classes have a culture of saving, care little for the deposit rate, and do not expect to borrow from a bank. In terms of investments, they would rather invest in land/property than stocks or bonds.
- 48% have internet access but only 2% shop online at least once a month. Most shop at open-air markets (73%) and convenience stores (62%). The report underscores the huge potential that internet shopping offers.
- Only 15% have traveled abroad, mostly to the UK.
- Average number of cars per middle-class household is 0.8, well below the levels in, say, Zimbabwe among other countries.
- Key areas of concern are the supply of electricity and unemployment, with crime and corruption seen as far less concerning.
- Three-quarters of the middle class are optimistic about the future of Nigeria.

continued ...

Box 3.1 continued

The report underscores the wealth of opportunity presented by burgeoning economic growth in Africa's most populous country. Nigeria's economy has quadrupled in size since 2000 with growth averaging 8.6% over 2000–2011. Its public or external debt is virtually zero and its private sector debt is very low. What is clear is the need for the government to step up its provision of infrastructure, and encourage the financial sector to expand the products it is offering this crucial segment.

Source: Renaissance Capital, *A Survey of the Nigerian Middle Class*, September 26, 2011.

spent on alcohol and tobacco proportionately decreases as households move into the middle class. Transportation costs and miscellaneous goods as a proportion of total consumption expenditure increase significantly for upper-middle-class households, as elaborated below.

While no noteworthy differences exist in housing and housing-related expenses between the deciles, further disaggregation of the figures shows that the middle class spends proportionately more than the poor on rent, water, electricity, general services related to the dwelling, and maintenance. On the other hand, expenses on liquid and solid fuels represent a much higher burden for the poor. The middle class spends more on furnishings, equipment, and maintenance, especially on furniture, furnishings, and major household appliances, suggesting better dwelling characteristics and more durable asset accumulation.

The better-off the household, the higher are the expenses on transportation. For the poor, the single most important component is transport services, especially payment for passenger transportation by road. The main difference between the poor and middle-class budget shares relates to vehicle purchases. While the poorest devote only 0.1 percent of their consumption to car purchases, the middle class spends between 0.2 percent and 2 percent of its consumption on automobiles and between 0.4 percent and 3.5 percent on fuels and lubricants.

Budget shares on communications, recreation, and culture are substantially higher for the middle class. In particular, spending is higher for telephone services, audiovisual and photographic equipment, newspapers and books, recreational and cultural services, and package holidays.

While health expenditure is stable across deciles, education expenditure is significantly higher for the middle class. Increasing expenditure on tertiary education largely accounts for the differences across the deciles. While the budget share for tertiary education is close to zero for the poorest deciles, it ranges between 0.4 percent and 1.2 percent for the middle class.

TABLE 3.6 Percentage of household spending on food and alcohol/tobacco in five African countries: rural vs. urban areas

	Food			Alcohol/Tobacco		
	< $2	$2–$4	$6–$10	< $2	$2–$4	$6–$10
Rural						
Côte d'Ivoire	67.1	65.8	60.0	3.2	3.2	3.5
Ghana	62.0	57.7	50.6	...	...	...
Morocco	55.8	57.3	57.0	0.4	0.4	0.4
South Africa	67.8	60.3	40.5	3.3	3.4	3.3
Tanzania	...	...	...	...	...	...
Urban						
Côte d'Ivoire	58.1	59.5	49.5	2.0	2.1	2.6
Ghana	56.1	50.2	45.0	...	...	...
Morocco	...	...	...	...	...	...
South Africa	56.8	51.6	37.8	5.1	5.2	3.9
Tanzania	...	...	...	...	...	...

Source: Pooreconomics.com.
Note: Empty cells denote missing data.

The miscellaneous goods category is particularly important for the middle class, accounting for between 10 percent and 14 percent of consumption. Within this category, the most important items for the middle class are insurance, social protection services, financial and other services. These items account for only about 3 percent of the consumption of the poor.

Ghana, Côte d'Ivoire, Morocco, South Africa, and Tanzania

For their 2011 book, *Poor Economics: A Radical Rethinking of the Way to Fight Global Poverty*, Banerjee and Duflo collected household survey data from a range of countries, including five African countries: Côte d'Ivoire, Ghana, Morocco, South Africa, and Tanzania. These data show spending and asset ownership patterns for those earning (i) below $2 a day, (ii) between $2 and $4 (the 'floating class'), and (iii) between $6 and $10 (the lower-middle class). The results are presented in Table 3.6. As has been noted from the previous Ghana data, lower-middle-class households typically spend a significantly smaller proportion of their household budget on food. This leaves more discretionary spending for other items. Spending on alcohol and tobacco makes up a very small proportion of most households' expenditure, regardless of income.

TABLE 3.7 Percentage of household spending on education and health in five African countries: rural vs. urban areas

	Education			Health		
	< $2	$2–$4	$6–$10	< $2	$2–$4	$6–$10
Rural						
Côte d'Ivoire	4.6	5.0	4.5	1.7	1.8	1.8
Ghana	4.0	4.0	4.0	3.6	3.7	4.0
Morocco	1.9	2.8	1.8	4.0	4.2	6.5
South Africa	0.9	0.9	1.0	0.1	0.1	0.2
Tanzania	...	...	...	...	...	...
Urban						
Côte d'Ivoire	14.8	27.4	12	2.2	2.3	2.3
Ghana	6.5	6.6	6.4	3.5	3.6	3.7
Morocco	...	...	...	...	...	...
South Africa	0.8	1.0	0.8	0.1	0.2	0.3
Tanzania	...	...	...	...	...	...

Source: Pooreconomics.com.
Note: Empty cells denote missing data.

For these five countries, the proportion of household budgets spent on education and health is similar across the classes, as shown in Table 3.7. The largest differences are seen in Morocco, where the rural lower-middle class spends a larger proportion of the household budget on health than the poor, and the urban middle class spends a smaller proportion on education than the poor and the floating middle. Across most of the countries, there is evidence of larger absolute amounts being spent by middle-class households on education and health.

Turning to asset ownership, Table 3.8 shows that in general, middle-class households are more likely to own a radio or a television than are poor households, and this applies to both rural and urban areas. Patterns in bicycle ownership and land ownership are more mixed, depending on local alternatives. Basic household amenities such as piped water, electricity, and latrines show a much more consistent pattern of adoption in middle-class households (see Table 3.9). In urban Ghana, only 35 percent of poor households have access to piped water, whereas more than 78 percent of the lower-middle class have such access. Similarly large differences apply for electricity and latrines.

TABLE 3.8 Percentage of households owning a radio, TV, bicycle, or any land, in five African countries: rural vs. urban areas

	Radio			TV			Bicycle			Land		
	< $2	$2–4	$6–10	< $2	$2–4	$6–10	< $2	$2–4	$6–10	< $2	$2–4	$6–10
Rural												
Côte d'Ivoire	45.5	59.3	70.1	8.0	22.7	40.5	38.7	37.1	23.0	55.1	55.0	48.5
Ghana	15.2	13.1	16.1	25.9	40.9	29.3	25.5	22.9	19.2	25.9	40.9	29.3
Morocco	67.4	72.7	84.1	54.5	70.6	79.4	10.5	10.8	16.0	66.8	79.7	89.3
South Africa	77.9	86.2	83.2	15.3	34.1	54.2	21.0	21.5	24.7	5.2	10.8	11.5
Tanzania	...	...	...	0.0	0.3	0.0	...	...	...	91.5	91.6	87.9
Urban												
Côte d'Ivoire	55.6	74.7	86.7	27.4	59.2	82.0	17.1	16.6	6.5	30.9	16.6	7.9
Ghana	16.0	13.6	15.5	17.9	20.1	26.5	14.7	12.9	12.8	17.9	20.1	26.5
Morocco	...	...	...	...	...	...	...	...	...	1.9	...	...
South Africa	76.8	81.1	90.0	39.8	64.2	83.7	15.7	15.9	28.9	1.9	0.8	0.5
Tanzania	...	...	...	0.7	2.9	4.6	...	...	...	66.9	48.9	37.9

Source: Pooreconomics.com.
Note: Empty cells denote missing data.

TABLE 3.9 Percentage of households with piped water, electricity, and latrines, in five African countries: rural vs. urban areas

	Piped water			Electricity			Latrine		
	< $2	$2–4	$6–10	< $2	$2–4	$6–10	< $2	$2–4	$6–10
Rural									
Côte d'Ivoire	2.6	10.7	21.0	15.1	29.4	43.4	13.0	20.6	30.3
Ghana	3.1	15.6	39.5	11.3	35.9	53.2	43.9	45.0	42.7
Morocco	13.3	11.2	23.4	38.9	44.7	41.2	3.8	7.8	21.1
South Africa	7.6	13.0	44.3	10.2	20.3	50.7	65.2	78.8	85.7
Tanzania	1.0	3.6	7.2	1.0	2.7	6.5	92.1	94.6	95.7
Urban									
Côte d'Ivoire	9.2	23.6	56.5	57.4	81.3	85.3	23.0	47.1	68.6
Ghana	35.0	55.7	78.1	55.2	89.0	93.4	26.5	35.8	47.3
Morocco	...	...	...	...	...	...	...	...	...
South Africa	57.6	81.9	95.7	35.2	59.6	87.3	70.1	86.0	95.9
Tanzania	15.4	38.6	65.5	16.9	41.4	74.1	96.7	97.8	97.5

Source: Pooreconomics.com.
Note: Empty cells denote missing data.

TABLE 3.10 Percentage of households with tile, thatch, and metal roofing, in five African countries: rural vs. urban areas

	Tile roofing			Thatch roofing			Metal roofing		
	< $2	$2–4	$6–10	< $2	$2–4	$6–10	<$2	$2–4	$6–10
Rural									
Côte d'Ivoire	...	...	...	38.1	19.3	16.4	59.7	63.7	75.8
Ghana	53.4	69.4	47.5	35.4	18.9	13.8	...	...	...
Morocco	...	...	...	...	...	...	...	...	...
South Africa	0.2	0.7	5.2	18.5	12.7	5.7	76.5	76.8	79.0
Tanzania	19.7	40.8	49.4	73.1	56.7	48.3	0.0	0.0	0.0
Urban									
Côte d'Ivoire	...	...	...	2.9	0.0	0.0	84.7	85.6	87.3
Ghana	72.4	65.2	55.2	8.4	0.6	0.2	...	...	..
Morocco	...	...	...	...	...	...	...	...	...
South Africa	2.1	7.7	35.3	0.1	1.3	0.2	62.3	60.1	48.6
Tanzania	62.9	83.4	91.0	32.7	11.9	2.5	0.0	0.0	0.5

Source: Pooreconomics.com.
Note: Empty cells denote missing data.

Table 3.10 provides details about the quality of housing based on type of roofing. Generally speaking, as households become wealthier, they are more likely to abandon their thatch roofs for tiled or metal roofing.

How the middle class view their own lives

This section examines how members of the African middle class see themselves and their future. In Monrovia, for example, an interviewee earning the Liberian equivalent of an upper-middle salary points out that she does not own a television or a car or many of the other amenities typically associated with being middle class (Estey, 2010). In Freetown, a generator mechanic for a UN compound points out that 'With the money they pay me, I'm able to sustain myself and my family, but I'm not able to save for a house' (Johnson, 2010). On the other hand, a university graduate with daily expenses of a little over $20 a day and living in a two-bedroomed flat in Nairobi's South C estate, putting him in the 'high income' or rich class (i.e. in the same ranks as a Nigerian businessman), points out that he is not rich. He suggests that he is somewhere in the middle (Mungai, 2011).

The Afrobarometer Values Survey is conducted in 20 Africa countries and provides quantitative data on the perceptions of Africans vis-à-vis their own living standards.[7] The survey does not collect data on income; however it does ask if people have a full-time job and, whether working or not, if they are currently looking for a different job. Those with full-time jobs who are not presently looking for a different job can reasonably be considered to be in stable permanent positions, and to belong to the middle class. Unsurprisingly, those with full-time jobs who are not looking for another job are more likely to be satisfied with their present living conditions compared with others, as shown in Tables 3.11 and 3.12.

TABLE 3.11 Perceptions of present living conditions according to job status, 2008 (%)

	No job (not looking)	No job (looking)	Part-time job (not looking)	Part-time job (looking)	Full-time job (not looking)	Full-time job (looking)
Very bad	20	24	18	22	13	20
Fairly bad	31	31	27	29	22	25
Neither good nor bad	21	21	30	24	30	23
Fairly good	23	20	21	21	29	27
Very good	4	4	4	4	5	5
Total	100	100	100	100	100	100

Source: Afrobarometer Values Surveys.

TABLE 3.12 Perceptions of own living conditions compared with others, 2008 (%)

	No job (not looking)	No job (looking)	Part-time job (not looking)	Part-time job (looking)	Full-time job (not looking)	Full-time job (looking)
Very bad	10	12	11	11	7	9
Fairly bad	28	31	27	29	20	24
Neither good nor bad	36	32	38	34	37	34
Fairly good	19	19	19	20	29	25
Very good	3	3	2	3	4	4
Total	100	100	100	100	100	100

Source: Afrobarometer Values Surveys.

TABLE 3.13 Perceptions of current living conditions compared with 12 months ago (%)

	No job (not looking)	No job (looking)	Part-time job (not looking)	Part-time job (looking)	Full-time job (not looking)	Full-time job (looking)
Very bad	9	11	9	9	6	8
Fairly bad	24	25	26	24	20	22
Neither good nor bad	30	29	31	32	33	30
Fairly good	31	29	31	30	35	34
Very good	4	4	3	4	6	5
Total	100	100	100	100	100	100

Source: Afrobarometer Values Surveys.

TABLE 3.14 Expectations with regard to living conditions in 12 months' time

	No job (not looking)	No job (looking)	Part-time job (not looking)	Part-time job (looking)	Full-time job (not looking)	Full-time job (looking)
Very bad	7	9	8	8	7	6
Fairly bad	10	11	12	10	10	9
Neither good nor bad	13	13	15	13	13	11
Fairly good	38	38	37	40	38	40
Very good	15	15	13	15	20	19
Total	100	100	100	100	100	100

Source: Afrobarometer Values Surveys.

Those with full-time jobs are also more likely to think that their living conditions are better than those of others and that they have improved over the last year (Table 3.13). Furthermore, they are generally more optimistic, believing that their living conditions will significantly improve over the next 12 months, and voicing less uncertainty about their future living conditions (Table 3.14).

The middle class as an engine of growth

There is considerable evidence of a link between the growth of the middle class and growth in consumption, which is a key component of aggregate demand and a major driver of output and income growth. Juliet Schor (1999) argues that it is a 'new consumerism' that defines the middle class: a constant, 'up-scaling of lifestyle norms; the pervasiveness of conspicuous, status goods and of competition for acquiring them; and the growing disconnect between consumer desires and incomes.' Murphy, Shleifer, and Vishny (1989) see the willingness of the middle-class consumer to pay a little extra for quality as a force that encourages product differentiation, thereby feeding investment in the production and marketing of new goods.

It is this latter role that has become more pronounced with the expansion of global trade. Moreover, new trade theories have evolved to explain the stylized fact that most trade expansion has been occurring at the extensive margin – that

BOX 3.2   CONSUMERISM AND THE BLACK MIDDLE CLASS IN SOUTH AFRICA

According to Brulliard (2010), South Africa has developed a sizable black middle class, with discretionary spending that may surpass that of the country's white population. The white population represents about 10% of South Africa's population of 48 million. However,

> ...now that blacks, who make up 79% of the population, are getting better education and employment opportunities, they are swelling the ranks.
>
> [...] South Africa's "black diamonds," as the Unilever Institute calls them, score seven or higher on a scale of living standards of 1 to 10. The scoring system includes income and education levels as well as the type of occupation. In terms of earnings, 61% of black diamonds earn at least $800 a month, but households have often more than one wage earner. The category has seen a steady growth in recent years with a 15% rise to reach 3 million black diamonds in 2008, according to the Unilever Institute.

Source: Brulliard (2010).

BOX 3.3 MIDDLE-CLASS CONSUMPTION AS A DRIVER OF INVESTMENT

According to their definition, the World Bank estimates that there will be 43 million middle-class Africans by 2030. Reflective of this is the increasing interest being shown by global firms seeking to tap this growing market.

For example, in June 2011, Wal-Mart Stores Inc. sealed a $2.4 billion deal to acquire a majority stake in Massmart Holdings Ltd., with an eye to using the South African retailer as a springboard for the continent (McGroarty, 2011). Ford Motor Co. is also planning to spend $500 million to expand production in South Africa, while Yum Brands Inc. intends to double the number of KFC restaurants in Africa by 2014 (McGroarty, 2011).

Middle-class consumption is considered to be the main driver of such foreign investment in Africa.

is, through the expansion of new goods rather than increased trade in existing products (Hummels and Klenow, 2002). During the 20th century, the middle-class consumers of North America and Europe were traditionally the source of demand, while low- and middle-income countries in Asia were the source of supply. More recently, however, the consumption role of the middle class in Asia and other emerging strong economies is being emphasized. All eyes are now turning to Asia, and specifically to the emerging middle class in China, as the next major global consumers in the wake of the declining middle class and/or consumerism in Europe and America.

On a similar note, the AfDB (2011: 14) reports that Africa's emerging consumers are likely to assume the traditional role of the US and European middle classes as global consumers, and to play a key role in rebalancing the

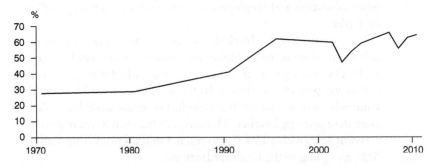

FIGURE 3.1 Domestic credit to the private sector in Africa, 1970–2010 (% of GDP) (source: World Bank (2011))

African economy.[8] This is lent credence by the fact that consumer spending in Africa, primarily by the middle class, remained reasonably resilient during the recession period of 2008/2009. It reached an estimated $680 billion in annual expenditures in 2008 (based on per capita consumption of more than $2) – or nearly a quarter of Africa's GDP. If consumption expenditure growth maintains its momentum, by 2020 Africa will likely reach $2.6 trillion in annual consumption expenditures and comprise a sizable proportion of worldwide consumption (AfDB, 2011).

Figure 3.1 shows that domestic credit to the private sector in Africa has grown significantly over time. This measure of the deepening and vibrancy of the private sector is also a good indication of the growth in entrepreneurial activities, which may also be linked to middle-class growth in Africa (see also Chapter 5 on 'Entrepreneurship'). Acemoglu and Fabrizio (1997), building on an earlier theory developed by Max Weber (1905), have also emphasized the role of the middle class as a source of entrepreneurship.

Conclusion

This chapter has investigated the overall change in consumption demand in selected African countries to determine how the middle class differs from the rest of the population in terms of its spending patterns.

The results suggest that, in most of the countries analyzed, consumption by the middle class has expanded considerably. This is due to an increase in the average consumption level of those in the middle class, combined with an increase in the size of the middle class itself. The overall growth is large for most of the African countries analyzed.

The country-specific analysis has identified some general patterns of middle-class consumption. We found a declining proportion of household expenditure spent on food as incomes increase. The middle class, by comparison with the poor, spends proportionately less on food and more on household assets, amenities, and better-quality dwellings. Middle-class households in Africa spend a similar proportion of their incomes on health and education as the poor, but this nonetheless represents a larger absolute expenditure value.

The middle class generally recognizes the higher quality of their living standards relative to others and are more confident about the future, but many are still reluctant to define themselves as rich or middle class, given that many 'middle-class' amenities are by no means guaranteed.

Notes

1 The methodological definitions of middle class used in the literature would benefit from more theoretical scrutiny which is beyond the scope of the present work. For reasons of cross-country comparability and data convenience, we adopt the conventional definition of per capita daily consumption of $2–$20 in 2005 PPP US$.

2 Due to data constraints, the time span of the data used may differ slightly across countries, therefore a two-year window is accepted here. For example, if no data are available for 1993, figures for 1992 or 1994 are considered instead. If none of the above is available, 1991 or 1995 figures are used as an alternative. The same rationale is followed for 2004 data. When there are no data available for 2004, 2003 figures are used instead, followed by 2005, 2002, and 2006, in order of preference.
3 Consider, for instance, that the top decile has an average consumption level of $15. While most of the households in this decile would be correctly classified as middle class as their consumption is lower than $20 per day, this represents only an approximation. It is likely that a small percentage of households at the top of this decile will have a level of consumption higher than $20.
4 However, note that the exact definition of consumption and the categories used as sub-components may vary across countries and over time.
5 The quintiles highlighted do not necessarily describe the middle class only. They are the best approximation available but the quintiles' boundaries may not exactly match the definition of poor, rich, and middle class used elsewhere in this book. They might also include households belonging to other categories. In the case of Ghana, for instance, the highest decile is likely to include households that belong to the 'rich' category. The same limitation applies at the lower boundary. However, despite this limitation, this approach successfully identified the main trend between categories.
6 Education and health are quite stable across classes, although as the middle-class total expenditure is higher than that of the poor, the amount spent is higher in absolute terms.
7 All data for Tables 3.11 to 3.14 derive from the Afrobarometer Values Surveys and relate to 2008 unless otherwise stated. They cover Benín, Botswana, Burkina Faso, Cabo Verde, Ghana, Kenya, Lesotho, Liberia, Madagascar, Malawi, Mali, Mozambique, Namibia, Nigeria, Senegal, South Africa, Tanzania, Uganda, Zambia, and Zimbabwe (2009).
8 See Box 3.2 on the growing consumerism of the middle class in South Africa.

References

Acemoglu, A., and Z. Fabrizio (1997). 'Was Prometheus Unbound by Chance?' *Journal of Political Economy*, vol. 105, no. 4, pp. 709–751.
AfDB (2011). 'The Middle of the Pyramid: Dynamics of the Middle Class in Africa.' Report published by the Complex of the Chief Economist (ECON). Tunis: African Development Bank.
Banerjee, A.V., and E. Duflo (2008). 'What Is Middle Class about the Middle Classes around the World?' *Journal of Economic Perspectives*, no. 22, pp. 3–28.
Banerjee, A.V., and E. Duflo (2011). *Poor Economics: A Radical Rethinking of the Way to Fight Global Poverty*. New York: Public Affairs Books.
Burger, R., S. Van Der Berg, and S. Nieftagodien (2004). 'Consumption Patterns of South Africa's Rising Black Middle-Class: Correcting for Measurement Errors.' Paper presented at the Conference of the Centre for the Study of African Economies (CSAE) on 'Poverty Reduction, Growth and Human Development in Africa.' Oxford, UK.
Deaton, A. (1997). *The Analysis of Household Surveys: A Microeconomic Approach to Development Policy*. Baltimore: Johns Hopkins University Press.
Deaton, A., and M. Grosh (1998). 'Guidelines for Constructing Consumption Aggregates for Welfare Analysis.' Paper no. 192, Princeton, NJ: Woodrow Wilson School of Public and International Affairs.

Deaton, A., and S. Zaidi (2002). *Guidelines for Constructing Consumption Aggregates for Welfare Analysis.* Washington DC: World Bank.

Estey, M. (2010). 'Rebuilding Liberia's Middle Class.' *GlobalPost* (online), May 19.

Hummels, D., and P.J. Klenow (2002). 'The Variety and Quality of a Nation's Trade.' Working Paper no. 8712. Cambridge, MA: National Bureau of Economic Research (NBER).

Johnson, K.S. (2010). 'Sierra Leone's Middle Class Gains Traction.' *GlobalPost* (online), May 19.

Kharas, H. (2010). 'The Emerging Middle Class in Developing Countries' Working Paper no. 285. Paris: OECD.

McGroarty, P. (2011). 'Africa's Middle Class to Boom.' *Wall Street Journal* (online), October 13.

McKinsey Report (2010) *Lions on the Move: The Progress and Potential of African Economies.* McKinsey Global Institute.

Mungai, C. (2011). 'Africa: East Africa's Growing Middle Class Hits 29 Million.' *The East African* (online).

Murphy, K.M., A. Schleifer, and R. Vishny (1989). 'Income Distribution, Market Size, and Industrialization,' *Quarterly Journal of Economics*, MIT Press, vol. 104, no. 3, pp. 537–564, August.

Renaissance Capital (2011). *A Survey of the Nigerian Middle Class.* September 26, 2011.

Schor, J. (1999). 'The New Politics of Consumption: Why Americans Want So Much More Than They Need,' *Boston Review*, Summer.

World Bank (2011). World Development Indicators. Washington DC: World Bank.

4

JOBS AND THE LABOR MARKET

Mary Strode, Lee Crawfurd, Simone Dettling, and Felix Schmieding

> ...nothing seems more middle class than the fact of having a steady well-paying job...
>
> Banerjee and Duflo (2008)

Introduction

The key to understanding the development of the African middle class is to examine how Africans earn their living. Defining the middle class as those spending between $2 and $10[1] per day, this chapter asks: what distinguishes someone who earns over $2 a day from someone who earns less?

In many ways they are similar, but there are two key differences. First, the middle class has moved away from agricultural self-employment toward non-agricultural wage employment (though this is a matter of degree, and many households and individuals engage in several types of work simultaneously). A second key distinction between the middle class and the poor consists in their terms of employment. Within the category of wage workers, there is a huge difference between casual laborers paid on a daily basis and regular salaried workers. Casual workers typically lack job security, have unpredictable hours and few benefits, whereas salaried employees enjoy steady and predictable working hours and payments with greater benefits (Banerjee and Duflo, 2008).

In the next section of this chapter, we identify the characteristics of a middle-class job in Africa and which sectors create such jobs. The analysis then moves on to identify the pathways through which Africans obtain middle-class jobs, focusing on the role of education and migration. Our research illustrates several trends which we believe will determine the growth of middle-class jobs in the region over the coming decades. The chapter concludes with a short summary of our main findings.

What is a middle-class job?

The strong economic annualized growth in Africa during the last decade of over 6 percent has been characterized by high labor intensity. The average employment–output growth elasticity of 0.6 has led to a rise in the ratio of employment to working-age population of 3.3 percent (IMF, 2011). However, such a rise will only translate into middle-class job growth if that employment is characterized by specific conditions.

According to Banerjee and Duflo (2008), what distinguishes a middle-class job is that it is steady and well paid. Steady means that working hours and salary payments are regular and foreseeable. A well-paid job signifies a consumption level above the poverty line of $2 a day. Furthermore, the economic risk associated with a job plays an important role in sustainably escaping poverty. Economic risk is far higher for own-account workers in the informal sector than for salaried employees in the formal sector (ILO, 2009).

How do the middle class earn their living?

Analyzing household-level data from 13 countries all over the world, Banerjee and Duflo (2008) conclude that what strongly characterizes middle-class jobs is their disconnection from agriculture. There are more middle-class jobs available in urban than in rural areas. The rural middle class tend to own less land and are less likely to work in agriculture. They either run a non-agricultural business or earn a salary outside agriculture. In urban areas, occupation patterns between the poor and the middle class are similar in terms of shares of entrepreneurs and wage workers. The main differences in these urban areas reside in the employment conditions, namely the regularity of payments and working hours, and the level of pay. Although the middle class is somewhat diversified, earning income from multiple sources, specialization increases with rising income.

Characteristics of middle-class jobs in Africa: Evidence from household-level data

Looking solely at a household-level data sample of African countries,[2] most of Banerjee and Duflo's (2008) conclusions hold in the African context. However, there is substantial variation in the sample, and for some characteristics the data do not support the findings of Banerjee and Duflo (2008) for African labor markets.

In rural areas, owning a non-agricultural business is clearly linked with higher consumption, as shown in Table 4.1. In urban areas, however, we see an increase in non-agricultural entrepreneurial activities only up to the floating middle class. Middle-class segments with higher consumption are less likely

TABLE 4.1   Percentage of households in selected African countries with at least one non-agricultural business: by per capita consumption level and rural/urban location

	Less than $1	Less than $2	$2–$4/day	$6–$10/day
Rural				
Côte d'Ivoire	16.7	23.7	28.8	39.5
Ghana	39.0	44.8	56.9	72.8
Morocco	41.1	37.2	35.1	29.3
Urban				
Côte d'Ivoire	47.3	64.6	57.0	35.8
Ghana	50.0	57.6	68.0	63.7

Source: Pooreconomics.com.

to derive their income from entrepreneurial activities and are more likely to receive a salary as an employee. For example, in Côte d'Ivoire, only 36 percent of the urban lower-middle class own a non-agricultural business, while 57 percent of the floating class and 65 percent of the poor (with consumption below $2) engage in non-agricultural entrepreneurial activities. Table 4.2 shows that in both urban and rural areas, the middle class is generally more likely to receive payment on a regular weekly or monthly basis. This indicates that an important characteristic of a middle-class job in Africa is the regularity and predictability of payments. At the same time, the middle class receives far fewer irregular payments (semester, piece rates, other) and is less likely to receive casual (hourly or daily) payment. For example, in Côte d'Ivoire, 93 percent of floating and 97 percent of urban lower-middle class households have at least one member who receives a weekly or monthly salary, compared with 77 percent of the poor households. At the same time, while 23 percent of the poor receive casual or other forms of payment, only 7 percent and 3 percent respectively of the floating and lower urban middle-class households are paid irregularly.

Contrary to Banerjee and Duflo's (2008) finding, the rural middle class in Africa is equally likely to be self-employed in agriculture as the poor, as shown in Table 4.3. In the limited sample of four African economies, the share of households with at least one member self-employed in agriculture increases with income in both Côte d'Ivoire and Morocco. Only in Ghana is the percentage of middle-class households with at least one member self-employed in agriculture lower than amongst poor rural households. In urban areas, all sample countries show a smaller share of agricultural self-employment in households with increasing income.

Table 4.4 shows that for the floating middle class and below, the share of households with one member self-employed outside agriculture generally increases with income in both urban and rural areas. The lower-middle class, however, seems less likely to be self-employed in the majority of countries, whether they work in agriculture or in other sectors.

TABLE 4.2 Per capita consumption levels and terms of payment in selected African countries: rural vs. urban areas (%)

	Casual payment (Hourly or daily)				Weekly or monthly				Other forms (Every trimester, semester, year, piece rates, other)			
	Less than $1	Less than $2	$2–$4	$6–$10	Less than $1	Less than $2	$2–$4	$6–$10	Less than $1	Less than $2	$2–$4	$6–$10
Rural												
Ghana	16.3	9.3	13.2	...	76.3	85.9	88.6	...	44.8	39.4	26.5	...
Côte d'Ivoire	...	4.3	6.2	5.2	...	83.5	84.6	86.8	0.0	12.2	9.2	8.0
Urban												
Ghana	16.3	7.0	12.5	11.6	81.6	92.5	89.1	88.4	23.3	12.3	4.2	4.8
Côte d'Ivoire	...	14.6	3.8	2.3	...	77.2	93.2	97.0	0.0	8.2	3.0	0.7
South Africa	...	34.7	29.3	...	...	...	98.6	...	...	...	...	...

Source: Pooreconomics.com.
Note: Empty cells denote missing data.

TABLE 4.3 Percentage of households in four African countries with at least one member self-employed in agriculture or other sector: by consumption level and rural/urban location

	In agriculture				In other sectors			
	Less than $1	Less than $2	$2–$4	$6–$10	Less than $1	Less than $2	$2–$4	$6–$10
Rural								
Ghana	85.4	80.4	62.1	42.2	53.1	60.2	72.4	76.8
Côte d'Ivoire	26.4	29.5	31.2	30.8	5.5	6.0	7.6	12.6
Morocco	66.4	74.0	83.8	91.2	76.3	81.7	89.0	90.2
South Africa	...	...	...	...	7.8	14.9	20.6	12.1
Tanzania	...	...	...	...	0.2	0.7	1.7	...
Urban	...	...	...	...	...	...	...	...
Ghana	54.3	41.1	14.6	15.4	71.0	79.1	78.9	69.3
Côte d'Ivoire	43.2	31.8	13.6	9.0	24.0	21.0	11.9	6.7
Morocco	...	...	...	...	...	...	...	...
South Africa	...	...	...	...	7.7	13.7	16.0	15.2
Tanzania	...	...	...	...	2.2	7.8	10.6	12.1

Source: Pooreconomics.com.
Note: Empty cells denote missing data.

The likelihood of earning a wage or salary in agriculture decreases with consumption levels in Côte d'Ivoire and South Africa, in both urban and rural areas. In Ghana, on the other hand, the percentage of households with at least one member working for a wage in agriculture increases concomitantly with rising consumption levels. In South Africa, the likelihood of working for a wage or salary outside agriculture decreases with rising consumption. However, in the poorer countries in our sample (Ghana and Côte d'Ivoire), a larger percentage of middle-class households earn a wage or a salary outside agriculture than is the case for poor households.

Generally, middle-class households in our sample countries seem to rely less on diversified income sources and to specialize more, as seen in Table 4.5. This specialization is less pronounced in rural areas than in urban areas. Over 50 percent of poor households in urban Côte d'Ivoire receive income from multiple sectors, while only 32 percent and 18 percent of urban middle-class households rely on diversified sources of income, indicating a far higher level of specialization which allows for the acquisition of sector-specific skills.

TABLE 4.4 Percentage of households in four African countries in which at least one member works for a wage or salary in agriculture and other sectors: by income level and rural/urban location

	In agriculture				In other sectors			
	Less than $1	Less than $2	$2–$4	$6–$10	Less than $1	Less than $2	$2–$4	$6–$10
Rural								
Côte d'Ivoire	93.4	86.0	73.4	57.8	22.7	30.6	42.7	55.0
Ghana	0.6	0.7	1.6	2.5	9.0	14.1	30.4	27.8
Morocco	...	...	...	...	...	...	...	...
South Africa	25.8	17.5	10.1	3.8	28.5	33.7	29.3	20.1
Urban								
Côte d'Ivoire	56.4	42.4	24.7	11.3	78.7	83.7	88.5	93.3
Ghana	1.7	2.1	4.8	4.4	18.8	31.0	46.9	48.3
Morocco	...	...	...	...	...	...	...	...
South Africa	7.6	6.7	3.1	0.6	52.4	40.9	32.0	13.4
Tanzania	...	...	...	...	...	...	...	...

Source: Pooreconomics.com.
Note: Empty cells denote missing data.

TABLE 4.5 Percentage of households in four African countries where at least one member receives income from multiple sectors: by income level and rural/urban location

	Less than $1	Less than $2	$2–$4	$6–$10
Rural				
Ghana	97.3	97.8	97.2	90.6
Côte d'Ivoire	38.1	42.3	42.1	39.8
Morocco	81.7	92.8	95.6	97.2
South Africa	1.6	0.7	0.1	1.5
Tanzania	...	...	...	...
Urban				
Ghana	95.5	95.6	94.7	89.8
Côte d'Ivoire	78.7	57.0	31.7	18.1
Morocco	...	...	...	...
South Africa	...	0.5	0.9	0.5
Tanzania	...	...	...	...

Source: Pooreconomics.com.
Note: Empty cells denote missing data.

Creating middle-class jobs in Africa: Evidence from macro-level data

We have seen that the 'typical' African middle-class job has certain characteristics: it is to be found outside agriculture; in urban areas; it brings in regular, foreseeable payments; and it requires a certain level of specialization. The question that next arises is: which sectors create such jobs?

Many SSA economies are still dominated by the agricultural sector; indeed in 2009, 59 percent of employment in SSA was in the agricultural sector. On average, only about one in ten workers was employed in the industrial sector (see Figure 4.1). The household-level data show that middle-class jobs are mainly created outside the agricultural sector. In this respect, the slow rate of industrialization in many African countries is impeding the growth of the middle class. The regional share of industrial employment has grown only marginally in the last 20 years, from 8 percent in 1990 to 11 percent in 2009 (ILO, 2011).

In several African countries, the services sector generates a high level of employment. However, a large share of this employment is informal. Only certain service industries create a substantial share of stable and well-paid jobs that enable employees to join the ranks of the middle class. The ILO data[3] presented in Table 4.6 show that skills-intensive sectors – such as communications, education, health and financial services – generate middle-class jobs that are steady and well paid. On the other hand, sectors such as wholesale and retail, hotels and restaurants, and construction largely employ informal labor.

In Ethiopia, only 27 percent of the workers in construction and 9 percent of those in hotels and restaurants enjoyed regular working hours and payment.

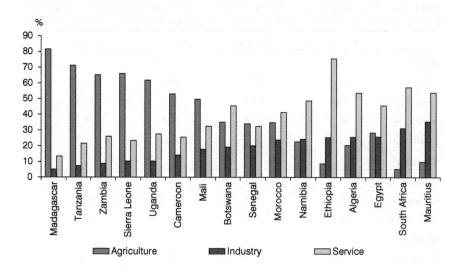

FIGURE 4.1   Percentage of male employment by sector in selected countries, 2009 (source: ILO (2011))

TABLE 4.6 Percentage of paid employment as a share of total labor in three African countries

	% of paid employment as share of total labor
Ethiopia (2005)	
Construction	26.5
Hotels and restaurants	8.5
Transport, storage and communications	56.6
Financial intermediation	56.0
Education, health and social work	61.9
Zambia (2000)	
Construction	37.6
Wholesale, retail, hotels and restaurants	27.5
Transport, storage and communications	86.9
Financing, insurance, real estate and business services	98.0
Botswana (2006)	
Construction	78.3
Hotels and restaurants	64.5
Transport, storage and communications	75.1
Financial intermediation	92.9
Education, health and social work	97.2

Source: ILO LABORSTA database.

In contrast, more than 60 percent of the workforce in education, health, and social services were employed formally with a steady income; while in financial intermediation and transport and communications, the figure was 56 percent.

Similarly, only 27 percent of those working in hotels and restaurants and 38 percent of construction workers in Zambia in 2000 were working as paid employees. On the other hand, 98 percent of Zambians working in finance, real estate, insurance and business services, and 87 percent of labor in transportation, storage and communications, reported being in regular, paid employment.

The overall share of well-paid, steady employment in SSA economies remains low, having increased by only four percentage points from 2000 to 2009, from 20 percent to 24 percent. This is significantly lower than all other global regions, except South Asia. Still, this increase is far stronger than in the 1990s, when the share of steady, well-paid employment increased by only 1.4 percentage points over the decade (ILO, 2011).

How do the poor become middle class?

The rise of the middle class in Africa at the aggregate level has been driven by broad-based economic growth, which has spurred incomes across a range of sectors. Mobility at the individual level may be due to a variety of factors, including various intangible differences; however, education and geographic mobility both play a key role, as examined below.

Education: The key to a middle-class job?

At the micro level, it is clear that education provides a financial return to individual investment. The expansion of education in Africa since independence has done much to lay the foundations for the emergence of a middle class.

How education increases earnings

The positive correlation between education and individual incomes is one of the most robust found in social science, and in Africa this is no exception.[4] Education can increase earnings through two main channels: either by increasing productivity within a current job or by allowing for the acquisition of a better job.

Kuepie, Nordman, and Roubaud (2006) have studied the returns to education in seven West African cities (see Figure 4.2). Their findings show significantly larger returns to individuals who work in the public sector and the formal private sector than in the informal sector, yet they also reveal a correlation with clear positive returns everywhere. These differentiated returns across sectors lead to a sorting effect, as educated individuals move where they can gain the highest return on their investment.

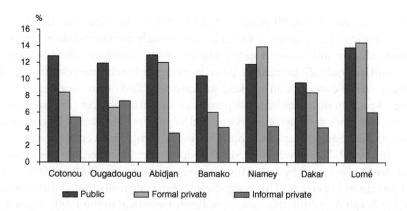

FIGURE 4.2   Percentage increase in earnings for an additional year of education, by sector, in urban West Africa (source: Kuepie, Nordman, and Roubaud (2006))

Figure 4.3 uses household survey data from 20 countries to show the relationship between education and employment status. Those with some education are much more likely to be in paid employment than those with no education.

Drawing on data from Ghana and Tanzania, Teal (2010) shows that workers in the public sector and in larger private firms have substantially higher levels of education than those in small-scale private firms or in self-employment. Higher-level education gives individuals the opportunity to move between sectors, as qualifications can provide employers with credible signs of higher productivity.

Fafchamps, Soderbom, and Benhassine (2008) show that this job-sorting occurs within individual sectors as well as between sectors. Focusing on manufacturing, they find that individuals with higher education procure the more skills-intensive, productive, and higher-income jobs.

Finally, there is also a linkage between education and location, with the returns being greatest in urban areas.

Will education continue to drive middle-class growth?

Although the individual returns from investments in education are clear, there exists something of a paradox at the aggregate level. In 2001, Pritchett wrote an article titled 'Where has all the education gone?,' examining why the massive expansion in education around the world had failed to boost economic growth

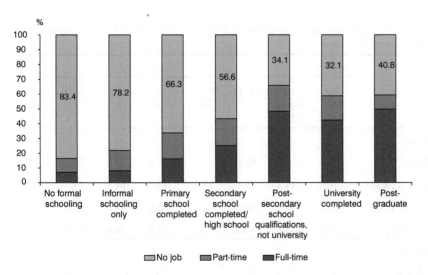

FIGURE 4.3 Employment status by educational level, 2008 (Question asked: 'Do you have a job paying cash income?') (source: Afrobarometer Values Surveys. All surveys from 2008 unless otherwise stated cover: Benín, Botswana, Burkina Faso, Cabo Verde, Ghana, Kenya, Lesotho, Liberia, Madagascar, Malawi, Mali, Mozambique, Namibia, Nigeria, Senegal, South Africa, Tanzania, Uganda, Zambia (2009), and Zimbabwe (2009))

at the national level. A major explanatory factor in Africa resides in the weak institutional environment. This means that while education can provide private gains to individuals, the counteracting context is a poorly governed public sector or parastatal organization, where scarce resources are wasted competing for government funding (known as 'rent-seeking'). Since 2000, the institutional environment has significantly improved in Africa, raising the prospect of a more productive and socially beneficial utilization of skilled labor in both the public and private sectors (Marshall and Jaggers, 2002).

These gains are being sustained and manifested in a variety of areas. In 2010/11, the World Bank's *Doing Business* report found that 36 out of 46 SSA governments had improved their economy's regulatory environment. This was a record improvement in reform since 2005. The growing middle class is also investing more in the education of the next generation. There is a clear and positive relationship between household earnings and investment in child education. Across four countries (Côte d'Ivoire, Ghana, South Africa, and Tanzania), both girls and boys from middle-class households have a better chance of being enrolled in school than children from poor households (see Tables 4.7 and 4.8).

The emerging consensus on the returns to education in Africa is that they are convex – meaning that the increase in income from an additional year of education is higher for tertiary or advanced education than it is for primary education.

TABLE 4.7 Percentage of girls in school in four African countries: by consumption level and rural/urban location

	Girls 7–12				Girls 13–18			
	Less than $1	Less than $2	$2–$4	$6–$10	Less than $1	Less than $2	$2–$4	$6–$10
Rural								
Ghana	69.4	76.5	86.0	...	45.8	50.8	58.4	...
Côte d'Ivoire	16.9	34.3	49.8	71.3	10.0	14.5	25.2	27.3
South Africa	87.2	89.1	86.6	...	85.6	84.7	84.5	...
Tanzania	45.3	52.1	60.5	...	47.6	55.6	65.8	...
Urban								
Ghana	81.9	83.9	86.0	...	58.0	62.2	60.5	...
Côte d'Ivoire	...	44.2	61.3	59.9	...	21.4	41.7	46.9
South Africa	83.6	92.7	93.5	94.1	...	91.4	89.5	94.5
Tanzania	62.3	64.2	70.0	68.1	45.8	54.6	69.4	76.3

Source: Pooreconomics.com.
Note: Empty cells denote missing data.

TABLE 4.8 Percentage of boys in school in four African countries: by consumption level and rural/urban location

	Boys 7–12				Boys 13–18			
	Less than $1	Less than $2	$2–$4	$6–$10	Less than $1	Less than $2	$2–$4	$6–$10
Rural								
Ghana	74.8	79.1	88.3	...	62.4	62.6	62.0	...
Côte d'Ivoire	29.3	48.4	67.9	73.3	17.5	28.6	51.4	53.4
South Africa	82.5	84.4	85.6	...	79.0	83.4	87.2	...
Tanzania	46.4	47.8	62.1	...	57.5	61.5	67.6	...
Urban								
Ghana	86.7	89.0	93.4	...	67.5	68.6	76.7	...
Côte d'Ivoire	...	55.0	77.5	71.8	...	34.5	64.6	67.3
South Africa	85.9	89.2	91.2	92.7	...	89.4	89.8	91.8
Tanzania	53.1	49.4	63.9	75.6	56.4	62.1	69.2	91.9

Source: Pooreconomics.com.
Note: Empty cells denote missing data.

Migration: How important is spatial mobility to securing a middle-class job?

Spatial mobility has the potential to play a key role in economic advancement, both internally within Africa and for those migrants who choose to leave the continent. Scale economies and agglomeration mean that when people are located densely together, they become more productive, particularly those with skills (World Bank, 2009). These differences in productivity lead to spatially differentiated earnings. Wages in cities and towns are typically higher than those in rural areas (though prices for most amenities are also higher). Moving from the village to the city provides an opportunity to seek out a better-paid job in a different sector or industry, and many of the new middle-class jobs created are in urban areas.

In their empirical analysis, Banerjee and Duflo (2008) report that the middle class in many countries are much more likely than the poor to move to a different area to find work. This supports the idea that, for those who were poor to begin with, moving to a new area can provide an opportunity to exit poverty and secure a middle-class job (see Figure 4.4).

Those who were middle class to begin with are also more likely to move for work reasons, compared with the poor. This is because their higher income allows them to explore opportunities and take the risk of relocating to a new area, even if this means leaving existing social networks and support structures behind. In a

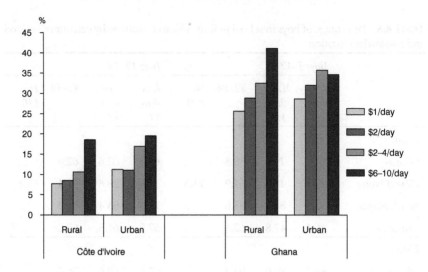

FIGURE 4.4   Percentage of households in Ghana and Côte d'Ivoire that have relocated for work reasons: by income level and urban/rural location (source: Pooreconomics. com)

field experiment in Bangladesh, Bryan, Chowdhury, and Mobarak (2011) found that offering rural villagers a free return bus ticket to the nearest city induced a large proportion of households (over one-fifth) to send a family member to the city in search of work. The migrant worker felt safe in the knowledge that they had the insurance policy of the return ticket in case things did not work out.

Beegle, De Weerdt, and Dercon (2011) discovered large returns to internal migration within Tanzania, as it added around 36 percentage points to consumption growth. Their findings reflect the same pattern of population relocating to areas with greater job opportunities.

International migration

For an individual willing to migrate abroad, the benefits are potentially even greater than would be gained by relocating within the same country. Clemens, Montenegro, and Pritchett (2008) document the huge wage differential between observably identical workers in different countries. Workers moving to the United States from Africa to do identical jobs may increase their wages massively. Estimates put the gain to a Nigerian male working in the urban formal sector to be at least 700 percent.

Perhaps unsurprisingly, polls have found that around a third of Africans would like to permanently emigrate to another country, almost regardless of their current employment status. The upper-middle class is slightly keener to migrate than the poor, perhaps reflecting their greater confidence, awareness of opportunities and capacity to take on risk (Gallup World, 2009). Figure 4.5

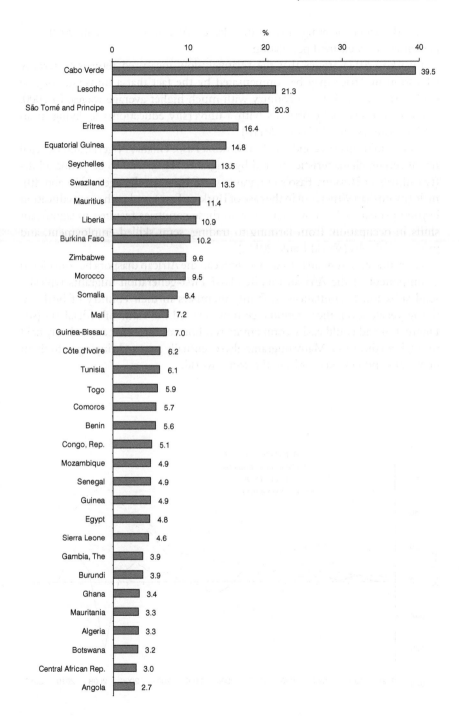

FIGURE 4.5 Stock of emigrants from Africa, 2010 (% of population) (source: World Bank (2011a))

shows the stock of emigrants from selected African countries in 2010, as a percentage of their total population.

Nyarko (2011) argues that the relatively low measured returns to tertiary education in Africa may be compensated by the fact that a university degree could provide a ticket to a country with much higher average wages. In 2000, one out of every eight Africans with a university education was living in an OECD country (World Bank, 2011b).

Household surveys conducted in Burkina Faso, Ghana, Nigeria, and Senegal reveal certain characteristics shared by migrants. They tend to be young adults (two-thirds of Burkina Faso's emigrants were between the ages of 15 and 40), male (more than 90 percent in the case of Burkina Faso), and with some education beyond primary school. Migration from these countries resulted in significant shifts in occupation: from farming to trading, semi-skilled employment, and professional jobs (World Bank, 2011a).

A key question remains: To what extent can the African diaspora be considered a component of the African middle class? First-generation migrants typically send substantial remittances to family members in their country of birth. At the aggregate level, these remittance flows exceed the value of official aid (see Figure 4.6) and could easily compensate sending countries for any subsidy paid for higher education. Many migrants also eventually return, bringing with them new skills and new networks to the wider world.

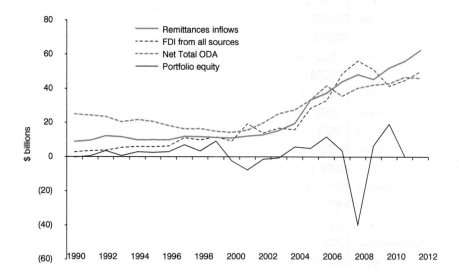

FIGURE 4.6 Remittances and other resource flows to Africa, 1990–2010 (source: World Bank (2011a))

Return migration, education, and leaders

The positive impact of return migration is illustrated to some extent by looking at African leaders. Around 40 percent of African leaders received a tertiary education abroad, and their skills and connections have contributed to increased foreign direct investment (Constant and Tien, 2010) and even to higher economic growth for their countries (Besley et al., 2011).

The diaspora is also contributing to building a new generation of schools and universities, such as the African Leadership Academy for 16 to 19-year-olds in Johannesburg and the Ashesi University College in Ghana, which were both founded by Africans educated in the US.

The question of a 'brain drain'

A common concern surrounding migration from poor to rich countries is that of a 'brain drain' of key skilled workers. There is, however, little evidence that skilled migration causes serious damage to sending countries. A paper by Gibson and McKenzie (2011) argues that there may in fact be a 'brain gain' effect, in which migration may increase the returns to education and could boost investment in secondary and tertiary education, leaving a higher total stock of educated individuals, even net of migration.

Future growth in middle-class jobs

Our analysis so far has identified private sector development in manufacturing and various service industries, as well as migration and urbanization, as determinants driving the growth of middle-class jobs. We now look ahead, to forecast the evolution of middle-class jobs in the coming decades.

The private sector in Africa is expanding rapidly and strong expansion in manufacturing and service industries such as telecommunications and financial intermediation is likely to translate into a sustained growth in middle-class jobs (Juma, 2011). The AfDB (2011) forecasts sustained economic growth for the region, doubling the average GDP per capita by 2030, despite strong population growth. While about a quarter of this growth will be driven by natural resources, continuing the trend of the recent decade, the McKinsey Global Institute (2010) expects consumer-facing industries, such as telecommunications and financial services, to grow at an annual rate of 7.8 percent and 8 percent respectively, and manufacturing at 4.6 percent annually over the next ten years (see Figure 4.7).

If we assume that the current labor-elasticity of growth in Africa will remain relatively constant, the expansion of the private sector should result in annual job growth of about 6 percent. Many of the jobs in telecommunications, financial services and to some extent manufacturing will demand a certain level of skills, providing increasing returns to education and raising the demand for skilled

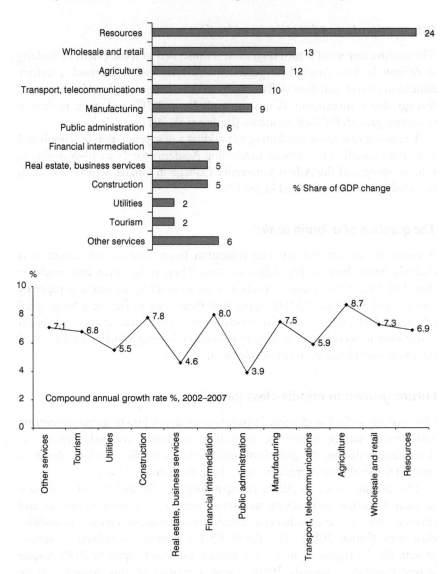

FIGURE 4.7   Sector shares of change in real GDP, 2002–2007 (100% = $235 billion)
(source: McKinsey Global Institute (2010))

labor. As access to schooling is expanding, literacy rates are expected to reach 96
percent by 2060, increasing the supply of skilled labor (IMF, 2011). With labor
productivity growth forecast to continue at a robust 3 percent, not only will
jobs in these new industries expand, but it is likely that wages will also increase
(McKinsey, 2010).

The new job opportunities will be located predominantly in urban areas. At
the same time, the agricultural sector in Africa is expected to contract, partly

due to the impact of global warming. As the rain-fed agriculture in Africa is extremely climate sensitive and the increased population pressure accelerates soil erosion, the AfDB (2011) forecasts a significant reduction in rain-fed land suitable for agricultural production.

With economic opportunities being concentrated in towns and cities, urbanization is expected to progress rapidly, increasing the share of city-dwellers from 40 percent in 2010 to 50 percent by 2050 and giving greater access to urban middle-class jobs. At the same time, productivity gains from agglomeration are expected to translate into greater labor productivity and wage growth. The AfDB (2011) estimates an increase in productivity of 4–8 percent when a city doubles its population.

Despite these positive trajectories, it needs to be borne in mind that the growth of well-paid, middle-class jobs starts from a comparatively low level. Even with forecasts of 10 percent annual growth in formal sector wage employment, the informal sector will continue to dominate the labor market, representing 60–70 percent of the workforce in 2020 (IMF, 2011). With the working-age population expected to triple by 2060, even a strong expansion of the formal sector will only translate into a moderate increase in the proportion of the population holding steady, middle-class jobs.

Conclusion

Analyzing household-level data from five African countries, this chapter has identified several characteristics of middle-class jobs. The 'typical' African middle-class job is to be found outside agriculture, in urban areas; it brings in a regular and predictable income stream and requires a certain level of specialized skills. Macro-level data show that the creation of middle-class jobs strongly depends on industrialization, especially the growth of manufacturing, as well as the expansion of certain service sectors, such as communications, transportation and financial services.

Two key factors to accessing middle-class jobs for Africans are: (i) to achieve a higher level of education, and (ii) to be willing to move in search of work, whether this is migration within the same country or overseas. As African governments and citizens continue to increase their investment in education at all levels, there is good reason to hope that the growth of the middle class during the past decade can be sustained.

With the private sector forecast to foster strong growth, especially in skills-intensive service industries, we expect the African economies to increasingly create new middle-class jobs. At the same time, African cities will continue to expand at a rapid pace, creating the dynamic environments conducive to innovation and higher labor productivity. Despite these positive trajectories, the informal sector will continue to dominate the African labor market in the coming decade, as the growth of steady, well-paid employment is starting from an extremely low level.

Notes

1 The definition used in this chapter differs from that of Chapter 1 due to the format of the data on which we have drawn. We distinguish between the floating middle class, with an income of $2–$4, and the lower-middle class, with an income of $6–$10.
2 The sample consists of data from Côte d'Ivoire, Ghana, Morocco, South Africa, and Tanzania. The country data used form part of Banerjee and Duflo's Poor Economics Dataset available at www.pooreconomics.com.
3 LABORSTA database, ILO, http://laborsta.ilo.org/.
4 For example, De Vreyer et al. (2010) on seven West African countries; Fonkeng and Ntembe (2009) on Cameroon; Kazianga (2004) on Burkina Faso; Siphambe (2000) on Botswana; Söderbom et al. (2005) on Kenya and Tanzania; and Uwaifo (2005) on Nigeria; and Appleton, S., G. Kingdon, J. Knight, M. Soderbom, and F. Teal (2003) on Uganda, Ghana, and South Africa.

References

AfDB (2011). *The Middle of the Pyramid: Dynamics of the Middle Class in Africa*. Tunis: African Development Bank.
Appleton, S., G. Kingdon, J. Knight, M. Soderbom, and F. Teal (2003). *Does Investing in Education Reduce Poverty? Evidence from Ghana, Uganda and South Africa*, id21 Development Research Reporting Service. Brighton, UK: ID21, Institute of Development Studies, University of Sussex.
Banerjee, A.V., and E. Duflo. (n.d.). Poor Economics Online Database. http://pooreconomics.com/data/country/home (accessed 18 September 2014).
Banerjee, A.V., and E. Duflo (2008). 'What is Middle Class about the Middle Classes around the World?' *Journal of Economic Perspectives*, vol. 22, pp. 3–28.
Beegle, K., J. De Weerdt, and S. Dercon (2011). 'Migration and Economic Mobility in Tanzania: Evidence from a Tracking Survey,' *Review of Economics and Statistics*, vol. 93, no. 3, pp. 1010–1033.
Besley, T., J. Motalvo, and M. Reynal-Querol (2011). 'Do Educated Leaders Matter?' *The Economic Journal*, vol. 121, no. 554, pp. 205–227.
Bryan, G., A.S. Chowdhury, and M. Mobarak (2011). 'Seasonal Migration and Risk Aversion: Experimental Evidence from Bangladesh.' BREAD Working Paper no. 319. Bureau for Research and Economic Analysis of Development.
Clemens, M., C.E. Montenegro, and L. Pritchett (2008). 'The Place Premium: Wage Differences for Identical Workers across the US.' Border Working Paper no. 148. Washington DC: Center for Global Development.
Constant, A., and B. Tien (2010). 'African Leaders: Their Education Abroad and FDI Flows.' DIW Berlin Discussion Paper no. 1087. Berlin: DIW.
Dercon, S. (2011). 'Social Protection, Efficiency and Growth.' CSAE Working Paper WPS/2011-17. Oxford, UK: Centre for the Study of African Economies.
De Vreyer, P., F. Gubert, and F. Roubaud (2010). 'Migration, Self-Selection and Returns to Education in the WAEMU,' *Journal of African Economies*. vol. 19, no. 1, pp. 52–82. Oxford, UK: Centre for the Study of African Economies.
Fafchamps, M., M. Soderbom, and N. Benhassine (2008). 'Wage Gaps and Job Sorting in African Manufacturing,' *Journal of African Economies*, vol. 18, no. 5, pp. 824–868.
Fonkeng, G.E., and A.N. Ntembe (2009). 'Higher Education and Economic Development in Africa: The Case of Cameroon,' *Educational Research and Reviews*, vol. 4, no. 5, pp. 231–246.

Gallup World (2009). '700 Million Worldwide Desire to Migrate Permanently.' November 2.

Gibson, J., and D. McKenzie (2011). 'Eight Questions about Brain Drain,' *Journal of Economic Perspectives*, vol. 25, no. 3, pp. 107–128.

ILO (2009). *Guide to the New Millennium Development Goals Employment Indicators*. Geneva: International Labor Organization.

ILO (2011). *Global Employment Trends*. Geneva: International Labor Organization.

IMF (2011). *Regional Economic Outlook: Sub-Saharan Africa*. Washington DC: International Monetary Fund.

Juma, C. (2011) 'Africa's New Engine,' *Finance & Development*, vol. 48, no. 4, pp. 6–11.

Kazianga, H. (2004). 'Schooling Returns for Wage Earners in Burkina Faso: Evidence from the 1994 and 1998 National Surveys.' Discussion Paper no. 892. New Haven, CT: Yale University Press.

Kuépié, M., C.J. Nordman, and F. Roubaud. (2006). 'Education and Labour Market Outcomes in Urban West Africa,' Working Document. Paris: DIAL.

Marshall, M.G., and K. Jaggers (2002). Polity IV Project: Political Regime Characteristics and Transitions, 1800–2002. Version P4v2002e [Computer File]. College Park, MD: Center for International Development and Conflict Management, University of Maryland.

McKinsey Global Institute (2010). *Lions on the Move: The Progress and Potential of African Economies*.

Nyarko, Y. (2011). 'The Returns to the Brain Drain and Brain Circulation in Sub-Saharan Africa: Some Computations using Data from Ghana,' Working Paper no. 16813, Cambridge, MA: National Bureau of Economic Research (NBER).

Poor economics http://pooreconomics.com/ (accessed 18 September 2014).

Siphambe, H.K. (2000). 'Rates of Return to Education in Botswana Households,' *Economics of Education Review*, vol. 19, no. 3, pp. 291–300.

Söderbom, M., F. Teal, A. Wambugu, and G. Kahyarara (2005). 'The Dynamics of Returns to Education in Kenyan and Tanzanian Manufacturing Employees in Manufacturing Firms.' CSAE Working Paper WPS/2003-17. Oxford: Centre for the Study of African Economies.

Teal, F. (2010). 'Higher Education and Economic Development in Africa: a Review of Channels and Interactions.' CSAE Working Paper WPS/2010-25. Oxford: Centre for the Study of African Economies.

Uwaifo, R. Oleyere (2005). *Africa's Education Enigma? The Nigerian Story*. Berkeley, CA: Berkeley University Press.

World Bank (2009). *World Development Report 2009: Reshaping Economic Geography*. Washington DC: World Bank.

World Bank (2011a). *Doing Business 2012: Doing Business in a More Transparent World*. Washington DC: World Bank.

World Bank (2011b). *Leveraging Migration for Africa: Remittances, Skills, and Investments*. Washington DC: World Bank.

5

ENTREPRENEURSHIP

Mohamed Ayadi and
Mohamed Safouane Ben Aïssa

Introduction

Small and medium enterprises (SMEs) constitute an important source of employment for both developed and developing economies. In some African countries, micro and small enterprises (MSEs) also play a vital role as subsistence for disadvantaged individuals (Liedholm, 2001).

In Africa, low income levels are associated with high levels of insecure self-employment due to a shortage of decent jobs. More than three-quarters of workers are vulnerable employees, with four out of five being counted among the working poor (ILO, 2011). Vulnerable employment is an even more serious issue for African women. Women are more likely than men to work in insecure jobs, either as own-account workers or as contributing family workers. More than 84 percent of women in Sub-Saharan Africa (SSA), compared with 71 percent of men, are engaged in this type of work (AfDB, 2011a).

When thinking about economic development and job creation, we need to distinguish between two kinds of entrepreneurship: creating jobs for outside workers or solely subsistence jobs (Charman and Peterson, 2009). In most SSA countries, people take refuge in activities that provide only minimal, subsistence support. This reflects a weakness in African economies to generate productive jobs. Africa creates significantly fewer opportunistic enterprises than other developing regions. Put differently, opportunity (as opposed to necessity) entrepreneurship is notably less prevalent in SSA than in other regions.

We may question the failure of the continent to mobilize the type of entrepreneurship that could create decent jobs in large numbers. When opportunities were created in the past through the privatization of state assets in the context of structural adjustment programs, few African entrepreneurs were in a position to take advantage of them (UNECA, 2005). On average, the number of firms currently being created in Africa is less than one-fifth the level being generated in other global regions. In addition, newly created African firms are smaller than those created elsewhere. A further constraint to entrepreneurship is the high level of unskilled workers in the continent as well as the lack of experienced commercial managers (Nkurunziza, 2011).

The positive relationship between human capital development and economic growth in Sub-Saharan Africa has come under close investigation in the past. McPherson (1992) concludes that owners of commercial enterprises who have undergone some vocational training grew their businesses 9 percent faster than those without such training. Similarly, Parker (1994) found that in Kenya, businesses with workers trained formally at vocational schools exhibit higher growth than those with untrained workers.

One way of explaining economic development is in terms of the education, entrepreneurial culture, psychological traits, and skills of economic agents (Barro, 1996; 1998). Past efforts by governments and donors to boost private sector development in SSA have often met with disappointing results. Schemes aimed at strengthening specific industries, groups of enterprises, or supporting institutions have rarely had a significant impact. The World Bank's 'Doing Business' agenda advocates minimal regulatory government intervention and a limited role in supporting particular economic actors (World Bank, 2006).

What does the middle class do?

Chapter 4 of this book revealed that middle-class individuals are more likely to hold salaried jobs and that they tend to have smaller families. They also spend more on the nutrition and schooling of their children than the poor (Chapter 1; AfDB, 2011b). In other words, the middle class have better educational and professional experiences than the poor. It has also been shown that Africa's middle class is strongest in countries that have robust and growing private sectors (Ramachandran, Gelb, and Shah, 2009).

Evidence from South African and Tunisian household surveys shows that middle-class populations tend to congregate in urban areas (2012 South African General Household Survey: Metadata/Statistics South Africa; 2010 Tunisian INS Household Survey).

There is a large proportion of the middle class in urban areas in both Tunisia and South Africa. By contrast 67 percent of the poor class in Tunisia and 52 percent of the poor in South Africa live in rural areas compared with only 15 percent of the middle class. In South Africa another 37 percent of the floating class also live in tribal areas. Over two-thirds of the middle class in Tunisia and South Africa are located in the largest cities. Similarly, there are more opportunities to become an entrepreneur in urban areas than in rural areas.

Middle-class household heads tend to have higher aspirations than their poorer counterparts, including those in the floating class (e.g., living on $2–4 a day). They tend to look for stable and permanent employment or entrepreneurial activities generating better revenues. Middle-class individuals are more qualified which helps them to have permanent and stable jobs and also to create 'entrepreneurial opportunity'. In Tunisia, 89 percent of formal activities are done by the middle-class households. On the other hand, 41 percent of the poor households and 22 percent of floating-class households are engaged in irregular or non-formal activities, compared with less than 8 percent of the middle class. Furthermore, 54 percent of the poor class are seasonal workers, working less than 12 months per year. Less than 10 percent of the middle class are in this same situation.

Middle-class households have better opportunities for productive entrepreneurship and even more opportunities for being managers in larger enterprises. The poor class households are more likely to be in 'subsistence entrepreneurship' often working alone as 'independent'.

It is no surprise then that middle-class people are generally considered suitable partners for private sector development and as agents of entrepreneurship. However, other conditions for doing business and entrepreneurship development are required. Julien (1989), Schumpeter (1934), and Shane (2003) make the case that entrepreneurs may be the agents of economic change but that their contribution is highly dependent on the environment in which they operate. Ginsburg (2000), Platteau (2001), and Putnam, Leonardi, and Nanetti (1993) argue that development can only be explained in terms of structure, social norms, regulations, and underlying administrative/fiscal conditions, such as those concerning legislation, taxation, and bureaucracy.

De Soto (1989) claims that the main obstacle for poor people seeking to become entrepreneurs is the legal system, which induces them to operate outside the law. 'Bad laws,' such as licensing, may force them to operate informally and so deprive them of opportunities to enjoy 'good laws' such as property rights. Richer countries are able to spend more on the bureaucracy to ensure that it works effectively, whereas poor countries are unable to sufficiently remunerate workers to assure high motivation. As a consequence, bureaucracies in poor countries tend to be ineffective and/or corrupt (Svensson, 2008). As a result, a large number of enterprises in developing countries have developed informally to avoid the burden of red tape and excessive regulation. The UNDP's Commission on the Private Sector and Development (UNDP, 2004) estimates that 80 percent of the non-agricultural workforce in SSA operates in the informal economy.

Targeted political initiatives to overcome constraints to doing business are sorely needed. A number of such initiatives in various African countries have contributed to the development of a thriving private sector and the emergence of modern opportunistic enterprises. In the analysis that follows, we look in detail at the Tunisian middle-class initiative since 1970, as well as the South Africa black middle-class political initiative. These success stories will help us to identify some of the political issues surrounding entrepreneurship development.

The role of entrepreneurship and the emergence of the middle class

In the mid-19th century, as industrialization was changing the structure of economies and societies in Europe, Marx defined two classes, namely capitalists and workers. However, since that time, sociologists and political theorists have identified a third group, namely those who *look forward to the future and consider savings and education as essential*. This group enjoys a comfortable income, job security, and opportunities for upward mobility. It represents neither the poor, nor the working class, nor the rich, but the *middle class* (Birdsall, Graham, and Pettinato, 2000).

The correlation between entrepreneurship and the middle class seems almost self-evident. The OECD (2011) concludes that the growth of a segment of the population with higher living standards than those of their poorer compatriots offers new – demand driven – markets and opportunities for entrepreneurship.

Opportunity versus necessity entrepreneurship

In poor economies, where paid employment opportunities are limited and social protection is non-existent or weak, people are driven mainly by survival needs. It is their inability to be hired as employees that pushes them into running their own businesses (Charman and Peterson, 2009), rather than a proactive identification of a new market opportunity. In contrast, a large proportion of the self-employed in OECD countries are motivated by a desire for greater independence (Hessels et al., 2008).

In developing countries, entrepreneurship and job status denote different things to poor and middle-class people. Combining a better education with job experience produces more highly skilled workers, capable of becoming productive entrepreneurs. On the other hand, a lack of skills leads to informal and subsistence entrepreneurship. Opportunities for self-employment in subsistence micro and small enterprises (MSEs) are largely restricted to activities with low entry barriers in terms of skills and capital (e.g. street trading, garment manufacture, etc.). These enterprises absorb a segment of the labor force that is not easily employable in the modern economy. These are the people with low levels of education, the handicapped, elderly people, single mothers, and persons who are temporarily unemployed.

There are established links between entrepreneurship, innovation, job creation, and the knowledge-based economy, and between entrepreneurship and economic growth. As we consider job creation, a distinction must be drawn between two classes of entrepreneurs (Van Stel, Carree, and Thurik, 2007), 'opportunity entrepreneurs' and 'necessity entrepreneurs', as defined below:

- *Opportunity entrepreneurs* or *Schumpeterian entrepreneurs* engage in business to pursue a perceived business opportunity. They create innovative change through the introduction of new products or technologies to conquer new markets. They generate jobs in the formal sector.

- *Necessity entrepreneurs* or *survival entrepreneurs* start their own business due to necessity (lack of other options) or survival. They create fewer jobs, and these are mainly in the informal sector, are vulnerable and low paid.

Schumpeterian entrepreneurs capitalize on ideas learned through previous employment to start their own business (Braguinsky, Klepper, and Ohyama, 2009). Necessity entrepreneurs, on the other hand, are unlikely to end up as future capitalists. If they ever find the right salaried job, they will close down their business (Banerjee and Duflo, 2008).

The boundaries separating 'survival' from 'opportunist' entrepreneurs are not clear-cut. Globally, we can say that the former are generally unsophisticated, small, and reliant on family labor. They operate essentially in the informal sector, particularly in trading, thanks to the low cost of entry to that sector. Opportunity entrepreneurs generally have high ambition and more capacity to take bigger risks. They use hired labor, enjoy higher incomes, have work experience prior to starting their businesses, and use networks and commercial knowledge for the betterment of their enterprises (Charman and Petersen, 2009).

Entrepreneurship in Africa

Empirical illustrations, based on the World Bank Enterprises Surveys and on national databases, depict divergences among countries and sectors.

Dual sectors

Sandefur (2006) provides data on changes in employment by firm size in the Ghanaian manufacturing sector between 1987 and 2003 (see Table 5.1). The data show a strong increase in employment at MSEs, stagnation at a low level in medium-sized firms, and a marked decrease in the employment share of large firms over this period. The average firm size decreased significantly between 1987 and 2003. This example, found in UNIDO (2008), shows that few MSEs manage the transition to large or even medium-sized firms.

In a study of nine countries in SSA, van Biesebroeck describes this lack of upward mobility as follows:

> Transitions between size classes or movements in the productivity distribution are very slow, especially at the top of the size or productivity distribution. Large firms remain large, and more productive firms remain at the top of the distribution. Smaller and less productive firms have a very hard time advancing in the size of productivity distribution.

(van Biesebroeck, 2005)

TABLE 5.1   Ghanaian census data on size of manufacturing firms, 1987 and 2003

		1987		2003	
	Employee size	Firms	%	Firms	%
Micro enterprises	1 to 4	2,884	35	14,352	55
Small enterprises	5 to 19	4,492	54	10,256	39
Medium enterprises	20 to 99	733	9	1,229	5
Large enterprises	100+	240	3	251	1
Total		8,351	100	26,088	100

Source: Ghana Statistical Service, National Industrial Census 1987, Phase I Report, and 2005 National Industrial Census Bulletin No.1. Cited in Sandefur (2006) and UNIDO (2008).

African countries are often characterized by a dual economy, where a small modern industrialized sector coexists with a large informal sector with little capital and low productivity of labor (Alby and Auriol, 2011). The coexistence of opportunity entrepreneurs and necessity entrepreneurs within the same economy suggests a nonlinear relationship between income level and entrepreneurship. Nkurunziza (2011) has identified a U-shaped relationship between entrepreneurship and per capita GDP. He argues that 'from a certain level of income, people are willing to take higher risk in order to pursue their passion, become more autonomous and achieve self-realization'. Thus, there will be an income threshold above which per capita income increases imply the increase of opportunity entrepreneurs.

Structure of enterprises by class

Table 5.2 suggests that countries with larger enterprises also tend to have a larger middle class. In Nigeria and Senegal, where more than 77 percent of firms have fewer than 20 employees, the proportion of the middle class is only 22 percent and 35 percent, respectively. By contrast, in Morocco, where less than 22 percent of enterprises are small, the middle class makes up around 85 percent of the population.

Table 5.3 shows that in 2007, public ownership of enterprises in four African countries (South Africa, Morocco, Côte d'Ivoire, and Cameroon) stood at only around 1 percent. By contrast, domestic private ownership constituted the predominant enterprise type (more than 80 percent on average).

Labor force characteristics

Firms in the hands of domestic private ownership tend to have a less educated labor force than other types of firms (see Table 5.4). Private foreign-owned firms have the highest levels of skilled workers and training programs (see Table

TABLE 5.2 Enterprise sizes in four African countries, 2007 (%)

Enterprise size	South Africa	Nigeria	Senegal	Morocco
Small (5–19 employees)	40.0	77.5	83.0	21.2
Medium (20–99 employees)	39.1	20.4	12.7	43.2
Large (100+ employees)	20.9	2.1	4.4	35.6
Middle-class size* 2010, $2–$20, % population	43.2	22.8	35.7	84.6

Source: Enterprise survey, 2007, World Bank.
Note: *Middle-class data from Statistics Department, African Development Bank, 2011.

TABLE 5.3 Percentage and type of enterprise in four African countries, 2007 (%)

Owner	South Africa	Morocco	Côte d'Ivoire	Cameroon
Private domestic	88.35	81.22	72.20	84.80
Private foreign	10.51	17.58	15.50	12.44
Government	0.07	1.01	0.09	0.58
Other	1.09	0.20	11.96	1.90

Source: Enterprise Survey 2007, World Bank.

5.5). When recruiting, private domestic firms are more likely to use friends and family members than external channels like placement offices or advertisements (see Table 5.6).

The relationship between education, employee skills, and enterprise ownership is a useful way to think about the connections between domestic opportunity enterprises and the education of their employees.

Enterprise owners differ in what they consider to be the greatest barriers to doing business, depending on their country of operation. South African firms

TABLE 5.4 Average employee's educational level, by type of enterprise in Africa (%)

	Private domestic firms	Private foreign firms	Public domestic firms	Total
0–3 years	11.5	8.7	3.8	10.9
4–6 years	30.3	22.6	11.5	28.6
7–9 years	48.6	53.8	61.5	7.0
10–12 years	6.1	11.1	19.2	28.3
13+ years	3.6	3.8	3.8	9.2

Source: Enterprise Survey 2007, World Bank.

TABLE 5.5 Formal training inside firms, by type of enterprise in Africa (%)

	Private domestic firms	Private foreign firms	Public domestic firms	Total
Firms offering training programs	30.8	50.8	58.3	35.2
Skilled production workers trained	37.5	39.7	31.2	37.7
Unskilled production workers trained	30.0	27.1	14.9	28.3

Source: Enterprise Survey 2007, World Bank.

TABLE 5.6 Recruitment methods, by type of enterprise in Africa (%)

	Private domestic firms	Private foreign firms	Public domestic firms	Total
Through family/friends	62.8	40.5	16.7	57.9
Placement office	7.3	10.8	13.0	8.0
Public announcement/ advertisement	17.0	32.4	63.0	20.4
Other	13.0	16.3	7.4	13.6

Source: Alby and Auriol (2011), using the Enterprise Survey databases of 31 SSA countries performed between 2002 and 2007.

are less constrained by workforce availability and labor regulation. Moroccan and Cameroonian enterprise owners view both workforce education and labor regulations as obstacles to doing business (see Tables 5.7 and 5.8).

Education and entrepreneurship

The relatively low literacy rate in Africa is an indication that the continent has a disproportionately large share of youth who either do not join the education system or who leave it early. These are the youth who end up in the labor market. The middle class has the lowest share of youth unemployment and the highest literacy rate, since they stay in school longer than the poor. Youth literacy is negatively related to youth unemployment and to survival enterprises.

Aggregate indicators

Low levels of education are still widespread in Sub-Saharan Africa. Although the proportion of people receiving secondary education doubled from 10 percent in 1980 to over 20 percent in 2000, SSA lags far behind East Asia (which

TABLE 5.7   Labor regulation reported as barrier to business in four countries, 2007 (%)

	South Africa	Morocco	Côte d'Ivoire	Cameroon
No obstacle	66.0	37.1	37.3	16.5
Minor obstacle	18.7	17.3	20.5	26.5
Moderate obstacle	9.6	28.4	14.1	29.2
Major obstacle	4.9	10.8	9.5	17.1
Very severe obstacle	0.9	4.7	6.5	6.1

Source: Enterprise Survey 2007, World Bank.

TABLE 5.8   Workforce education reported as barrier to business in two countries, 2007 (%)

	South Africa	Morocco
No obstacle	59.6	20.4
Minor obstacle	19.1	18.8
Moderate obstacle	13.0	28.5
Major obstacle	6.4	22.3
Very severe obstacle	1.9	8.1

Source: Enterprise Survey 2007, World Bank.

has an almost 40 percent level of secondary enrollment) and South America (about 30 percent) (World Bank, 2004). According to the World Development Indicators: (i) gross tertiary enrollment was on average lower than 6 percent in 2003 in SSA; (ii) basic education indicators were also disappointing, with a primary education completion rate of only 61 percent in 2004; and (iii) literacy rates are below 60 percent for those aged 15 and above (World Bank, 2006). This lack of education partly accounts for the low number of firms being created in Africa.

Household individual indicators

Inequalities in educational endowments are more critical when we look at class divisions within countries. Inequalities become apparent between poor, middle, and upper classes. There is also a sharp distinction in educational achievement between North African and SSA countries.

In general, North African countries have larger middle-class populations, with higher incomes and better levels of health and education (Ayadi et al., 2010). However, greater inequalities emerge within countries across the income distribution. In SSA countries (e.g. Benin and Mali), households with higher incomes help their children to acquire a better education (see Chapter 6 for more on the linkage between education and household income levels).

Education distribution curves show the weakness of middle-class education in SSA, which correlates with the lack of skilled work and the predominance of necessity entrepreneurship. SSA youth consider a lack of skills and support to be the main obstacles to entrepreneurial intention. Inequality in access to education is potentially a major constraint for dynamic entrepreneurship growth in SSA.

Enterprise individual indicators

Education is crucial for the growth of enterprises, especially in middle-income countries such as South Africa. The educational level of managers is higher in South Africa than in Côte d'Ivoire (see Figure 5.1). Managers in South Africa are more likely to hold a degree and to have received better training, indicative of the larger opportunist entrepreneurship in the country. A similar pattern is seen in employees' education levels (see Figure 5.2).

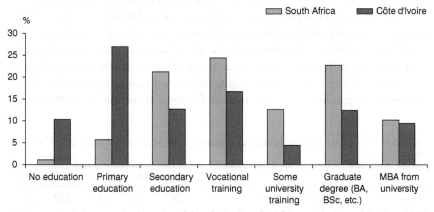

FIGURE 5.1 Managers' educational levels in South Africa and Côte d'Ivoire, 2007 (%) (source: Enterprise Survey 2007, World Bank)

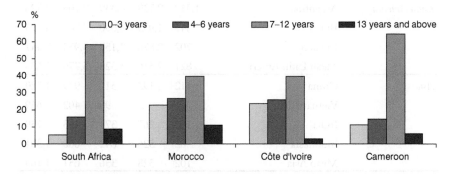

FIGURE 5.2 Employees' educational levels in four African countries, 2007 (%) (source: Enterprise Survey 2007, World Bank)

Figure 5.2 also shows that more than 40 percent of employees completed primary school, having received between 7 and 12 years of education, especially in Cameroon (65 percent) and South Africa (58 percent). However, the number of employees with tertiary education is generally low, especially in Côte d'Ivoire and Cameroon.

Comparing entrepreneurship in Africa with the rest of the world

Africa represents 10 percent of the world's population, yet its GDP is only 1 percent of global GDP. Africa is facing a raft of challenges impeding the growth of dynamic businesses. The volume of firms created in Africa is less than one-fifth of the average number in other regions. New enterprises are also smaller than those created elsewhere (Nkurunziza, 2011), while business conditions are the worst worldwide. For example, start-up fees represent 20 percent of total investment in Africa, compared with just 8 percent in China (Bigsten et. al., 2004). African enterprises employ more unskilled workers, while African managers are generally less experienced than those in other developing regions.

Although salaries are higher in China, their enterprises are more attractive as investment destinations as the country enjoys higher productivity and better governance. As a consequence, per capita income is steadily increasing in China, creating an expanding domestic market for local firms and contributing to

TABLE 5.9 Per capita income in Africa compared with other global regions, 1970–2005 (2000 PPP $)

		1970	1980	1990	2000	2005
Africa	Poor countries	288	267	205	192	211
	Lower income countries	458	492	541	494	531
	Middle income countries	1,985	2,483	2,174	2,983	3,569
	Mean Africa	793	928	816	1,020	1,193
Latin America	Argentina	1,318	2,739	4,339	7,703	4,728
	Brazil	441	1,933	3,090	3,700	4,723
	Mexico	702	2,876	3,157	5,935	7,447
	Mean Latin America	821	2,516	3,528	5,779	5,633
Asia	China	112	192	312	949	1,720
	Vietnam	...	...	98	402	639
	India	112	267	374	453	739
	Indonesia	82	526	642	800	1,301
	Mean Asia	102	328	356	651	1,100

Sources: WDI Database, Ayadi et al. (2010).
Note: Empty cells denote missing data.

entrepreneurship. Table 5.9 shows that per capita income has increased by 50 percent over the last 35 years in Africa, but with a decrease in poor countries. By contrast, per capita income increased by 700 percent in Latin America and by a massive 1,500 percent in China and Indonesia, creating huge opportunities for local firms. In part due to entrepreneurship as well as other factors, in China and other East Asian countries, the share of the middle class increased from 8 percent in 1981 to 61 percent in 2005. By comparison, in SSA it rose only slightly from 26 percent in 1981 to 30 percent in 1999 (see Table 5.10 and Figure

TABLE 5.10   Size of the middle class as a percentage of total population by global region, 1981–2005 (%)

	1981	1990	1999	2005
East Asia and Pacific	7.5	20.6	38.6	61.4
Europe and Central Asia	88.6	87.6	83.0	84.5
Latin America and the Caribbean	68.8	71.1	71.4	74.9
Middle East and North Africa	71.8	78.9	79.3	81.9
South Asia	14.0	17.9	23.4	26.7
SSA	26.2	23.8	22.4	27.1
Africa*	26.2	27.0	27.0	30.5

Sources: PovcalNet, World Bank, * Statistics Department, AfDB (2011a).

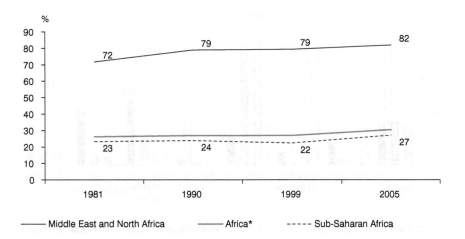

FIGURE 5.3 Size of the middle class across three regions, 1981–2005 (% of population) (sources: PovcalNet, World Bank; Statistics Department, AfDB (2011a))

5.3). The emergence of competitive modern firms in East Asia has increased both per capita income and the size of the middle class.

Structural barriers and challenges to entrepreneurship

SMEs may generate employment and innovation, but they generally are less productive than larger firms. They also find it more difficult to access official finance (UNDP, 2004). An unwieldy regulatory burden in commodity and labor markets, combined with an excessive tax burden and low quality of institutions and governance, have all conspired to drive workers and firms in Africa into the informal economy (IMF, 2011). Finally, excessive or inappropriate government regulations also act as a major constraint to entrepreneurship (Loayza, 1996; Botero et al., 2003).

Questioned about their most serious obstacles to doing business, managers in different countries gave diverse answers. In Côte d'Ivoire, inadequate access to finance and political instability were cited as key constraints. In South Africa, managers cited crime, theft, and disorder reduction as the top challenges. In Nigeria and Senegal, lack of access to electricity at a reasonable price emerges as the main obstacle. For Cameroonian entrepreneurs, competition from the informal sector and tax administration represent hurdles to doing business. In Morocco, high tax rates are a huge disincentive for opportunity enterprise development (see Figure 5.4).

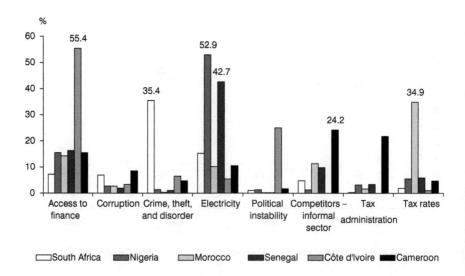

FIGURE 5.4   Serious obstacles to doing business in selected African countries, 2007 (source: Enterprise Survey 2007, World Bank)

Entry barriers to the formal sector

Lengthy, expensive, and complicated procedures to start up and operate businesses, stringent labor regulations, high labor costs, and high taxes have increased the costs of operating in the formal economy, and hence have provided strong incentives for workers and firms to operate informally (IMF, 2011).

North African countries have a higher proportion of the middle class compared with East Asian countries, but they also have a greater prevalence of informal enterprises, due to a lack of appropriate institutions. The size of the informal economy in these countries (as a share of formal, officially measured GDP) is large compared with emerging economies. The informal sector is estimated at 30 percent in Tunisia, 34 percent in Egypt, and 44 percent in Morocco, compared with just 15 percent in China (see Figure 5.5).

In Sub-Saharan Africa, the informal sector is even larger. The UNDP's Commission on the Private Sector and Development (UNDP, 2004) estimates the share of the non-agricultural workforce that is informal to be 80 percent in SSA. Xaba, Horn, and Motala (2002) estimate that 61 percent of urban employment and as much as 93 percent of new jobs in SSA are created in the informal economy. As a consequence, the size of the informal economy continues to expand relative to the formal economy.

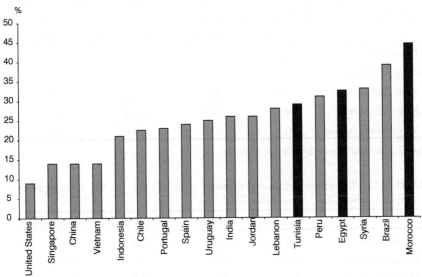

FIGURE 5.5 Size of informal economy in various countries worldwide (% of GDP), 2008 (source: Regional Economic Outlook: Middle East and Central Asia, IMF (2010))

Note: African countries shaded black.

Flodman Becker (2004), citing various International Labour Organization (ILO) documents, reports that the informal economy represents 92 percent of total non-agricultural job opportunities for women in Sub-Saharan Africa. Furthermore, 95 percent of these are self-employed jobs, compared with just 5 percent with paid-employee status.

Enterprises operate informally because the cost, time commitment, and effort involved in formal registration are perceived to be too high. Alby and Auriol (2011) consider that an important determinant of informality, and thus of opportunistic enterprise growth, is the existence of fixed entry costs to the formal sector. These costs are proportionally higher in poor countries than in advanced economies. In developing countries (especially small ones), formalization entails fixed costs that are beyond the reach of poor entrepreneurs (Djankov et al., 2002; Auriol and Warlters, 2005). The OECD (2009) reports that informal sector development may reduce the credibility of public institutions. It may generate a poor allocation of human capital, reducing efficiency and productivity.

Even large and modern enterprises sometimes join the informal economy if they lose significant market share (De Soto, 1989). Mead (1994) differentiates the informal economy between (1) poor people who are pushed into self-employment by a lack of employment alternatives (so-called 'necessity entrepreneurship'), and (2) those that have identified promising business

TABLE 5.11 Tax rates: perception as an obstacle to the formalization of enterprises in four African countries, 2007 (%)

	South Africa	Morocco	Côte d'Ivoire	Cameroon
No obstacle	77.6	7.3	24.7	7.9
Minor obstacle	10.8	17.9	17.5	15.7
Moderate obstacle	7.1	18.7	14.6	27.6
Major obstacle	4.1	30.6	22.4	31.1
Very severe obstacle	0.5	24.8	10.1	15.4

Source: Enterprise Survey 2007, World Bank.

TABLE 5.12 Tax administration: perception as an obstacle to the formalization of enterprises in four African countries, 2007 (%)

	South Africa	Morocco	Côte d'Ivoire	Cameroon
No obstacle	84.0	33.8	23.0	4.7
Minor obstacle	9.0	27.9	19.8	7.7
Moderate obstacle	4.5	20.4	20.2	20.9
Major obstacle	2.0	11.5	22.1	39.7
Very severe obstacle	0.6	5.4	8.6	26.7

Source: Enterprise Survey 2007, World Bank.

TABLE 5.13 Corruption: perception as an obstacle to the formalization of enterprises in four African countries, 2007 (%)

	South Africa	Morocco	Côte d'Ivoire	Cameroon
No obstacle	51.8	44.6	7.0	5.2
Minor obstacle	21.1	9.9	9.1	9.6
Moderate obstacle	11.0	8.9	12.2	19.8
Major obstacle	11.6	12.9	26.2	24.8
Very severe obstacle	4.4	10.9	41.8	38.3

Source: Enterprise Survey 2007, World Bank.

TABLE 5.14 Crime, theft, and disorder: perception as obstacles to the formalization of enterprises in four African countries, 2007 (%)

	South Africa	Morocco	Côte d'Ivoire	Cameroon
No obstacle	16.6	69.0	2.7	22.6
Minor obstacle	23.9	4.2	2.9	25.9
Moderate obstacle	24.0	1.6	3.4	16.8
Major obstacle	22.1	1.1	18.8	15.7
Very severe obstacle	13.3	0.8	70.3	15.4

Source: Enterprise Survey 2007, World Bank.

opportunities and are pulled into self-employment by market opportunities ('opportunity entrepreneurship'). His research in Southern and Eastern Africa suggests that necessity entrepreneurship explains the major share of informality in the region.

Tables 5.11 to 5.14 reveal differing perceptions regarding barriers to enterprise formalization, depending on the national context. All African enterprise owners consider high tax rates to represent a burden, with the exception of those in South Africa. Insecurity is more critical in South Africa and Côte d'Ivoire, but seems to be less important in Morocco.

The investment climate

Although there is evident talent and nascent entrepreneurship in Africa's agriculture sector, it is easier to start a new business in the services sector (SEED Initiative, 2010). Improving the region's business environment should reduce the costs of doing business and strengthen its competitiveness (IMF, 2011). In this respect, it is critical not only to improve the underlying legal framework, but also to make access to government services more equitable. For example, in Egypt it can take some firms nearly six months to obtain an operating license, while others can do so in about two weeks (IMF, 2011).

Incentives for firms to transition from the informal to the formal economy are undermined when the quality of public institutions is low (North, 1990). Weak institutional quality can take the form of low quality of public services or weak enforcement of regulations. It can also take the form of corruption, which may limit access to government services to a privileged few or favor a few large 'protected' or 'connected' firms at the expense of many small ones. Corruption can also reduce the costs of informality, thereby increasing the incentives to continue to operate informally (IMF, 2011).

Access to finance

Start-up conditions and available financial resources play a crucial role in the evolution of enterprises. Difficulty in accessing finance at competitive rates is a key business constraint and may prevent firms from developing and expanding to their full potential. As we have seen, the majority of African firms are informal and lack the legal status that would help them to access official finance. Better financial services are needed to address the problem of missing competitive and growth-oriented SMEs in SSA (UNDP, 2004).

Peruvian economist De Soto (1989) argues that even the poorest people in the informal economy may own assets that could be formally registered as collateral in order to be eligible for bank credits. As long as assets are not registered, they remain 'dead capital.' The state should therefore provide title deeds and secure property rights effectively.

Empirical research shows that in developing countries, only a limited number of entrepreneurs use credit in order to start their businesses. Instead they tend to use their own funds, sometimes with the help of family or friends. Credit is mostly accessed once the business has become established and proven to be viable. Firms starting with a less binding budget constraint usually have a larger

TABLE 5.15 Financial characteristics of SMEs in four African countries, 1990s (%)

	Kenya	Tanzania	Zambia	Zimbabwe
Firms receiving supplier credit	30.3	11.8	19.2	66.4
Avg. years of supplier relation	8.5	7.9	8.6	12.0
% with title to property	37.4	37.1	47.9	43.2
% receiving any bank loan at start-up	24.6	8.2	11.4	11.2

Sources: Enterprise Surveys 1990s, Regional Program on Enterprise Development, World Bank. Cited in: Biggs and Shah (2006: 3051) and UNIDO (2008).

start-up size and grow faster than financially constrained start-ups (Nkurunziza, 2011). Firms in Africa finance about 68 percent of their investment needs with internal funds, a small share with bank credit, a low number of investments with equity finance, and a few with trade finance (Honohan and Beck, 2007).

There is a clear lack of affordable meso-finance solutions for SMEs (see Table 5.15). Interest rates charged by microfinance institutions are too high for medium- and long-term investments. Furthermore, there is a gap between the maximum loans provided by microfinance institutions and the minimum loans available from commercial banks. More sophisticated and diversified financial products such as leasing, factoring, and risk capital are largely unavailable for SMEs in the region (UNDP, 2004).

Lack of skills

Skills are increasingly recognized as a barrier to entrepreneurship, often amplified by other obstacles such as financial illiteracy, which prevents access to credit from formal financial institutions (Fatoki and Chindoga, 2011).

Political initiatives, entrepreneurship, and the middle class

The middle class is generally conceived as the source of entrepreneurship and innovation – they create the small businesses that drive a modern economy. Middle-class values also emphasize education and hard work. Thus, the middle class is the source of all the needed inputs for growth in a neoclassical economy – new ideas, physical capital accumulation, and human capital development (OECD, 2011).

In the sections below, we look at two case studies illustrating successful national political initiatives aimed at boosting private sector engagement and enlarging the middle class. The featured case studies are from the very different subregions of Northern and Southern Africa.

Tunisia: Modernization and middle-class growth to create stability

At the beginning of the 1970s, a political strategy was formulated to grow the private sector in order to increase wages and create a social base for political stability. The growth of the middle class was targeted by the then Prime Minister Hedi Nouira to contribute to the country's modernization, as requested by the political elite. This goal was framed as a political initiative to reduce social and political tensions in the country (Khiari, 2003).

The middle class has a historical base in Tunisia, composed of the petite-bourgeoisie, artisans, intellectuals, and government employees. Its development embodies economic, social, and political objectives. From an economic standpoint, increasing wealth helps to boost local demand for emergent industries. From a social standpoint, it contributes to the reduction of inequalities between classes. The original political objective was to reduce social tension after the 1960s' unpopular political experience. The public and the government reacted positively to this strategy and helped develop the middle class as well as the private sector in Tunisia (El Baz, 2005).

However, the success of the political initiative to develop the middle class in Tunisia was largely due to the popularization of education and modernization,

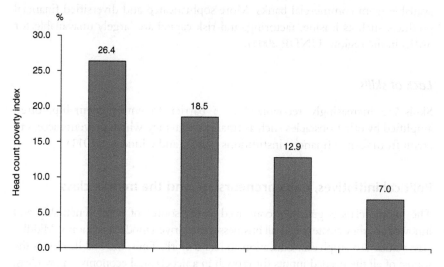

FIGURE 5.6a: Tunisia: Headcount Poverty Index, 1981–2005 (source: PovcalNet, World Bank)

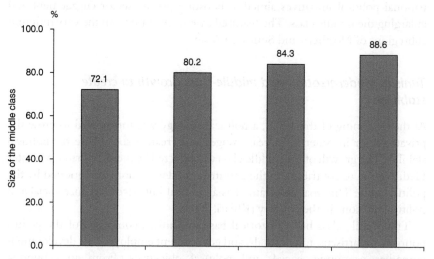

FIGURE 5.6b: Tunisia: size of the middle class, 1981–2005 (source: PovcalNet, World Bank)

thereby stimulating private sector-led development. In the early 1970s, a development strategy was also put in place that relied on financial and fiscal incentives to attract foreign and domestic capital to export-oriented light industries (Ayadi et al., 2005).

Such initiatives resulted in a sharp decline in the poverty headcount for the whole country from over 26 percent in 1981 to just 7 percent in 2005 (see Figure 5.6a). In less than three decades, Tunisia succeeded in cutting the overall poverty rate by 70 percent, while the middle class increased from 72 percent to 89 percent (Figure 5.6b).

Growth has also been relatively high, averaging 5.3 percent in total GDP and 3.2 percent in per capita terms over the period 1962–2000. In the two decades of the 1980s and 1990s, total GDP rose at over 4 percent per year and per capita GDP growth averaged 2 percent (see Figure 5.7). Although lagging behind East Asian countries, this performance places Tunisia above the average GDP recorded for developing countries (Ayadi et al., 2005).

At the national level, the sectoral composition of employment has radically changed in favor of labor-intensive and export-oriented manufacturing. The share of agricultural employment to total employment has halved, from almost 46 percent in the 1960s to 23 percent in the 1990s. Meanwhile, employment in the manufacturing sector has risen by almost ten percentage points over the same period, from 14 percent to 24 percent. The textiles and clothing subsector accounts for about half of manufacturing employment. Construction and clothing, which are intensive in low-skilled labor, together account for more than one-fifth of the nation's total employment. Tourism also relies heavily on relatively low-skilled labor and this sector has increased at a rapid pace.

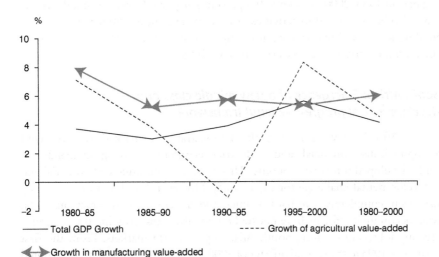

FIGURE 5.7 Tunisia: GDP, agricultural, and manufacturing growth, 1980–2000 (%) (source: Calculations based on household consumption surveys and National Accounts (Ayadi et al., 2005))

The growth of these activities has increased job opportunities for low-income workers, many of whom come from rural areas. In this way, the shift to labor-intensive industries and services has contributed to the reduction of poverty, although unemployment remains relatively high at around 15 percent of the active population from 2005 until 2012.

Increases in the size of the middle class have been correlated with entrepreneurship and sound social and political initiatives. Economic growth has certainly boosted incomes and reduced poverty; however, social policies and government commitment have also played a crucial role. Social programs have targeted the poor since the mid-1970s, but more trenchantly since the early 1990s. Rural roads have played an important role in connecting the poor to urban goods and labor markets, urban services, and to generally improving their living conditions. The housing component of social programs has not only ameliorated the living conditions of the poor but has also freed up incomes and savings, which can then be spent on food and non-food items. This has had positive effects on poverty alleviation. Overall, social policy has been an important instrument in reducing poverty (Ayadi et al., 2005).

On the other hand, enterprise development is heavily reliant on education, and this is also an area where major progress has been made in Tunisia. Enrollment ratios have significantly increased for both males and females. Universal primary enrollment was achieved by the early 1990s, and secondary and tertiary enrollment has sharply increased.

The labor market has been a catalyst in allowing the poor to share in the country's growth. Agriculture has hardly created any new jobs for decades, while minimum agricultural wages increased only moderately in real terms over the period 1980–2000 (averaging 0.5 percent per year). However, small farmers have also been engaged in activities other than agriculture; 50 percent of those holding less than 5 hectares are also employed in sectors such as construction, the food industry, and services (Ayadi et al., 2005).

South Africa: Emergence of a new middle class and development of progressive legal framework

South Africa's development path demonstrates a marked duality, with a sophisticated financial and industrial economy growing alongside an underdeveloped informal economy. This presents both untapped potential and a developmental challenge for the country. However, South Africa's economy has been completely overhauled since the advent of democracy in 1994. Macroeconomic reforms have boosted competitiveness, growing the economy, creating jobs, and opening South Africa up to world markets. From the first quarter of 1993 to the second quarter of 2008, the country enjoyed uninterrupted economic growth (SAinfo, 2011).

Several initiatives have been undertaken in the legislative and the political areas. South Africa has a world-class and progressive legal framework. Legislation governing commerce, labor, and maritime issues is particularly well developed, while laws on competition policy, copyright, patents, trademarks, and disputes conform to international norms and conventions.

South Africa has developed a sizable black middle class, which is estimated to have more spending power than the country's white population (Brulliard, 2010). The black middle class has emerged partly as a result of a government program called the BEE (Black Economic Empowerment) Act, initiated after the first democratic elections in 1994. Despite allegations of cronyism and corruption, South Africa's black middle class grew by 30 percent over a single year (between the last quarter 2005 and the first quarter 2007), with numbers increasing from 2 million to 2.6 million. The collective spending power of this population segment rose from R130 billion to R180 billion (SAinfo, 2011).

South African economist Mike Schuster notes that 'SA's overall employment picture was positive, with Statistics SA's latest figures showing not only that jobs were increasing, but that workers were moving from the informal to the formal sector and that earnings were up sharply.' According to the labor force survey, formal sector employment – where workers are more likely to have a regular salary and a pension or provident fund – has been rising steadily since 2001. In March 2007, formal sector jobs accounted for 67 percent of South Africa's total employment, while the informal sector accounted for just under 17 percent, with domestic work taking 7 percent (SAinfo, 2011).

The new generation of African entrepreneurs

At the start of the new millennium, a group of entrepreneurs decided that the time was ripe to establish a system of regional enterprise networks in response to liberalized economic and political conditions. Consequently, in 2000, the pan-African Enterprise Network was formed at the Millennium Conference in Addis Ababa.

This group of entrepreneurs are highly educated men and women who have gained work experience in formal sector firms in Africa and elsewhere. Importantly, they demonstrate a global outlook, which is crucial for Africa's deeper integration into the global economic marketplace.

Most middle- and upper-class urban residents attend universities, lead cosmopolitan lives, and hold professional occupations. Network members fall into this category. Those members in agribusinesses may work in offices on their farms, but they reside in the nearby cities. Social and professional relationships among members are formed across kinship, ethnic, and spatial lines.

With donor-funded assistance, these members organized 31 national, three regional, and one pan-African business networks in West, East, and Southern Africa. The objective of these networks is to expand intra-African business activity and investment, and to create a more favorable climate for the private sector.

McDade and Spring (2005) have looked at this small but potentially influential segment of the business community, who describe themselves as the 'new generation of African entrepreneurs.' Forty (70 percent) of the network members interviewed by McDade and Spring had worked in managerial positions in other firms before starting their own enterprises. Of these, 42 percent had been employed as managers or had held executive positions in major national firms in their own countries, 25 percent had worked in a family-owned business before starting their own enterprise, 23 percent had been employed in managerial positions in a foreign firm before returning to Africa, and 10 percent had worked (two were still employed) in the Africa office of a multinational firm.

Network members incorporate modern management practices in their business operations. They carry out market research to expand their customer base, use data for planning business ventures, provide training to develop staff capacity, and delegate responsibilities among employees. One of the main concerns expressed by network members was the low quality of job applicants in terms of skills-sets. A few network members sought to address this by setting up commercial schools that offered training in business management and computer skills.

Currently, the end of donor funding has led to the closing of some regional secretariats, while interregional conferences have ceased. In a special arrangement with the South African Enterprise Network, donor funding continues along with intraregional meetings and conferences. Most network members maintain their social and professional relationships in spite of the cessation of official activities in some of the national and regional networks. They continue to engage in commercial and investment activities. In addition, they continue to advocate on behalf of the private sector with governments.

Major expansion of regional trade and regional economic integration remains a future goal rather than a current reality. However, this small but growing segment of the African entrepreneurial landscape may serve as a catalyst to improve economic conditions and stimulate private sector-led development (McDade and Spring, 2005). The next step for African development may be the creation of long-term networks looking for intraregional business activities and investment. Although the network may not be efficient in the short term, it is a longer-term project.

Conclusion

Middle-class entrepreneurs are more qualified to increase opportunistic entrepreneurship as they are better qualified to manage larger enterprises. They live in urban areas where there are more incentives to create enterprises. Middle-class qualifications facilitate emergence of innovative enterprises.

Enhancing productive entrepreneurial activities in Africa will be crucial for growth and poverty eradication (Mead, 1999). However, enterprise development is inextricably linked to economic development and to income levels. In this context, a distinction must be drawn between two classes of entrepreneurs: opportunity entrepreneurs and necessity/subsistence entrepreneurs.

In poor economies, where paid employment opportunities are limited and social protection is nonexistent or weak, people who engage in small businesses are mainly driven by survival needs. Lack of education and skills is another factor that may lead to informal and subsistence entrepreneurship. African countries are characterized by a 'dual' economy, where a small modern industrialized sector coexists with a large informal sector characterized by little capital and low marginal productivity of labor. Few MSEs manage the transition to become medium-sized or large firms.

The proportion of the middle class increases across countries when the size of medium and large firms increases. The middle class has the lowest share of youth employment and the highest literacy rate, which indicates that they pursue their studies for a longer period and end up as better candidates for opportunistic entrepreneurship.

Per capita income has increased by 50 percent over the last 35 years in Africa, though with some decrease in the poorest countries. Nonetheless, this does not compare well with the performance of other global regions during the same period. For example, per capita income increased by 700 percent in Latin America and by 1,500 percent in China and Indonesia, creating huge opportunities for local firms. In East Asian countries, the share of the middle class increased from 7.5 percent in 1981 to 61 percent in 2005. However, in Sub-Saharan Africa, the middle class decreased from 26 percent in 1981 to 22 percent in 1999. Some correlation has been established between the growth of the middle class and enterprise creation.

The emergence of opportunity entrepreneurship in East Asia has contributed to increases in per capita income and the growth of the middle class. This has been facilitated by conducive institutional conditions for doing business. In Africa, however, a heavy regulatory burden in product and labor markets, an excessive tax burden, and low quality of institutions and governance have all conspired to drive workers and firms into the informal economy. This has increased the costs of operating formally, and provided strong incentives for firms to operate informally, where they can avoid those costs. Four-fifths of the non-agricultural workforce in Sub-Saharan Africa operate in the informal economy. Informal enterprises do not hold a legal status, which effectively denies them access to formal finance at competitive rates. The issuance of property titles could help to provide capital for informal businesses.

A limited number of African entrepreneurs use credit in order to start their businesses. Most use their own funds, sometimes relying on family or friends. Business credit is mostly accessed once a business has been established and proven to be viable. To promote a credit culture in Africa, reforms must be made to the banking system, the collateral and bankruptcy laws, and financing instruments for SMEs. Closer collaboration among banks, microfinance institutions, and non-financial service providers could help to facilitate enterprise development.

In Tunisia and South Africa, the development of the middle class has been partly a political initiative, as much as a social one. The development of a middle class has scaled up local demand for emergent industries and has helped to address inequalities. The Tunisian middle class has emerged through successful government efforts to increase education and encourage modernization. In South Africa, the black middle class has emerged through a government program called the BEE (Black Economic Empowerment), initiated in 1994, as well as through the development of a progressive legal framework.

Most middle- and upper-class urban residents attend universities, lead cosmopolitan lives, and have professional occupations. A segment of entrepreneurs in this category have founded a system of regional enterprise networks in response to liberalizing economic and political conditions, which they perceive as providing economic and professional opportunities in Africa. These entrepreneurs are highly educated men and women who have prior work experience in formal sector firms in Africa and elsewhere, and pursue a global outlook. Their hope is that expanded opportunities may be generated by greater cooperation among African entrepreneurs.

Currently, interregional conferences of the network have ceased but some donor funding continues, along with intraregional meetings and conferences. Most network members maintain their social and professional relationships in spite of the cessation of official activities in some of the national and regional networks. They continue to engage in commercial and investment activities and to advocate on behalf of the private sector with governments. This small but growing segment of the African entrepreneurial landscape may serve as a catalyst to improve economic conditions and stimulate private sector-led development.

References

AfDB (2011a). *Gender, Poverty and Environmental Indicators on African Countries 2011*, Statistics Department. Tunis: African Development Bank.

AfDB (2011b). 'The Middle of the Pyramid: Dynamics of the Middle Class in Africa.' Report by the Chief Economist Complex of the AfDB. Tunis: African Development Bank.

Alby, P., and E. Auriol (2011). 'Social Barriers to Entrepreneurship in Africa: The Forced Mutual Help Hypothesis'. Toulouse School of Economics (ARQADE). Available online at: www.csae.ox.ac.uk/conferences/2011-edia/papers/592-alby.pdf (accessed 18 September 2014).

Auriol, E., and M. Warlters (2005). 'Taxation Base in Developing Countries', *Journal of Public Economics*, vol. 89, pp. 625–646.

Ayadi M., M. Amara, A. Lahga, and R. Belhaj Kacem (2010). 'Développement Economique et Social, Croissance Pro-Pauvres et Convergence vers les OMD des Pays Africains.' Addis Ababa: African Union.

Ayadi, M., G. Boulila, M. Lahouel, and P. Montigny (2005). 'Pro-poor Growth in Tunisia.' Paris, France: International Development and Strategies.

Banerjee, A.V., and E. Duflo (2008). 'What is Middle Class about the Middle Classes around the World?' *Journal of Economic Perspectives*, vol. 22, no. 2, pp. 3–28.

Barro, R.J. (1996). *Health, Human Capital, and Economic Growth*. Washington DC: Pan American Health Organization.

Barro, R.J. (1998). 'Human Capital and Growth in Cross-Country Regressions,' in *Can Education Foster Growth?* Stockholm: Economic Council of Sweden.

Biggs, T., and M.K. Shah (2006). 'African SMEs, Networks, and Manufacturing Performance,' *Journal of Banking & Finance*, vol. 30, pp. 3043–3066.

Bigsten, A. et al. (2004). 'Do African Manufacturing Firms Learn from Exporting?', *Journal of Development Studies*, vol. 40, no. 3, pp. 115–141.

Birdsall, N., C. Graham, and S. Pettinato (2000). 'Stuck in the Tunnel: Is Globalization Muddling the Middle Class?', Center on Social and Economic Dynamics Working Paper no. 14, August.

Botero, J., S. Djankov, R. La Porta, F. Lopez-de-Silanes, and Al Shleifer (2003). 'The Regulation of Labor,' *Quarterly Journal of Economics*, vol. 119, no. 4, pp. 1339–1382.

Braguinsky, S., S. Klepper, and A. Ohyama (2009). 'Schumpeterian Entrepreneurship,' Atlanta Competitive Conference Paper.

Brulliard, N. (2010). 'South Africa's "Black Diamonds" Overtake Whites,' *Global Post* (online), May 19.

Charman, A.J., and L.M. Peterson (2009). 'An Investigation of Characteristics Distinguishing Entrepreneurs from the Self-employed in South Africa.' Paper presented at the Second Annual International Conference on Entrepreneurship. Johannesburg: WITS Business School.

De Soto, H. (1989). *The Other Path: The Invisible Revolution in the Third World.'* New York: Harper Collins.

Djankov, S., R. La Porta, F. Lopez-de-Silanes, and A. Shleifer (2002). 'The Regulation of Entry,' *Quarterly Journal of Economics*, February, vol. CXVII, Issue 1, pp. 1–37.

El Baz, S. (2005). 'La Tunisie, pays émergent?', FASoPo, Fond d'Analyse des Sociétés Politiques.

Fatoki, O., and L. Chindoga (2011). 'An Investigation into the Obstacles to Youth Entrepreneurship in South Africa,' *International Business Research*, vol. 4, no. 2, pp. 161–169.

Flodman Becker, K. (2004). *The Informal Economy: Fact Finding Study*. Stockholm: Swedish International Development Cooperation Agency (SIDA).

Ginsburg, T. (2000). 'Does Law Matter for Economic Development? Evidence from East Asia,' *Law & Society Review*, vol. 34, pp. 829–856.

Hessels, J., K. Suddle, and M. Mooibroek (2008). *Global Entrepreneurship Monitor 2008: the Netherlands*. Zoetermeer: EIM.

Honohan, P., and T. Beck (2007). *Making Finance Work for Africa*. Washington DC: World Bank.

ILO (2011). *Global Employment Trends 2001: the Challenge of a Jobs Recovery*. Geneva: International Labor Organization.

IMF (2010). *Regional Economic Outlook: Middle East and Central Asia*. Washington DC: International Monetary Fund.

IMF (2011). *Regional Economic Outlook: 2011*. Washington DC: IMFJulien, P.-A. (1989). 'The Entrepreneur and Economic Theory,' *International Small Business Journal*, vol. 7, pp. 29–38.

Kharas, H., and G. Gertz (2010) 'The New Global Middle Class: A Cross-Over from West to East', in Cheng, l. (ed.) *China's Emerging Middle Class: Beyond Economic Transformation*. Washington, DC: Brookings Institution.

Khiari, S. (2003). *Tunisie, le délitement de la Cité, coercition, consentement, résistance*. Paris: Éditions Karthala.

Liedholm, C. (2001). 'The Impact of Training on the Performance of Micro and Small Enterprises Served by Microfinance Institutions in Tanzania.' *Research Journal of Business Management*, vol. 4, pp. 103–111.

Liedholm, C. and D.C. Mead (1999). 'Small Enterprises and Economic Development: The Dynamics of Micro and Small Enterprises'. London and New York: Routledge.

Loayza, N. (1996). 'The Economics of the Informal Sector: A Simple Model and Some Empirical Evidence from Latin America.' *Carnegie-Rochester Conference Series on Public Policy*, vol. 45, pp. 129–162.

McDade, B., and A. Spring (2005). 'The "New Generation of African Entrepreneurs": Networking to Change the Climate for Business and Private Sector-led Development,' *Entrepreneurship & Regional Development*, vol. 17 (January), pp. 17–42.

McPherson, M.A. (1992). 'Growth and Survival of Small Southern African Firms.' PhD Dissertation, Michigan State University, East Lansing, Michigan.

Mead, D.C. (1994). 'The Contribution of Small Enterprises to Employment Growth in Southern and Eastern Africa,' *World Development*, vol. 22, no. 12, pp. 1881–1894.

Mead, D.C. (1999). 'MSEs Tackle both Poverty and Growth (but in differing proportions),' in K. King and S. McGrath (eds), *Enterprise in Africa: Between Poverty and Growth*. London: Intermediate Technology Publications, pp. 61–70.

Nkurunziza, F. (2011). 'Entrepreneurship and Job Creation in Africa.' Paper presented at IDRC Workshop, 'West and Central African Labour Markets,' Dakar, Senegal.

North, D. (1990). *Institutions, Institutional Change and Economic Performance*. Cambridge: Cambridge University Press.

OECD (2009). 'L'Emploi informel dans les pays en développement: une normalité indépassable ?' Paris: OECD.

OECD (2011). 'How Middle-Class Is Latin America?', *Latin American Economic Outlook*. Paris: OECD.

Parker, J. (1994). 'Micro and Small scale Enterprises in Kenya: Results of the 1993 National Baseline Survey.' GEMINI Technical Report No 75. New York: PACT Publications.

Platteau, J.P. (2001). *Institutions, Social Norms, and Economic Development*. London and New York: Routledge.

Putnam, R., R. Leonardi, and R. Nanetti (1993). *Making Democracy Work: Civic Traditions in Modern Italy*. Princeton, NJ: Princeton University Press.

Ramachandran, V., A. Gelb, and M.K. Shah (2009). *Africa's Private Sector: What's Wrong With the Business Environment and What to Do about It*. Washington DC: Center for Global Development.

SAinfo (2011). 'South Africa: Economy Overview.' Online at: www.SouthAfrica.info (accessed 18 September 2014).

Sandefur, J. (2006). 'Explaining the Trend toward Informal Employment in Africa: Evidence from Ghanaian Manufacturing.' Oxford: Centre for the Study of African Economies (CSAE).

Schumpeter, J. (1934). *The Theory of Economic Development: An Inquiry into Profits, Capital, Credit, Interest, and the Business Cycle*. Cambridge, MA: Harvard University Press.

SEED Initiative (2010). 'An Investigation into the Triple Bottom-line Performance of Micro and Small Social and Environmental Enterprises in Developing Countries: Establishing a Baseline for a Longitudinal Study.' Nairobi: United Nations Environment Program.

Shane, S.A. (2003). *A General Theory of Entrepreneurship: The Individual–Opportunity Nexus*. Northampton: E. Elgar.

Svensson, F. (2008). 'Entrepreneurship and Bureaucracy: Explaining Economic Development across Countries Applying the Actor-Structural Approach to Economic Development,' *Journal of Asia Entrepreneurship and Sustainability*, vol. IV, no. 1, June.

UNDP (2004). *Unleashing Entrepreneurship: Making Business Work for the Poor.* Report of the Commission on the Private Sector and Development. New York: UNDP.

UNECA (2005). *Economic Report on Africa 2005: Meeting the Challenges of Unemployment and Poverty in Africa*. Addis Ababa: United Nations Economic Commission for Africa.

UNIDO (2008). *Creating an Enabling Environment for Private Sector Development in Sub-Saharan Africa*. Vienna: United Nations Industrial Development Organization.

Van Biesebroeck, J. (2005). 'Firm Size Matters: Growth and Productivity Growth in African Manufacturing,' *Economic Development and Cultural Change*, vol. 53, no. 3, pp. 545–583.

Van Stel, A., M. Carree, and R. Thurik (2007). 'The Effect of Entrepreneurship Activity on National Economic Growth,' *Small Business Economics*, vol. 24, no. 3, pp. 311–321.

World Bank (2004). *World Development Report 2005: A Better Investment Climate for Everyone*. Washington DC: World Bank and Oxford University Press.

World Bank (2006). *Doing Business in 2006 – Creating Jobs*. Washington DC: World Bank and the International Finance Corporation.

Xaba, J., P. Horn, and S. Motala (2002). 'The Informal Sector in Sub-Saharan Africa' Working Paper on the Informal Economy – Employment Sector 2002/10. Geneva: International Labor Organization.

6

EDUCATION

Benedict Kunene, Maurice Mubila,
and Oluyele A. Akinkugbe

The blurring of class divisions and the growth in the size of the middle class are generally recognized as two positive effects of an expansion in education. Indeed, there exists a mutually reinforcing and virtuous relationship between the two. Education creates a broad middle class by opening up new avenues for upward mobility, while the middle class provides the support to further strengthen and expand education and national development.

The dynamism of educational expansion continues to dominate sociopolitical and economic discourse across the world. In the last decade or so, a belief that the sustained growth in G7 economies over the period 1965–2005 may be attributable to the large middle class in those countries has gained ground. On a similar note, accelerating growth in India, China, South Korea, Taiwan, Hong Kong, and Brazil is also associated with dramatic increases in the size of their middle classes (Ravallion, 2009; Banerjee and Duflo, 2007, 2008; Kharas and Gertz, 2010).

In a recent study, the African Development Bank (AfDB, 2011) also stressed a linkage between the growing middle class – what Ravallion (2009) calls 'the bulging middle' – and economic growth on the African continent. It reports that the region's economic growth over the past two decades has not only been accompanied by an expanding middle class but is also being spurred by it. The middle class therefore contributes significantly to poverty reduction and robust growth in consumption expenditure (AfDB, 2011: 1).

This chapter examines whether or not the assumed positive and bi-directional correlation between education and the middle class in Africa is consistent with the evidence. We look at the expansion of the education systems in Africa over the last four decades; their financing – both public and private; the concomitant growth of the middle class as well as its increasing influence over the years. We then explore the dynamics of the relationship between education and the middle class on the continent. The final section offers some policy recommendations.

Africa's bulging middle class and the demand for education

Africa's middle class has increased in size and purchasing power over the last two decades, as strong economic growth rates have lifted previously poor households onto a higher-income pathway. By 2010, the size of the middle class in Africa (including the floating class) had risen to 34 percent of the population (see Figure 6.1). This strong growth has helped to stimulate the demand for private education on the continent since the 1980s.

This is particularly evident in such countries as Nigeria and Kenya, which have vibrant private sectors, and where public (i.e. state) education is not favorably perceived by the middle and upper classes of society. This may be partly attributed to the insufficient supply of school places and/or a lack of up-to-date instructional materials in many public schools across African countries. Such schools are also often viewed as overcrowded and lacking discipline and rigor on the part of poorly paid teachers.

This perception leads families with the financial means to seek an alternative form of education, which they believe will enhance their children's life chances. In other words, they would rather pay to have their children educated in private schools, in the expectation that their offspring will receive a higher-quality education and a job placement on completion of their studies. In addition, the middle class also goes the extra mile to ensure that after their children have obtained a first degree at home, they should travel to Europe or North America for higher degree programs.

In this respect, concerns have been raised about a possible 'brain drain' from Africa, as many emigrants do not return home after their studies. However, on a more positive note, this phenomenon has led to important remittance flows to

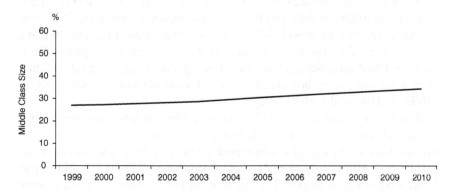

FIGURE 6.1 Growth in Africa's middle class (% of total population), 1999–2010 (source: African Development Bank, Statistics Department (2011))

Nigeria, Kenya, Ethiopia, Tanzania, Senegal and other African countries. Many national economies have significantly benefited from these inflows in the last decade or so. In addition, return migration and circular migration can stimulate trade, foreign investment, and skills transfer.

Financing education in Africa

Macroeconomic and demographic context

Recent data released by the World Bank indicate that one reason why African countries managed to weather the global economic crisis of 2008/2009 reasonably well was due in part to improved economic and structural policies implemented in many countries. As a result, Africa remains one of the fastest-growing developing regions in the world. Output is estimated to have expanded by about 4.2–4.7 percent in 2010 (World Bank, 2011a), which represents a vigorous rebound from the 1.7 percent growth achieved in 2009. The recovery was strongest among exporters of metals, minerals, and oil, which benefited from higher commodity prices. GDP grew at 3.4 percent in 2011 and is expected to reach 4.5 percent in 2012.

UNESCO (2011a) indicates that approximately 1 billion people were living in Africa in 2010, representing about 14 percent of the world's population of 6.9 billion. Moreover, unlike the demographics characterizing much of Europe, Asia, and North America, the population of Africa is young (48 percent were under the age of 15 in 2010), with an estimated growth rate of 2.4 percent between 2005 and 2010. This means that there is a large and rising demand for education for the burgeoning population. This places a heavy burden on the working-age cohorts to help fund schooling needs.

Africa continues to be confronted by a number of developmental challenges. Cardinal amongst them is poverty – about half of the population lives on $1.25 or less a day (see Chart 20: The Size of the Poor Class, AfDB, 2011), although this percentage is falling (World Bank, 2011a). Health is another major challenge. Maternal mortality rates are still a cause of grave concern, with an average of 590 deaths per 100,000 live births (WHO, 2010), although this represents a 26 percent decline from 1990. Progress is being made on other health fronts, but not at a rate to achieve the majority of health-related Millennium Development Goals by 2015. Child mortality rates are also showing a declining trend but children from rural and poorer households remain disproportionately affected (AfDB, UNECA, AUC, and UNDP, 2012).

Africa's long-term growth will be impacted by emerging macroeconomic, social, and demographic changes. Among these trends, we can identify growing urbanization, an expanding and better-educated labor force, and the rise of the middle-class African consumer. An expanding urban middle class should help to boost productivity, as workers become more skilful and move from subsistence rural agricultural work into urban employment, thereby increasing demand and boosting investment.

Expansion and diversification of education systems in Africa

While national and international support for education has grown since the Millennium Development Goals (MDGs) Summit and World Education Forum of 2000, education systems in African countries have also expanded substantially. According to the Education For All (EFA) Report of 2011 (UNESCO, 2011c), enrollment in primary education has increased more than fivefold in four decades – from 23 million in 1970 to 129 million in 2010. Secondary school enrollment increased more than tenfold, from 4 million to 42 million, over the same period. Figure 6.2 shows the increase in primary and secondary enrollments in Africa over the period 2000–2005. Enrollment at the tertiary level also grew significantly between 1970 and 2008. Although considerably smaller in absolute terms, it increased 22-fold, from 0.2 million in 1970 to 4.5 million in 2008 (see Figure 6.3).

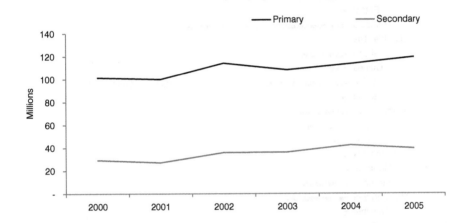

FIGURE 6.2   Primary and secondary enrollments in Africa in millions, 2000–2005 (sources: UNESCO (UIS online); AfDB Data Portal)

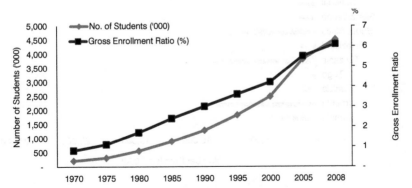

FIGURE 6.3   Tertiary enrollments in Africa, 1970–2008 (sources: UNESCO (UIS online); World Bank (WDI online); AfDB Data Portal)

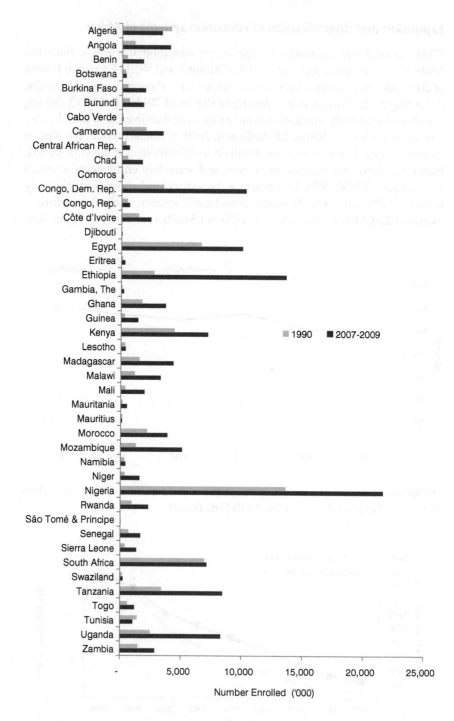

FIGURE 6.4 Primary school enrollments in selected African countries, 1990–2009 (source: UNESCO (UIS online))

This rapid enrollment growth has been supported by government policies in many African countries; for instance, the abolition of school fees, introduced in the 1990s (e.g. in Cameroon, Ethiopia, Ghana, Malawi, and Uganda) and in the 2000s (e.g. Benin, Burundi, Lesotho, Liberia, Mozambique, Rwanda, Sierra Leone, Tanzania, and Zambia). While budgetary constraints often represent a barrier to the provision of free primary education, most African countries allocated more resources to the education sector during the 2000s. As shown in Figure 6.4, several African countries recorded dramatic increases in primary school enrollments over the period 1990–2009, notably the Democratic Republic of Congo, Kenya, South Africa, Tanzania, and Uganda.

Types of education financing in Africa

In many African countries, education is provided largely by the government, especially at the primary level. Consequently, the financing of education usually constitutes a significant proportion of the government's annual expenditure. Other stakeholders that complement government financing of education include: households, the private sector, international development partners, NGOs, community-based organizations, associations, religious institutions, communities, etc. Funding from these sources has continued to grow in importance over the years in most of Africa, due to the increased demand for education and requests for all stakeholders to assist in its financing.

Public financing

This is most commonly measured by examining: (i) public education expenditure as a percentage of total government expenditure and (ii) public expenditure as a percentage of GDP. Figure 6.5 shows the trends in public education expenditure over the period 1980–2009 using both indicators. Africa allocated around 4 percent of its total GDP to education during this period. In

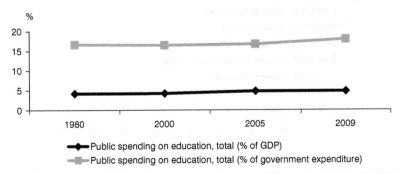

FIGURE 6.5 Public spending on education in Africa, 1980–2009 (sources: UNESCO (UIS online); AfDB Data Portal)

relation to total government expenditure, on average 18 percent was channeled to educational development between 1980 and 2009. However, this is still short of the EFA target on expenditure, which had been set at 20 percent in 2000. This may explain why, in the face of rising enrollments, the quality of education at all levels continues to fall far below expectations across Africa (UNESCO, 2011a).

At the country level, Figures 6.6 and 6.7 show the trend in educational expenditure as a percentage of total public expenditure and GDP for the years 1999 and 2009. Figure 6.6 presents total government expenditure as a percentage of GDP for selected African countries. This shows that most

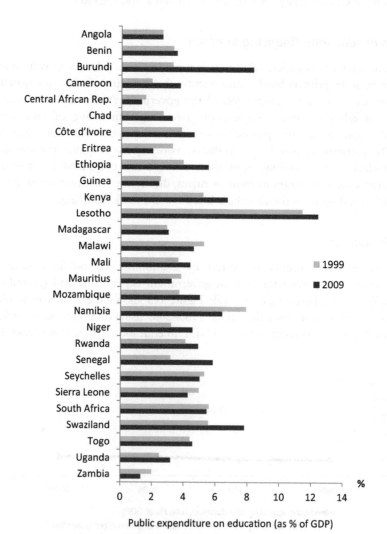

Public expenditure on education (as % of GDP)

FIGURE 6.6 Public expenditure on education in selected African countries, 1999 and 2009 (source: UNESCO (UIS online))

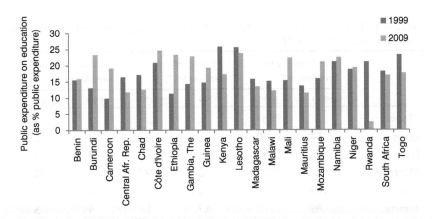

FIGURE 6.7 Public expenditure on education in selected African countries, 1999–2009 (% of total public expenditure) (source: UNESCO (UIS online): http://stats.uis.unesco.org/unesco)

countries allocated less than 5 percent of GDP to education in 2009. The exceptions were Burundi (8 percent), Lesotho (12 percent), Senegal (6 percent), South Africa (5.5 percent), and Swaziland (8 percent). It should be highlighted that increases in this ratio were recorded for most countries between 1999 and 2009. Figure 6.7 reveals that education expenditure during this period represented between 4 percent and 12 percent of total government spending. We can identify the high-performing countries as Lesotho, Burundi, Côte d'Ivoire, Swaziland, and Namibia.

Private financing

Though governments are the major financiers of education in Africa, the private sector fulfills a complementary role in a number of ways, including supporting public education institutions, and private schools that are created and managed by private operators through the payment of out-of-pocket fees by households in various forms.

UNESCO (2011a) notes that the proportion of household spending on education varies across the three levels (primary, secondary, and tertiary). As a proportion of total education expenditure, it stood at around 29 percent at the primary level in 2009 (despite many African countries abolishing school fees for primary education). The growing dissatisfaction of the middle class with the quality of primary education has led to a growing demand for private schools and private tuition. This explains why household contributions to this level of education remain high. UNESCO (2011a) further notes that the household contribution declines to 22 percent at the tertiary level, and the high unit cost indicates elevated public subsidies to tertiary students in Africa.

TABLE 6.1 Increasing private enrollment in education at pre-primary, primary, and secondary levels, 1999 and 2007

	Pre-primary private enrollments*		Primary private enrollments*		Secondary private enrollments*	
	1999	2007	1999	2007	1999	2007
Algeria	...	34	...	...	...	51
Egypt	54	30	...	8	4	...
Libya	...	17	...	5	3	2
Mauritania	...	...	2	9	13	17
Morocco	100	96	4	8	5	5
Tunisia	88		0.7	1	5	5
Benin	...	...	7	13	25	35
Botswana	...	96	5	...	4	...
Burkina Faso	34		11	13	39	43
Burundi	49	46	0.8	1	12	7
Cabo Verde	...	...	...	0.4		12
Comoros	100	62	12	10	41	41
Côte d'Ivoire	46	46	12	12	...	...
Ethiopia	100	95	...	...	6	...
Gambia	...	100	14	18	39	25
Ghana	33	19	13	17	14	16
Kenya	10	35	...	19	6	11
Liberia	39	24	38	30	...	...
Madagascar	93	94	22	19	...	41
Mauritius	85	82	24	26	...	...
Namibia	100		4	4	5	5
Niger	33	29	4	4	11	15
Nigeria	...	...	4	5		12
Rwanda	...	...	...	2	44	41
São Tomé	...	0.5	...	...	...	...
Senegal	68	51	12	12	23	23
Seychelles	5	6	5	6	4	6
South Africa	26	6	2	2	3	3
Togo	53	55	36	42	28	31
Uganda	100	100		10	45	...
Tanzania	...	10	0.2	1	...	...
Zambia	...	...	...	3	4	...
Zimbabwe	...	...	88	...	...	...

Sources: UNESCO, Global Education Digest, Various editions (2005–2011); UNESCO, EFA Monitoring Report, Various editions (2005–2010).

Growing enrollment in private schools

The proportion of children attending private schools in Africa ranged from a small percentage in Burundi, South Africa, and Tanzania, to more than 30 percent in Congo, Equatorial Guinea, and Mali in 2009 (see Table 6.1). In these countries, community schools play a particular role in the provision of education (UNESCO, 2011b). The number of private schools is on the increase in numerous countries, at both primary and secondary levels. In the 33 countries listed in Table 6.1, enrollments in private schools at pre-primary, primary, and secondary levels trended upward throughout most of the period 1999–2007. Many of these countries recorded enrollment levels far above the SSA average for all three levels. Significant increases in private schools could also be observed in secondary education. From 2000 to 2007, 12 of the 33 countries in Table 6.1 experienced an increase in the proportion of children attending private secondary schools. In 2007, the proportion surpassed 40 percent in Algeria, Burkina Faso, Comoros, Madagascar, and Rwanda.

Relationship between education and the middle class

Conceptualizing the dynamics

Weir (2002) notes that the expansion of education and higher education, in particular in the United States, has helped to blur class stratification in several ways. By promoting occupational mobility, enhanced suburban lifestyles, and enjoyment of consumer goods that have become the hallmark of a middle-class lifestyle, higher education has to some extent leveled the life chances, choices, and opportunities of children from very different backgrounds. Access to higher education has also meant fewer children following in their parents' occupational footsteps, as new career choices have opened up to them.

The expansion of higher education has also helped to blur the lines of the occupational prestige hierarchy. Many occupations have instituted new credentials. Furthermore, a new lexicon of semi-professional categories has helped soften the rigid demarcations of occupational stratification and is contributing to the notion of one big middle class.

As Figure 6.8 shows, better education (e.g. post-secondary education – technical and vocational, university and college in particular) and the growth of the middle class can spur economic growth through both private and public channels. The private benefits for individuals are well documented and include better employment prospects, higher salaries, and an enhanced ability to save and invest. These benefits may result in better health and improved quality of life, triggering a virtuous spiral in which increased life expectancy enables individuals to work more productively over a longer time, boosting lifetime earnings.

Education can bring other benefits for society. By producing well-trained teachers, it can enhance the quality of primary and secondary education systems and give secondary graduates greater opportunities for economic advancement. Furthermore, by training physicians and other health workers, education can improve a society's wellbeing and raise productivity at work. And by nurturing governance and leadership skills, it can provide countries with the talented leaders they need to establish a policy environment favorable to growth. Setting up robust and fair legal and political institutions and making them part of a country's fabric, and developing a culture of job and business creation, for example, calls for advanced knowledge and decision-making skills. Similarly, addressing environmental problems and improving security against internal and external threats places a premium on the skills that higher education is best placed to deliver.

Although none of these outcomes is inevitable, the framework presented in Figure 6.8 suggests many possible routes through which education can benefit economies. In the next section, we assess the evidence that supports these linkages and present new evidence of our own.

The role of education in creating the middle class

If the experience of the US and Europe is anything to go by, the positive role played by education in the growth of the middle class cannot be over-emphasized (AfDB, 2011). Figure 6.8 shows how the enhancement of a country's human resources through greater access to education can stimulate middle-class growth. Countries that have higher levels of educational attainment, improved health, and human development tend to have larger middle-class populations (AfDB, 2011).

Tables 6.2 and 6.3 show how educational attainment levels in Africa have increased since 1960, accelerating the expansion of the middle class, as well as spurring urbanization, consumption, and economic growth. Table 6.2 shows

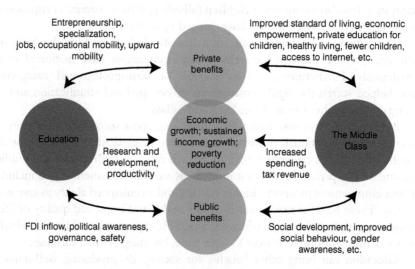

FIGURE 6.8 Education and the middle class: the dynamics of interconnectedness

TABLE 6.2 Improved adult and youth literacy rates in Africa, 1985–2015 (%)

	Adult Literacy Rate (15 and over) %			Youth Literacy Rate (15–24) %		
	1985-1994	2000-2007	2015 (est.)	1985-1994	2000-2007	2015 (est.)
Algeria	50	75	81	74	92	95
Benin	27	41	47	40	52	60
Botswana	69	83	87	89	94	95
Burkina Faso	14	29	36	20	39	45
Burundi	37	59	...	54	73	...
Cabo Verde	63	84	89	88	97	98
Central African Rep.	34	49	...	48	59	...
Chad	12	32	39	17	44	52
Côte d'Ivoire	34	49	...	49	61	...
Egypt	44	66	73	63	85	93
Ethiopia	27	36	...	34	50	...
Gabon	72	86	91	93	97	98
Ghana	...	65	71	...	78	84
Kenya	...	74	...	...	80	...
Liberia	41	56	64	51	72	80
Libya	76	87	91	95	99	100
Malawi	49	74	79	59	83	90
Mali	...	26	38	...	39	55
Mauritania	...	56	61	...	66	71
Mauritius	80	87	90	91	96	97
Morocco	42	56	62	58	75	83
Mozambique	...	44	49	...	53	57
Namibia	76	88	90	88	93	94
Niger	...	29	36	...	37	46
Nigeria	55	72	79	71	87	92
Rwanda	58	65	...	75	78	...
São Tomé	73	88	91	94	95	95
Senegal	27	42	47	38	51	56
Seychelles	88	91	...	99	99	...
Sierra Leone	...	38	47	...	54	67
South Africa	...	88	91	...	95	98
Swaziland	67	84	89	84	94	96
Tanzania	59	72	74	82	78	77
Tunisia	...	78	83	...	96	98
Uganda	56	74	81	70	86	91
Zambia	65	71	72	66	75	74
Zimbabwe	84	91	94	95	91	99

Sources: (i) UNESCO, Global Education Digest, Various editions (2005–2011); (ii) UNESCO, EFA Monitoring Report, Various editions (2005–2010).

TABLE 6.3 Educational attainment of population aged 25 and above, 1960–2000

| Region (no. of countries) | Year | Pop. over 25 (mill.) | No school | Highest level attained (% of the population 25 and over) | | | | | | | Average years of school |
| | | | | Primary | | Secondary | | Higher | | | |
				Total	Full	Total	Full	Total	Full		
World (109)	1960	1,013	34.7	43.5	21.2	18.0	7.3	3.7	2.4		4.6
	1970	1,197	32.7	40.7	20.7	21.3	9.2	5.3	3.5		5.1
	1980	1,455	31.1	33.4	14.4	27.2	13.2	8.3	5.3		5.8
	1990	1,803	27.6	31.0	13.5	29.5	13.0	11.9	7.7		6.4
	1995	1,905	26.7	32.2	13.7	28.0	12.6	13.0	8.3		6.5
	2000	2,109	24.7	33.2	13.9	27.8	12.4	14.3	9.1		6.7
All developing (73)	1960	469	68.0	26.2	8.3	5.1	1.9	0.8	0.5		1.8
	1970	585	62.1	29.3	10.5	6.9	2.8	1.7	1.2		2.3
	1980	752	55.7	28.0	8.6	13.0	5.3	3.2	2.2		3.1
	1990	1,004	46.9	31.5	11.2	16.3	7.3	5.3	3.6		4.0
	1995	1,157	41.8	33.5	11.9	18.3	8.2	6.3	4.3		4.5
	2000	1,327	37.2	35.9	12.8	19.7	8.8	7.2	4.9		4.9

Middle East/North Africa (11)									
1960	19	82.3	12.9	5.0	3.7	1.8	1.1	0.6	1.1
1970	25	78.3	13.9	5.1	5.9	3.0	1.8	1.1	1.5
1980	34	67.3	18.4	6.5	10.4	5.5	3.9	2.4	2.5
1990	50	51.6	25.4	8.8	17.1	9.3	5.9	3.7	3.8
1995	59	43.9	28.7	9.9	20.0	10.8	7.4	4.7	4.5
2000	68	37.0	31.6	10.9	22.2	12.1	9.1	5.9	5.1
Sub-Saharan Africa (22)									
1960	41	76.0	17.9	5.8	5.9	1.5	0.2	0.1	1.4
1970	52	71.9	20.1	4.4	7.1	1.7	0.9	0.7	1.6
1980	66	61.8	28.6	6.7	9.0	2.5	0.7	0.5	2.1
1990	90	51.5	35.3	8.1	11.5	3.3	1.5	1.2	2.8
1995	104	45.6	32.5	7.3	19.0	6.8	2.6	2.0	3.6
2000	120	43.5	34.2	7.7	19.2	6.6	3.0	2.4	3.8

Source: Barro and Lee (2000).
Notes: 'Total' refers to the percentage of the population for whom the indicated level is the highest attained. 'Full' refers to those who had the completion of the indicated level as the highest attained.

that with the dramatic increases in investment in education across Africa, adult and youth literacy rates improved significantly over the period 1985–2007. This trend is projected to continue to 2015; by which time most African countries would be close to 82 percent for youth literacy and 72 percent for adult literacy. Again, this development has the potential for a further expansion and strengthening of the middle class in Africa.

Figure 6.9 shows the growth in GDP per person employed in Africa over the period 1990–2008. Enhanced labor productivity triggered by higher levels of educational attainment could be one of the many factors to explain this.

Figure 6.10 shows the expansion of telephone and internet users in Africa from 1970 to 2009. This highlights the increased demand for information and modern technology by the bulging middle class in Africa.

Figure 6.11 supports the findings of AfDB (2011), namely that the enhancement of human resources in Africa through greater access to education over the years has expanded the size of the middle class, with significant positive secondary effects. Since a large proportion of the middle class enjoy steady and predictable incomes, they can afford secondary and tertiary education for their children and affluent urban lifestyles, including improved access to ICT. Furthermore, the middle class continues to drive the growth of the private sector through entrepreneurial activities. In this way, Figure 6.11 shows positive and very strong correlations between these socioeconomic indicators and the size of the middle class in Africa. That is, as enrollment in secondary and tertiary education grows over time, so too does the size of the middle class.

The role of the middle class as co-funder of education

As highlighted in earlier sections of this chapter and in AfDB (2011), human capital investments in education and health rise as affluence increases. Table 6.1 and Figure 6.12 reveal that enrollments in private schools – at pre-primary, primary, and secondary levels – have witnessed appreciable increases over the years across most African countries. This indicates a sizable and strong middle class, who lack confidence in the ability of public schools to offer quality education for their children and so would rather pay for private schools and tutoring.

Conclusion

Since the end of World War II, governments across the world have pursued a strategy to expand access to education, particularly higher education. This was largely driven by the need to unlock the potential of all members of society to live long, healthy, and productive lives, through the creation of a middle class of professional workers.

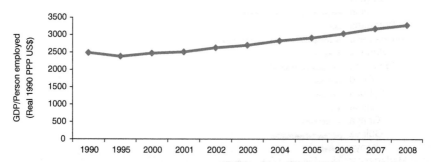

FIGURE 6.9 GDP per person employed in Africa (real 1990 PPP$), 1990–2008 (source: World Bank (2011a))

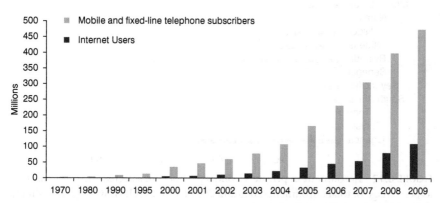

FIGURE 6.10 Growth fixed line/mobile and internet users in Africa, 1970–2009 (million) (sources: World Bank (2011b); AfDB Data Portal)

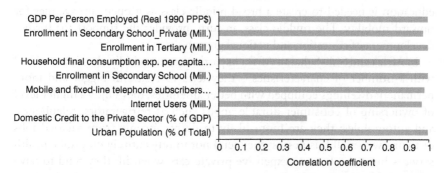

FIGURE 6.11 Correlation of an educated population/workforce with other socioeconomic indicators in Africa (sources: UNESCO (UIS online); World Bank (WDI online); AfDB Data Portal; World Bank EDSTATS)

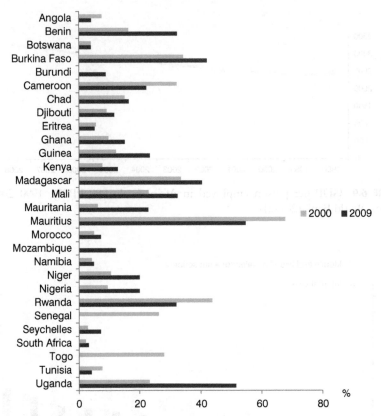

FIGURE 6.12   Enrollment in private secondary schools in selected African countries as percentage of total enrollment, 2000 and 2009 (sources: UNESCO/(UIS online); AfDB Data Portal; World Bank EDSTATS)

The growth of the middle class and the expansion in education seem to be intertwined in a mutually reinforcing and virtuous relationship. Expanded education is needed to create a broad middle class as it opens up avenues for upward mobility. The middle class, in turn, provides the support for further development of education and national growth.

In Africa and Sub-Saharan Africa in particular, the middle class is associated with a number of characteristics – they tend to reside in bigger and more permanent dwellings equipped with better amenities; they enjoy a higher level of ownership of consumer durable goods such as refrigerators, telephones, and automobiles; they are more likely to derive income from salaried jobs or their own small businesses; they tend not to rely entirely on public health services but to seek more expensive private care when ill; they tend to have fewer children and generally spend more on their nutrition and schooling; they are better educated; and they are more geographically concentrated in urban areas or along coasts.

In this chapter, we have examined the relationship between education and the middle class in Africa. We have looked at the expansion of the education systems over the last four decades, the financing – both public and private – of the system, as well as the concomitant growth and rising influence of the middle class over the years. We have also examined the dynamics of the relation between the growth of education and that of the middle class on the continent. Available data generally support the proposition that the enhancement of human resources in Africa through greater access to education over the years has significantly increased the size of the middle class. This is supported by results of earlier studies, as well as by the findings of the African Development Bank (AfDB, 2011).

The sustained growth of Africa's middle class will require governments to ensure that those in the 'floating' class (i.e. those earning between $2 and $4 per day) do not slip back into poverty. According to Birdsall (2007), 'inclusive growth' – i.e., growth conducive to increasing the size and economic influence of the middle class – is fostered by many of the same policies that reduce poverty, namely fiscal discipline (e.g. good debt management and a fair tax and redistribution system), lack of trade volatility, sound monetary policy (resulting in low and stable inflation), and improved infrastructure. Furthermore, sustained investment will be needed in the education, health, and other social sectors to ensure that the middle class in Africa continues to thrive, and to scale up job creation and poverty reduction across the continent.

References

AfDB (2011). 'The Middle of the Pyramid: Dynamics of the Middle Class in Africa.' Report by the Chief Economist Complex. Tunis: African Development Bank.

AfDB, UNECA, AUC, and UNDP (2012). *Assessing Progress in Africa toward the Millennium Development Goals: Emerging Perspectives from Africa on the post-2015 Development Agenda* (MDG Progress Report for Africa).

Banerjee, A., and E. Duflo (2007). 'The Economic Lives of the Poor,' *Journal of Economic Perspectives*; vol. 21, no. 1, pp. 141–167.

Banerjee, A., and E. Duflo (2008). 'What Is Middle Class about the Middle Classes around the World?,' *Journal of Economic Perspectives*, vol. 22, no. 2, pp. 3–28.

Barro, R., and Jong-Wha Lee (2000). 'International Data on Educational Attainment: Updates and Implications.' CID Working Paper no. 42. Center for International Development at Harvard University.

Birdsall, N. (2007). 'Reflections on the Macro Foundations of the Middle Class in the Developing World.' Working Paper no. 130. Washington DC: Center for Global Development.

Bloom, D., D. Canning and K. Chan (2006). 'Higher Education and Economic Development in Africa.' Human Development Sector, African Region, World Bank. Washington DC: World Bank.

Bruillard, N. (2010). 'South Africa's "black diamonds" overtake whites,' *Global Post*, 19 May www.globalpost.com/dispatch/south-africa/090630/black-middle-class-townships-economy (accessed 18 September 2014).

OECD (2010). *The Emerging Middle Class in Developing Countries*. Paris: OECD, DEV/ DOC 2.

Ravallion, M. (2009). 'The Developing World's Bulging (but Vulnerable) Middle Class,' Policy Research Working Paper no. 4816. Washington DC: World Bank.

UNESCO (2011a). *Financing Education in Sub-Saharan Africa: Meeting the Challenges of Expansion, Equity and Quality*. UNESCO Regional Bureau for Education in Africa. Paris: UNESCO.

UNESCO (2011b). *Global Education Digest 2011/ Comparing Education Statistics Around the World*. Paris: UNESCO.

UNESCO (2011c). *Education For All (EFA) Monitoring Report 2011*. Paris: UNESCO.

Weir, M. (2002). 'The American Middle Class and the Politics of Education.' In O. Zunz, L. Schoppa, and N. Hiwatari (eds), *Social Contracts under Stress*. New York: Russell Sage Foundation.

WHO (2010). *Trends in Maternal Mortality: 1990 to 2008*. Estimates developed by WHO, UNICEF, UNFPA and the World Bank World Bank/ EDSTATS.

World Bank (2011a). *Africa Regional Brief*. Washington DC: World Bank.

World Bank (2011b). *Learning for All: Investing in People's Knowledge and Skills to Promote Development*. Washington DC: World Bank.

World Bank (2011c). World Development Indicators (WDI online) http://databank. worldbank.org/ddp/home.do?Step=12&id=4&CNO=2 (accessed 18 September 2014).

7

GENDER

Abena Oduro and Alice Nabalamba

The share of the middle-class population in developing countries has expanded rapidly during the last decade (Ravallion, 2010) and this trend is expected to continue (Kharas, 2010). This trend has also been observed in Africa, as documented in Chapter 1. However, recent studies that have 'counted' the middle class in Africa have been unable to disaggregate this segment of the population by gender. This chapter makes the case that the methodology used to identify and count the middle class, such as growth of income or consumption, does not lend itself to such disaggregation.[1] We then look at the factors that are likely to lift individuals out of poverty and into the middle class. This is followed by an analysis of the opportunities and constraints faced by women and men when they make this transition. The final section addresses the question of whether an expansion in Africa's middle class can help to reduce gender inequality.

Gender and the middle class: conceptual issues

Who exactly makes up Africa's middle class? Several studies that have set out to answer this question utilize income or consumption expenditure per capita as the indicator (Birdsall, 2010; Ravallion, 2010; Banerjee and Duflo, 2008). Income or consumption expenditure per capita is obtained by dividing aggregate household income or consumption expenditure by the number of household members.

This method of identifying the middle-class status of individuals appears to be an improvement on alternative methods that classify women using the occupational status of the (generally male) head of household. According to that methodology, women – irrespective of their occupational status – derive their class status from their husband, father, brother, or other male relative who is the official head of the household – unless, that is, they are themselves heads of households. This method of identifying the class status of women has been roundly criticized, as it effectively renders women invisible (Acker, 1973; Sorenson, 1994). On this basis, they are not considered as 'social beings with identities and existence of their own' (Acker, 1973: 25).

There are several difficulties with the current practice of identifying the middle-class status of individuals. First, by dividing aggregate household income equally among household members, we lose sight of the fact that adults in a household are unlikely to be earning equivalent incomes. Thus, a household comprising one working adult, one non-working adult, and two children will classify all its adults as middle class if the per capita income falls within the critical range.[2] This methodology sweeps under the carpet the disadvantages and constraints that some groups, including women, face in the labor market. A second problem with this method of identifying the class status of individuals is that it assumes household resources are pooled and shared equally.

There is a large body of literature showing that the 'unitary model' of household behavior does not always hold (Schultz, 1990; Hoddinott and Haddad, 1995; Doss, 2006). In several African countries, the domestic sexual division of labor is extended to household provisioning. Amongst fishing communities along the coast of Ghana's Central Region, for example, husbands sell fresh fish to their wives who then process it for sale. Profit from the sale of the processed fish is then used by the wives to provision the household. 'Fishermen husbands believe they have fulfilled their household provisioning responsibilities once they provide fresh fish for processing' (Britwum, 2009: 75). To cite another example, couples in Kenya's Central Province retain separate sources of income and very few of them pool their incomes (Johnson, 2004). In northern Ghana, because wives are not considered to be permanent members of the household, they must bargain with men who are the custodians of communal resources in order to gain access to their subsumed interests and rights (Apusigah, 2009).

The current practice of attributing middle-class status to individuals based on aggregate household income or consumption expenditure provides little or no information that can be used to conduct a gender analysis. Since all women and men in a household have identical class status, a gender analysis of the middle class is limited to comparing individuals based on the sex of the household head.[3] However, this ignores the circumstances of the large proportion of women who live in male-headed households.

Is a gender analysis of the middle class necessary? The answer is 'yes' for at least two reasons. First, women and men do not have equal opportunities to participate in the labor market. Even when women do participate, their terms of engagement are quite different and usually inferior to those of men. Norms, rules, regulations, and institutions create gender inequalities both within and outside the household. There is another principal reason why gender analysis is crucial, in that a person's class status is influenced by gender (Witz, 1995; Wright, 1997).

Women and men face differentiated opportunities also in acquiring education and skills. This results in women being crowded in specific occupations and at the lower end of the income scale. These unequal opportunities are determined to a large extent by gender relations. The middle class is not homogeneous. The divisions into a floating class, lower-middle class, and upper-middle class also have gendered dimensions. Third, within households, resources are not always pooled and or shared equally.

Factors that explain the growth of the middle class

Growth that is poverty reducing can explain the expansion in the absolute numbers and the share of the population in African countries that is middle class. The trend in the African GDP growth rate was positive from 2000 until 2008, when it began to slow down. The average growth rate for African countries was estimated at 6 percent in 2007 but declined to 3 percent in 2009 before picking up to just under 5 percent in 2010 (AfDB, 2011). Ravallion's study finds that the 'pace at which the middle class expands tends to be higher in more rapidly growing economies' (Ravallion, 2010: 451). In a simulation exercise, countries with growth rates below the mean of the survey countries recorded an increase in the middle-class proportion of the population when the growth rate in those countries was pegged at the survey mean rate (Ravallion, 2010).

To earn an income level that can be classified as middle class, a person must be employed in the labor market and/or own financial and physical assets. Second, the person must be employed in an activity or activities and/or own assets that generate the required level of income. To remain in the middle class, incomes must be sustained above the minimum critical level. In addition to introducing policies that will foster growth, governments need to implement social protection measures that will safeguard the most vulnerable from falling below the minimum threshold, if the middle class is to expand.

Participation in the labor market depends on the characteristics of the individual, including age, sex, marital status, agency, and physical location. Cultural norms and practices also have a mediating influence. Whether or not the activities that the individual is employed to do, or the assets the individual owns, will generate the requisite level of income to be classified as middle class depends on a number of factors. These include: the time the individual spends on these activities; his or her level of access to, and efficiency in, the use of inputs; as well as his or her sector of employment.

To have comparable chances to move out of poverty and join the ranks of the middle class, women and men must have equal opportunity to participate in, increase, and sustain income-generating activities. Both women and men must be equipped with the requisite skills and have access to relevant knowledge, factors of production, and inputs. Norms, rules, laws, and practices will have to be changed to provide both men and women with the economic and social space to scale up their incomes and take advantage of the opportunities that growth provides.

TABLE 7.1 Female and male labor market participation rates, 2000 and 2009 (%)

Country	2000		2009	
	Women	Men	Women	Men
Algeria	32.7	82.2	38.8	82.8
Angola	76.9	91.1	76.4	89.1
Benin	65.2	81.6	68.8	78.2
Botswana	71.8	81.7	75.5	82.1
Burkina Faso	79.5	91.5	80.2	91.4
Burundi	91.4	90.5	91.6	88.1
Cabo Verde	48.7	85.1	57.0	82.8
Cameroon	52.2	82.7	54.5	82.0
Central African Republic	70.6	87.1	71.7	87.1
Chad	65.2	79.9	63.5	77.8
Comoros	71.6	84.1	75.3	85.9
Congo, Dem. Rep.	56.7	87.6	57.7	87.0
Congo, Rep.	60.9	84.0	62.8	83.5
Côte d'Ivoire	49.9	82.4	51.5	82.6
Djibouti	58.4	82.3	63.6	80.0
Egypt	25.2	77.1	23.9	79.1
Eritrea	56.6	83.6	63.9	84.6
Ethiopia	75.5	92.1	83.1	90.9
Gabon	67.2	84.9	72.1	82.8
Gambia, The	71.2	85.9	71.1	85.1
Ghana	73.9	77.1	75.3	75.8
Guinea	82.1	90.5	82.6	89.9
Guinea-Bissau	61.7	85.1	61.3	85.6
Equatorial Guinea	34.8	95.2	40.7	93.8
Kenya	77.0	89.0	78.2	88.8
Lesotho	70.4	81.0	72.4	78.5
Liberia	68.4	77.9	69.1	76.8
Libya	23.7	77.6	26.1	81.6
Madagascar	85.9	90.4	86.0	89.4
Malawi	75.4	78.2	74.4	77.9

Country	2000		2009	
	Women	*Men*	*Women*	*Men*
Mali	37.0	69.9	38.7	68.3
Mauritania	57.4	82.5	60.9	82.0
Mauritius	44.2	84.7	45.4	79.8
Morocco	29.5	84.3	28.3	83.7
Mozambique	86.5	87.2	85.6	86.6
Namibia	49.9	65.0	53.5	63.9
Niger	38.6	88.6	39.4	88.0
Nigeria	38.7	75.4	39.9	74.7
Rwanda	87.5	87.3	88.4	86.0
São Tomé and Principe	44.0	76.6	47.1	78.5
Senegal	63.6	90.4	65.7	89.7
Sierra Leone	69.2	68.5	66.8	67.9
Somalia	59.8	86.1	57.9	86.1
South Africa	46.9	63.1	50.8	66.6
Sudan	30.0	75.3	32.2	74.0
Swaziland	50.4	79.0	55.5	75.8
Tanzania	89.1	91.5	88.8	91.2
Togo	61.3	86.9	65.0	86.4
Tunisia	25.8	76.0	27.8	73.8
Uganda	81.1	91.8	80.5	91.2
Zambia	62.5	78.7	60.0	79.3
Zimbabwe	64.7	79.0	61.2	75.4

Source: World Bank, Gender Statistics Database.

Factors that explain the inclusion of women and men in the middle class

Factors determining the inclusion of women and men in the middle class fall under three main headings: (i) variables that explain participation in the labor market and ownership of assets; (ii) variables that explain incomes generated from factors of production owned by women and men, and (iii) redistribution of income or social protection.

Participation in the labor market

Although female participation rates in the formal labor market have risen in many African countries over the course of the last decade, they remain below 50 percent in a number of countries (see Table 7.1). In contrast, male participation rates average 80 percent and only fall below 70 percent in a few African countries.

Women tend to be concentrated in particular industries and occupations (Assad and Arntz, 2005; Kolev and Robles, 2010; Siphambe and Thokweng-Bakwena, 2001). In contrast, men are more likely to hold managerial and professional positions (Ghana Statistical Service, 2008; Siphambe and Thokweng-Bakwena, 2001). Women are less likely to be wage or salaried workers (see Table 7.2). A number of countries have seen some improvement in the incidence of female salaried employees, but in others there has been a decline. In Ghana, women are largely found in lower-paid occupations.

The other side of the coin is the high incidence of women who are contributing family workers or own-account workers. Contributing family workers usually do not receive a fixed remuneration for their services. The data in Table 7.3 do not differentiate between contributing family workers and own-account workers. This is because the ILO classifies this category of workers as vulnerable. In Ghana, 27 percent of women in employment in 2005/6 were unpaid family workers, compared with 9 percent of men. In Rwanda, about 58 percent of employed women and 20 percent of employed men were recorded as unpaid workers (Strode, Wylde, and Murangwa, n.d.).

Understanding participation rates

The variations in female participation rates across countries are framed by the social norms defining women's scope for geographical mobility (Assad and Arntz, 2005). Women's responsibilities for child care and the household economy help to explain female labor market participation rates.

Women who are married and/or who have children are less likely to participate in the labor market than single females since they have competing demands on their time. Moreover, women's participation rates in the labor market respond positively to wage increases and negatively to the price of child care (Lokshin, Glinskaya, and Garcia, 2004).

Working hours that make it difficult to combine market work and domestic work can explain these patterns. A project on promoting decent work for women in the banking and domestic sectors in Ghana found that the introduction of longer opening hours and weekend opening made working in the banking sector increasingly difficult for women.[4]

Education and skills are important in explaining labor participation rates (Sackey, 2005; Yakubu, 2010). The level of education and training are also

TABLE 7.2 Proportion of wage and salary workers amongst employed women and men, 1995–2005 (%)

Country	1995		2000		2005	
	Female	Male	Female	Male	Female	Male
Algeria	...	...	57.7	61.4	51.1	36.0
Benin	...	...	...	...	4.2	16.3
Botswana	64.9	67.2	67.9	71.2	58.6	62.2
Burkina Faso	1.4	5.8	...	...	3.0	8.4
Burundi	...	...	2.3	9.6	...	...
Cabo Verde	...	...	33.0	43.8	...	...
Cameroon	5.7	22.3	8.7	29.3	...	...
Chad	0.8	8.8	...	...	...	...
Congo, Rep.	...	...	...	...	8.6	35.5
Côte d'Ivoire	...	...	12.2	25.4	...	...
Djibouti	30.1	72.8	...	...	...	...
Egypt	52.9	58.1	57.2	60.6	50.8	62.2
Ethiopia	4.0	7.0	6.4	9.5	6.2	9.3
Gabon	29.2	58.6	...	...	34.5	52.2
Kenya	...	...	19.3	46.4	...	...
Lesotho	43.7	32.4	29.9	22.5	...	...
Madagascar	10.5	14.5	...	...	10.8	16.0
Mali	1.8	4.9	...	...	6.2	14.7
Mauritius	85.5	78.8	90.9	79.1	84.1	78.6
Morocco	52.7	47.5	73.7	58.2	31.6	39.5
Mozambique	...	...	...	...	3.0	15.7
Namibia	43.4	65.2	56.1	67.7	68.8	76.0
Niger	...	...	...	...	3.9	5.9
Rwanda	3.3	9.4	...	...	...	...
Senegal	...	...	15.1	26.1	...	...
Sierra Leone	...	...	...	...	3.7	11.3
South Africa	...	...	80.0	81.7	80.0	81.7
Swaziland	67.4	82.7	...	...	...	...
Tanzania	...	...	4.0	9.8	6.1	15.3
Togo	...	...	...	...	5.7	16.6
Tunisia	69.1	70.5	...	...	...	...
Uganda	...	...	8.2	20.3	7.5	22.2

Source: World Bank, Gender Statistics Database.
Note: ... denotes missing data.

TABLE 7.3 Proportion of contributing family workers and own-account workers by gender, 1995–2005 (%)

Country	1995		2000		2005	
	Female	Male	Female	Male	Female	Male
Algeria	...	...	35.8	30.0	48.9	32.0
Botswana	33.8	30.7	15.1	12.6	38.9	32.9
Cabo Verde	...	...	44.0	35.9	...	...
Cameroon	91.4	69.5	87.8	64.4	...	...
Congo, Rep.	...	...		...	89.4	60.0
Côte d'Ivoire	...	...	84.0	69.5	...	...
Egypt	41.5	22.3	38.3	19.4	45.4	20.5
Ethiopia	93.7	88.4	92.8	88.8	93.3	89.3
Gabon	62.7	36.5	...	...	63.8	45.0
Madagascar	86.6	82.9	...	...	85.6	78.9
Mali	97.8	93.5	...	...	92.8	81.9
Mauritius	...	...	7.1	15.7	14.7	17.7
Morocco	44.7	48.2	22.3	32.2	66.9	54.3
Mozambique	...	...	...	...	95.9	78.1
Namibia	54.2	31.7	36.2	19.9	28.2	17.0
Niger	...	...	...	...	89.2	83.2
Rwanda	95.5	88.9	...	...	...	...
Senegal	...	...	84.1	73.2	...	...
South Africa	...	...	3.8	3.2	16.5	15.3
Tanzania	...	...	95.5	88.8	92.9	82.1
Uganda	...	...	91.8	79.5	92.3	77.4
Zambia	90.4	67.4	90.8	73.7	...	...

Source: World Bank, Gender Statistics Database.
Note: ... denotes missing data.

major factors determining the likelihood of a woman being a paid or salaried worker, and the sector in which she is employed. Skills can be acquired through training in formal institutions, apprenticeships, and on-the-job training. Basic education, in particular being able to read and write in a language that exposes the individual to a wide knowledge base, is critical in determining the skills that can be acquired. Reading and writing skills are usually acquired by attending formal schools.

The gender gap in primary education (measured by the Gender Parity Index) has narrowed in many African countries over the last two decades and is virtually non-existent in several others (see Figure 7.1). The gender gap, however, remains wide at the secondary and tertiary education levels, despite an increase in the gross enrollment rates of both sexes (see Table 7.4). Girls are more likely than boys to be used for household domestic work and to look after younger siblings, and this social practice hinders female enrollment. As girls grow older, they often face social pressure to marry early and have children, which may reduce their ability to enroll for higher education and vocational training.

There remains a sizable gender difference in adult literacy rates in Africa (see Figure 7.2). Women are therefore more likely to be excluded from acquiring professional skills because they cannot satisfy the entry requirements for polytechnics and technical schools.

The traditional apprenticeship system is the route to acquire skills for most youth who have never attended school or who have failed to complete primary and/or secondary school. Traditional apprenticeships are more common in West Africa than in the rest of the continent. Since having a certificate from a formal education institution and being able to read and write is not a requirement for enrollment in an apprenticeship program, this is one less hurdle for women seeking to acquire skills. However, another barrier to entry exists in terms of occupational segregation. Traditional apprenticeships do not provide young women with the opportunity to diversify their skills acquisition. In Ghana, for example, female apprentices are concentrated in three trades: textiles and apparel; personal services (for example, hairdressing); and food preparation, processing, and beverages. Males, on the other hand, are found in trades such as building, automotives, and mechanics, where there is little female presence (Ghana Statistical Service, 2013).

Data from the industrial surveys of Africa[5] reveal a high correlation between the sex of apprentices and the sex of entrepreneurs. Male entrepreneurs are unlikely to train female apprentices, and female entrepreneurs are unlikely to train male apprentices. This pattern of segregation in the provision of apprenticeship training perpetuates the occupational segregation by sex observed in the distribution of enterprises across sectors.

The range of opportunities open to women through on-the-job training is therefore quite limited. Women are less likely than men to hold the necessary educational qualifications for skilled jobs, while the traditional apprenticeship system restricts the skills they can acquire. It is no great surprise therefore that women are concentrated in occupations that do not require skills upgrading. Women who do qualify for professional and skilled jobs may find that they have fewer opportunities for on-the-job skills upgrading.

FIGURE 7.1 Gender parity gap at the primary education level (source: World Bank, Gender Statistics Database)

Note: The Gender Parity Index is measured as the ratio of gross enrollment rate of girls to the gross enrollment rate of boys.

TABLE 7.4 Secondary education: gross enrollment rates for girls and boys, 2000 and 2009 (%)

Country	2000		2009	
	Girls	*Boys*	*Girls*	*Boys*
Algeria	...	...	97.3	95.7
Angola	12.9	15.7	...	...
Benin	14.3	30.7	...	...
Botswana	78.1	74.3	...	...
Burkina Faso	8.2	12.5	16.8	22.6
Burundi	...	...	17.8	24.6
Cabo Verde	...	...	88.2	74.7
Cameroon	...	...	37.7	45.2
Central African Republic	...	...	9.8	17.5
Chad	4.7	16.5	14.0	34.1
Comoros	26.1	31.9	...	...
Congo, Dem. Rep.	...	...	26.2	47.0
Congo, Rep.	28.9	41.0	...	...
Côte d'Ivoire	16.2	29.9	...	...
Djibouti	10.9	16.6	25.8	35.1
Egypt	72.8	78.6	66.0	68.4
Equatorial Guinea	18.2	41.4	...	...
Eritrea	20.2	29.1	26.4	37.1
Gabon	44.7	51.9	...	...
Gambia, The	...	...	56.1	58.2
Ghana	35.6	43.7	53.6	60.5
Guinea	8.6	22.9	27.4	46.3
Guinea-Bissau	14.1	25.6	...	...
Kenya	38.3	40.2	56.5	62.4
Lesotho	34.5	26.3	52.3	37.8
Liberia	30.6	43.1	...	...
Madagascar	...	...	30.6	32.5
Malawi	26.6	35.5	27.6	31.5
Mali	12.5	22.7	30.1	46.4

continued ...

Table 7.4 continued

Country	2000		2009	
	Girls	*Boys*	*Girls*	*Boys*
Mauritania	15.8	20.8	...	...
Mauritius	75.7	78.1	88.3	86.1
Morocco	33.7	42.4	...	...
Mozambique	4.7	7.5	20.6	26.2
Namibia	64.1	57.2	...	...
Niger	5.0	8.3	8.8	14.5
Nigeria	22.4	27.3	...	...
Rwanda	10.3	11.0	26.0	27.5
Senegal	12.5	19.2	...	...
Seychelles	107.7	101.1	107.5	102.6
South Africa	89.7	81.3	96.1	91.6
Sudan	...	...	35.5	40.3
Swaziland	41.9	41.7	...	...
Tanzania	5.7	7.0	24.1	30.7
Togo	18.9	42.6	...	...
Tunisia	78.0	73.9	93.8	86.8
Uganda	14.0	18.1	24.9	29.8

Source: World Bank, Gender Statistics Database.
Note: ... denote missing data.

Earnings and productivity

Average earnings for females in paid employment are lower than those of men (Agesa, Agesa, and Dabalen, 2008; Kolev and Robles, 2010; Siphambe and Thokweng-Bakwena, 2001). In Ethiopia, women's average wage rate is only 66 percent that of men (Kolev and Robles, 2010). However, Siphambe and Thokweng-Bakwena (2001) found that the gender wage gap narrowed among professionals. The difference in the characteristics between women and men (e.g. skills) can explain a proportion of the gender wage gap, for example in the public sector in Botswana (Siphambe and Thokweng-Bakwena, 2001). Job characteristics also help to explain the gender wage gap (Kolev and Robles, 2010).

However, a gender wage gap does exist, even allowing for the difference in human capital between women and men. Siphambe and Thokweng-Bakwena

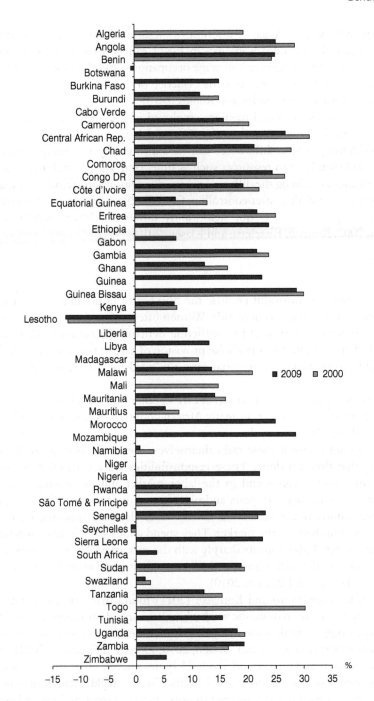

FIGURE 7.2 Gender gap in adult literacy rates, 2000 and 2009 (source: World Bank, Gender Statistics Database)

(2001) reveal some evidence of discrimination against women in Botswana's private sector. The gender wage gap in Egypt can be explained by women being crowded into particular low-wage occupations (Assad and Arntz, 2005). Meanwhile in Ethiopia, there is some evidence of discriminatory practices in the private formal sector (Kolev and Robles, 2010).

Most African women and men are employed in the informal sector. Even there, we can find evidence of gender differentials in terms of both earnings and productivity. These differences can be explained by the unequal access women and men have to resources such as time, land, agricultural inputs, and credit. Studies examining the difference in productivity among female and male farmers have found that, after controlling for differences in access to resources and inputs, productivity is not significantly different (Gilbert, Sakala, and Benson, 2002; Kumase, Bisseleua, and Klasen, 2010).

Time

Time is a binding constraint because the number of hours in a day is fixed, yet subject to multifarious demands. Women often suffer from time poverty because their time is subject to conflicting demands: between work in the labor market; work in the household; provision of care to the sick, the elderly, and children; provision of personal care; the need for leisure activities and sleep.

Domestic work and the provision of care to other household members tend to be the preserve of women in many African countries. These are traditional responsibilities that society has come to expect them to perform. Even if women do not perform these tasks themselves, they are still responsible for ensuring that they get done. These responsibilities are a constraint on how much time women can spend in the labor market and on making money. In Guinea, women aged 15 years and older spend on average 17.5 hours per week performing domestic chores, i.e. cooking, cleaning, washing, ironing, and making purchases at the market. They spend another 4.5 hours collecting wood and water. This contrasts sharply with the average of 2.5 hours per week spent by men on domestic chores and 1.7 hours they spend on collecting wood and water (Bardasi and Wodon, 2010).

In South Africa, Floro and Komatsu (2011) found that women spend on average 5 hours a day on domestic work whilst men spend on average 3.1 hours. Not surprisingly, in both these countries women devote less time to working in the labor market (Bardasi and Wodon, 2010; Floro and Komatsu, 2011).[6] In Rwanda, women and girls spend about 21 hours a week on domestic duties, whereas men and boys spend about 7 hours (Strode, Wylde, and Murangwa, 2010). Amongst the Guji-Oromo in Ethiopia, there is a strict division of labor. Women perform a wide range of tasks and 'in general women have little leisure time during the day, except soon after they have given birth to children' (Debsu, 2009: 26).

Women in agricultural households experience an additional constraint on their time, often being expected to provide labor on their husband's farm. However, they are not always compensated for this extra work. The practice varies from one country to another across the continent and can also vary within a country (Koopman, 2009; Kevane and Gray, 1999). Men in some societies have 'priority use of women's labor whether on farm or off farm' (Apusigah, 2009: 65). Not only does this reduce the time women have available to spend on their own farms, it can also result in their failing to apply fertilizers and other inputs at the right time. This reduces the yield of their crops and thus the income over which women have control.

Land

Gender relations and land in Africa manifest different dimensions. Land is an integral part of patriarchy in most African societies. For example, among some ethnic groups in Ethiopia, male identity is linked to ownership of land (Hultin, 1984, cited in Torkelsson and Tassew, 2008). In patrilineal societies, land tends to be handed down from father to son (Debsu, 2009; Wrigley-Asante, 2008). Gender relations define access to, ownership, and control of land and determine the incentives to invest in producing greater yields.

In many parts of the continent, women's access to land is only made possible through men. In some countries, married women can access and gain ownership of land through their husbands (Duncan, 2010; Kumase, Bisseleua, and Klasen, 2010). Unmarried women can sometimes access land by virtue of membership of a family or lineage, as happens among the Akan of Ghana (Amanor, 2001). A second dimension concerns the quality and size of the plots to which women have access. Women are not always allocated the best-quality (i.e. most fertile) land (Apusigah, 2009; Koopman, 2009; Torkelsson and Tassew, 2008). They also tend to be allocated small plots, partly because they do not have the inputs to farm larger plots.

Women are less likely to own land because inheritance norms transfer land from one male relative to another. This is the case also in matrilineal systems of inheritance. Among the Akan in Ghana, for example, a man's inheritance is passed to his uterine brother or the nephew of his sister (Awusabo-Asare, 1990). However, the practice of husbands gifting land to their wives as a reward for their labor contribution is one pathway to land ownership for women. Another is the practice of fathers gifting land to their daughters. In Ghana, excluding land reported as family land, 64 percent of agricultural plots are owned by men individually and 29 percent of plots are owned by women individually (Oduro, Baah-Boateng, and Boakye-Yiadom, 2011). There is increasing evidence of women accessing land through purchase (Kevane and Gray, 1999; Oduro, Baah-Boateng, and Boakye-Yiadom, 2011). Among cocoa-farming communities in southern Cameroon, women are less likely than men to inherit land, yet a

TABLE 7.5 Asset ownership by gender in Ghana (%)

Asset	% of men who own	% of women who own
Principal residence	30.0	15.8
Agricultural land	14.2	7.3
Other real estate	17.2	8.5
Livestock	36.6	23.5
Large stock	4.7	0.6
Small stock	25.1	13.5
Poultry	27.4	17.1
Agricultural equipment & installations	65.5	49.3
Large equipment	14.0	2.7
Small equipment	65.1	49.1
Businesses	20.4	40.0
Savings	53.6	41.7
Formal	35.6	20.7
Informal	21.9	24.5

Source: Oduro, Baah-Boateng, and Boakye-Yiadom (2011).

greater proportion obtain land through purchase, marriage, and gifts (Kumase, Bisseleua, and Klasen, 2010).

Land reform programs have failed to significantly reduce the gender inequality in land ownership, as many allocate land to households rather than to individuals (Obeng-Odoom, 2012). In some instances, when the head of the household is a woman, she is assumed to be linked to a man and is not included in the allocation (Koopman, 2009).

Lack of ownership implies lack of security of tenure. In Ghana, this causes women to make production decisions that adversely impact on soil fertility (Goldstein and Udry, 2008). In Burkina Faso, landlords are willing to rent land to women because women cannot claim permanent rights to the land. These tenure conditions can restrict women's options to choose the farming practices that will generate high yields (Kevane and Gray, 1999).

Access to support services

Access to extension advice can increase the take-up of new technologies and contribute to increased productivity. Extension services are, however, generally directed less to women than to men. Women farmers are also less likely than men to have contact with extension officers, who tend to be male (Kumase, Bisseleua, and Klasen, 2010; World Bank and IFPRI, 2010). This can create a gender barrier, particularly where cultural norms restrict interaction between the sexes.

Another issue to be considered is the high level of illiteracy among women farmers, which may deter them from applying for any training that involves reading material. Another disincentive for women may be the timing of extension services. If meetings are not held at times that suit women, many will not be able to attend.

Access to credit

Most women start businesses with their own money and loans from friends and family because they do not have the collateral required by formal institutions (Stevenson and St-Onge, 2005a). In Tanzania, most women entrepreneurs in an ILO study used their own savings to start their businesses (66 percent), followed by assistance from their spouse (33 percent), credit from family and friends (21 percent), credit from a microfinance institution (9 percent), credit from a bank (4 percent), and credit from a moneylender (1 percent) (Stevenson and St-Onge, 2005b).

Women are less likely than men to meet the collateral requirements demanded by formal finance institutions. The lack of asset ownership is not restricted to women by any means – it is a problem for both sexes. Data from Ghana show the incidence of asset ownership used as collateral to be quite low for both sexes (see Table 7.5). Not having an account with a formal financial institution excludes the possibility of accessing credit from these sources. In Ghana, about 36 percent of male respondents and 21 percent of female respondents reported owning an account with a formal savings institution (see Table 7.5). In South Africa, the incidence of ownership of a formal account is higher, i.e. 38 percent and 44 percent of black women and men respectively have bank accounts (Naidoo and Hilton, 2006).

The three most common barriers cited by women to accessing credit from commercial banks are cumbersome procedures, high interest rates, and collateral requirements. In Tanzania, women are often denied control over property. In Ethiopia, similar problems are cited, including lack of property ownership rights coupled with women's limited ability to build cash reserves in their smaller enterprises, which eliminates commercial banks as a financing option for them. Only 4 percent of the 123 women in the ILO study (2003) accessed finance from a commercial bank for their initial start-up.

Women's general low educational level, limited access to networks, and the lack of technical skills are also handicaps to their accessing formal credit. Women are less likely to prepare financial records and have limited capacity to prepare business plans. These are all requirements if they are to access loans from formal financial institutions (Stevenson and St-Onge, 2005a, 2005b; Naidoo and Hilton, 2006). There is also evidence of bias against women borrowers on the part of the financial institutions (Stevenson and St-Onge, 2005a; Naidoo and Hilton, 2006).

Microfinance is a possible solution for some women, but loan sizes are sometimes considered too small and women do not always want to be part of group loans (Naidoo and Hilton, 2006). Because of all these difficulties in procuring financial support, women's businesses are less likely to grow into large-scale enterprises capable of generating employment for outside workers.

Conclusion

There are very few data on the gender composition of the middle class in Africa. This is largely because the mainstream methods employed to count the middle class have not been designed with this in mind. An alternative method that has been used in the industrialized countries and that might be used in the African context is the classification of individuals on the basis of their occupations.

Our examination of the data and review of the literature have found evidence of barriers to women's entry into the middle class in Africa. Although some gender gaps are closing, women's average educational level is still lower than that of men, and they tend to be unskilled workers, segregated into a narrow set of occupations. The education gap partly explains gender differences in labor participation rates, occupational segregation, and wage differentials. Cultural norms and practices also play a key role. Gender biases in access to and ownership of land, extension advice, and other inputs result in lower productivity among women farmers and entrepreneurs. Women also suffer from a considerable time constraint that limits the hours they can devote to income-generating work. When in work, there are further limitations on the earnings over which they have direct control.

An increase in the size of Africa's middle class will reduce some dimensions of gender inequality but not others. There is some evidence of a correlation between rising incomes and school enrollment. However, evidence from Kenya (Lokshin, Glinskaya, and Garcia, 2004) suggests that as mothers' wages increase, girls are less likely to be sent to school. This is because they are required to stay at home to look after their younger siblings. If rising incomes are to be accompanied by an equitable increase in enrollment of both boys and girls, then policies to tackle this problem need to be considered. For example, the provision of child-care centers that can be accessed by a broad spectrum of the population could help to narrow the gender education gap. The evidence on the gender wage gap and occupational segregation suggests that these differentials can be reduced as more women become better educated. Educational policies that encourage girls to stay in school and to study a range of subjects could also help to close the gender gap.

Evidence from developed countries suggests that rising incomes do not always even out the time spent by men and women on unpaid domestic work (Sevilla-Sanz, Gimenez-Nadal, and Fernandez, 2010). Gender norms may become more entrenched when women earn more than men; this may result in women being forced to compensate by spending more time in unpaid work. International evidence also indicates that with rising incomes, there is a decline in self-employment among women and a rise in paid employment, although occupational segregation remains.

The gender asset gap could narrow as middle-income status is attained. This depends to a large extent on the introduction of laws that recognize women's contribution to asset ownership and that protect their access to assets. In countries with a partial community property regime, the gender gap in asset ownership is virtually non-existent (Deere and Diaz, 2011).

This chapter has argued that the attainment of middle-class status is not sufficient in itself to bring about full gender equality. What is also needed are changes in cultural practices and norms that will treat women as equals, together with the introduction of rules and laws designed to correct existing biases.

Notes

1 A bottom-up approach, utilizing household surveys, would allow for such dissagregation.
2 The class status of children is derived from their parent(s).
3 The appropriate unit of analysis should depend on the research question. In this study, the objective is to examine the factors that determine women's inclusion in the middle class. The appropriate unit of analysis is therefore the individual.
4 'Promoting Decent Work for Women in the Banking and Domestic Sectors in Ghana' is a project funded by the IDRC and implemented by the Centre for Gender Studies and Advocacy of the University of Ghana.
5 Conducted by the Centre for the Study of African Economies at the University of Oxford.
6 Conducted by the Centre for the Study of African Economies at the University of Oxford.

References

Acker, J. (1973). 'Women and Social Stratification: A Case of Intellectual Sexism,' *American Journal of Sociology*, vol. 78, no. 4, pp. 936–945.
AfDB (2011). 'The Middle of the Pyramid: Dynamics of the Middle Class in Africa.' Report by the Chief Economist Complex. April. Tunis: African Development Bank.
Agesa, R.U., J. Agesa, and A. Dabalen (2008). 'Changes in Wage Distributions, Wage Gaps and Wage Inequality by Gender in Kenya,' *Journal of African Economies*, vol. 18, no. 3, pp. 431–460.
Amanor, K.J. (2001). *Land, Labour and the Family in Southern Ghana. A Critique of Land Policy under Neo-liberalism.* Uppsala: Nordiska Afrikainstitutet.

Apusigah, A.A. (2009). 'The Gendered Politics of Farm Household Production and the Shaping of Women's Livelihoods in Northern Ghana,' *Feminist Africa*, vol. 12, pp. 51–68.

Assad, R., and M. Arntz (2005). 'Constrained Geographical Mobility and Gendered Labor Outcomes under Structural Adjustment: Evidence from Egypt,' *World Development*, vol. 33, no. 3, pp. 431–454.

Awusabo-Asare, K. (1990). 'Matriliny and the New Intestate Succession Law,' *Canadian Journal of African Studies*, vol. 24, no. 1, pp. 1–16.

Banerjee, A.V., and E. Duflo (2008). 'What is Middle Class about the Middle Classes around the World?,' *Journal of Economic Perspectives*, vol. 22, no. 2, pp. 3–28.

Bardasi, E., and Q. Wodon (2010). 'Working Long Hours and Having No Choice: Time Poverty in Guinea,' *Feminist Economics*, vol. 16, no. 3, pp. 45–78.

Birdsall, N. (2010). 'The (Indispensable) Middle Class in Developing Countries,' in R. Kanbur and M. Spence (eds), *Equity and Growth in a Globalizing World*. Washington DC: International Bank for Reconstruction and Development/World Bank.

Britwum, A.O. (2009). 'The Gendered Dynamics of Production Relations in Ghanaian Coastal Fishing,' *Feminist Africa*, Issue 12, pp. 69–85.

Debsu, D.N. (2009). 'Gender and Culture in Southern Ethiopia: An Ethnographic Analysis of Guji-Oromo Women's Customary Rights,' *African Study Monographs*, vol. 30, no. 1, pp. 15–36.

Deere, C.D., and J.C. Diaz (2011). *Asset Accumulation: The Challenge for Equity*. FLACSO, Sede Ecuador.

Doss, C. (2006). 'The Effects of Intrahousehold Property Ownership in Expenditure Patterns in Ghana,' *Journal of African Economies*, vol. 15, no. 1, pp. 149–180.

Duncan, B.A. (2010). 'Cocoa, Marriage, Labour and Land in Ghana: Some Matrilineal and Patrilineal Perspectives,' *Africa*, vol. 80, no. 2, pp. 301–321.

Floro, M.S., and H. Komatsu (2011). 'Gender and Work in South Africa: What Can Time-Use Data Reveal?,' *Feminist Economics*, vol. 17, no. 4, pp. 33–66.

Ghana Statistical Service (GSS) (2013). 2010 Population and Housing Census Report: Women and Men in Ghana, July 2013. GSS: Accra.

Gilbert, R.A., W.D. Sakala, and T.D. Benson (2002). 'Gender Analysis of a Nationwide Cropping System Trial Survey in Malawi,' *African Studies Quarterly*, vol. 6, Nos. 1 & 2, pp. 223–243.

Goldstein, M., and C. Udry (2008). 'The Profits of Power: Land Rights and Agricultural Investment in Ghana,' *Journal of Political Economy*, vol. 24, no. 1, pp. 45–63.

Hoddinott, J., and L. Haddad (1995). 'Does Female Income Share Influence Household Expenditures? Evidence from Côte d'Ivoire,' *Oxford Bulletin of Economics and Statistics*, vol. 57, no. 1, pp. 77–96.

Johnson, S. (2004). 'Gender Norms in Financial Markets: Evidence from Kenya,' *World Development*, vol. 32, no. 8, pp. 1355–1374.

Kevane, M., and L.C. Gray (1999). 'A Woman's Field is Made at Night: Gendered Land Rights and Norms in Burkina Faso,' *Feminist Economics*, vol. 5, no. 3, pp. 1–26.

Kharas, H. (2010). 'The Emerging Middle Class in Developing Countries.' Working Paper no. 285. Paris: OECD Development Centre.

Kolev, A., and P.S. Robles (2010). 'Exploring the Gender Pay Gap through different Age Cohorts: the Case of Ethiopia,' in J.S. Arbache, A. Kolev, and E. Filipiak (eds), *Gender Disparities in Africa's Labor Market*. Washington DC: Agence française de développement and World Bank.

Koopman, J.E. (2009). 'Globalization, Gender, and Poverty in the Senegal River,' *Feminist Economics*, vol. 15, no. 3, pp. 253–285.

Kumase, W.N., H. Bisseleua, and S. Klasen (2010). 'Opportunities and Constraints in Agriculture: A Gendered Analysis of Cocoa Production in Southern Cameroon' Courant Research Centre, Discussion paper no. 27. Göttingen, Germany: Georg-August-Universitat.

Lokshin, M.M., E. Glinkskaya, and M. Garcia (2004). 'The Effect of Early Childhood Development Programmes on Women's Labour Force Participation and Older Children's Schooling in Kenya,' *Journal of African Economies*, vol. 13, no. 2, pp. 240–276.

Naidoo, S., and A. Hilton (2006). *Access to Finance by Women Entrepreneurs in South Africa*. Washington DC: International Finance Corporation, World Bank Group.

Obeng-Odoom, F. (2012). 'Land Reforms in Africa: Theory, Practice and Outcome,' *Habitat International*, vol. 36, pp. 161–170.

Oduro, A.D., W. Baah-Boateng, and L. Boakye-Yiadom (2011). *Measuring the Gender Asset Gap in Ghana*. Accra: Woeli Publishing Services and University of Ghana.

Ravallion, M. (2010). 'The Developing World's Bulging (but Vulnerable) Middle Class,' *World Development*, vol. 38, no. 4, pp. 445–454.

Sackey, H.A. (2005) *Female Labour Force Participation in Ghana*. AERC Research Paper 150. Nairobi: African Economic Research Consortium.

Schultz, T.P. (1990). 'Testing the Neoclassical Model of Family Labor Supply and Fertility,' *Journal of Human Resources*, vol. 24, no. 4, pp. 599–634.

Sevilla-Sanz, A., J.I. Gimenez-Nadal, and C. Fernandez (2010). 'Gender Roles and the Division of Unpaid Work in Spanish Households,' *Feminist Economics*, vol. 16, no. 4, pp. 137–184.

Siphambe, H.K., and M. Thokweng-Bakwena (2001). 'The Wage Gap between Men and Women in Botswana's Formal Labour Market,' *Journal of African Economies*, vol. 10, no. 2, pp. 127–142.

Sorenson, A. (1994). 'Women, Family and Class,' *Annual Review of Sociology*, vol. 20, pp. 27–47.

Stevenson, L., and A. St-Onge (2005a). *Support for Growth-Oriented Women Entrepreneurs in Kenya*. Geneva: ILO.

Stevenson, L., and A. St-Onge (2005b). *Support for Growth-Oriented Women Entrepreneurs in Tanzania*. Geneva: ILO.

Strode, M., E. Wylde, and Y. Murangwa (2010). *Labour Market and Economic Activity Trends in Rwanda. Analysis of the EICV2 Survey*. Kigali: National Institute of Statistics, Rwanda.

Torkelsson, A., and B. Tassew (2008). 'Quantifying Women's and Men's Rural Resource Portfolios – Empirical Evidence from Western Shoa in Ethiopia,' *European Journal of Development Research*, vol. 20, no. 3, pp. 462–481.

Witz, A. (1995). 'Gender and Service-Class Formation,' in T. Butler and M. Savage (eds), *Social Change and the Middle Classes*. London: University College of London.

World Bank and IFPRI (2010). *Gender and Governance in Rural Service: Insights from India, Ghana and Ethiopia*. Washington DC: Gender and Governance Author Team, International Food Policy Research Institute and World Bank.

Wright, E.O. (1997). *Class Counts*. Cambridge: Cambridge University Press.

Wrigley-Asante, C. (2008). 'Men Are Poor but Women Are Poorer: Gendered Poverty and Survival Strategies in the Dangme West District of Ghana,' *Norsk Geografisk Tidsskrift- [Norwegian Journal of Geography]*, vol. 62, pp. 161–170.

Yakubu, A.Y. (2010). 'Factors Influencing Female Labor Force Participation in South Africa in 2008,' *Africa Statistical Journal*, vol. 11, November, pp. 85–104.

8

HEALTH

Alice Nabalamba and Helen Johansen

Introduction

Health in Africa is an integral part of development. Poor health impedes productivity and economic development, while a poor economy lacks the finances needed to enhance health systems.

The health sector cannot be viewed in isolation, as there are multiple interlinkages with other sectors. For example, access to clean water and well-managed sanitation systems cost money but decrease the risk of waterborne diseases and epidemics. Maternal and infant mortality rates, as well as women's health in general, are linked to education rates for women. Good infrastructure – including modern health care centers and roads linking populations to clinics – increases the chances of timely health care. Food security has positive influences on children's health and school performance, which in turn help to build the basis for a better economy. However, ill health can push people into poverty and make it very difficult for them to transition to the ranks of the middle class. Health influences all sectors of government and all facets of society.

This chapter reviews emerging issues relating to Africa's growing middle class and health. We look at the state of the health of the middle class, including health outcomes, risk factors, and needs. The emerging issue of non-communicable diseases and its correlation to the growth of the middle class in Africa is discussed. Other topics include access to and use of health services, current and future health infrastructure, and health financing. We also look at the gendered dimension of health, in particular women's health status, fertility rates, child delivery care, and preventive health care.

Data sources

Two main sources of data were drawn upon for this chapter. The first is the World Health Survey (WHS) 2002, conducted by the World Health Organisation. The second is a comparison by country of the percentage of the population in the middle class, from the original 2011 AfDB report, 'The Middle of the Pyramid' (on which Chapter 1 is based). This source derives health and infrastructure data by country from the WHO Atlas of Health Statistics: *Health Situation Analysis in the African Region 2011*. The latter gives more recent (mainly 2008) statistics than the 2002 WHS data.

The WHS 2002 was designed to collect information on the health of populations and health care systems worldwide. It covered the population aged 18 and over living in private households. The sample design of the survey was intended to extend to 90 percent coverage in each country that participated. The response rate for the household component was high, exceeding 90 percent in most of the African countries.

The WHS is a cross-sectional survey undertaken in 20 African countries: Burkina Faso, Chad, Comoros, Congo Republic, Côte d'Ivoire, Ethiopia, Ghana, Kenya, Malawi, Mali, Mauritania, Mauritius, Morocco, Namibia, Senegal, South Africa, Swaziland, Tunisia, Zambia, and Zimbabwe. The survey instrument used was identical in all countries worldwide, but with additional modules for developing countries (e.g. in Africa) in order to capture the unique character of health care systems and issues of the region. The survey measured a number of dimensions, namely: major health risk factors; health care coverage; self-rated health of individuals; health system responsiveness; health care expenditure of households; and stress and social capital in Africa's population.

Although the WHS covered only 20 of the total 53 African countries, the sample included Western, Central, Northern, Eastern, and Southern African countries, Anglophone and Francophone countries, and middle- and lower-income countries. Thus, the sample countries are broadly representative of the whole of Africa. In some instances in this analysis, a smaller representative sample of ten countries is used, namely Chad, Côte d'Ivoire, Ethiopia, Kenya, Malawi, Mali, Mauritius, Namibia, South Africa, and Tunisia.

Methodology

This chapter uses the 2002 World Health Survey to explain differences in health needs and health outcomes, health care services utilization, health care costs as a proportion of household income, and health outcomes of the African middle class in 20 countries at the beginning of the 21st century. It adopts the relative definition of income or economic class. For Africa and other developing regions, the WHS used household assets or household wealth as a proxy for income. Respondents were asked about the physical size of their home (i.e. the number of rooms) and whether they owned items or amenities such as electricity, table, chairs, washing machine, dishwasher, TV, clock, telephone, etc.

As a result, five income groups were computed, from quintile 1 (poorest) to quintile 5 (richest). This chapter uses quintiles 3 and 4 as the measure of middle income or middle class. Quintiles 1 and 2 represent the poor population and quintile 5 represents the rich. Countries are listed by decreasing GDP per capita.

A linear regression by country of the percentage of the population in the middle class taken from 'The Middle of the Pyramid' paper (AfDB, 2011a) versus health and infrastructure data from the Health Situation Analysis in the *African Region Atlas of Health Statistics, 2011* was also carried out.

Appendix 8.1 presents the slope, intercept, standard error, 95 percent probability and R^2 values for linear regressions on scatter plot charts. R-squared can be thought of as the fraction of variance explained by a model. For linear regression with one explanatory variable like this analysis, R-squared is the same as the correlation coefficient.

Health outcomes

Life expectancy

Life expectancy at birth, i.e. the average number of years that a newborn is expected to live, reflects the overall mortality level of a population. It summarizes the mortality pattern that prevails across all age groups: children and adolescents, adults, and the elderly. As seen in Figure 8.1, life expectancy increases alongside an increase in the proportion of the middle-class population. Research shows that people who live in a prosperous country tend to live longer than those

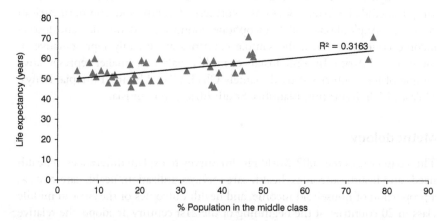

FIGURE 8.1 Life expectancy is higher in countries with a larger middle class, 2008 (sources: WHO: Regional Office for Africa, 2011; middle-class data from AfDB (2011a))

in a poor country. It has been calculated that improving the population's life expectancy by one year is associated with a 4 percent improvement in GNP, and that this relationship is strongest in Sub-Saharan Africa (Bloom, Canning, and Sevilla, 2004).

A similar relationship holds for Healthy Life Expectancy (HALE) at birth, i.e. the average number of years that a person can expect to live in good health (see Appendix 8.1). This measure takes into account years lived in less than full health due to disease and/or injury; as a result, it captures both fatal and non-fatal health outcomes and disabilities. HALE also increases as the middle class grows. This has the overall effect that there are more healthy people of working age in the total population.

Mortality

Given the increasing life expectancy that accompanies the growth of the middle class, one would expect a concomitant decrease in overall mortality rates. Indeed, Figure 8.2 shows that mortality rates for adults and for children under the age of 5 do decline as the size of the middle class increases across Africa. The mortality rates are age-standardized to WHO's World Standard Population to adjust for differences in the population age distribution between countries. Jamison, Lau, and Wang (2005) have estimated that reductions in adult mortality explain 10–15 percent of the economic growth that occurred from 1960 to 1990. This is consistent with Figure 8.2, which shows death rates declining as the proportion of the middle-class population increases.

Years of Life Lost

The indicator Years of Life Lost (YLL) is a summary measure of premature mortality which provides an explicit way of weighting deaths occurring at

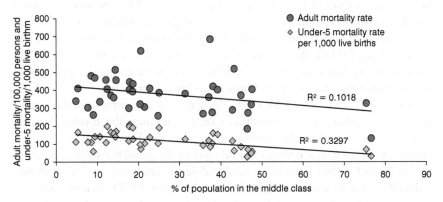

FIGURE 8.2 Adult mortality rate and under-5 mortality rate, 2008 (sources: WHO: Regional Office for Africa, 2011; middle-class data from AfDB (2011a))

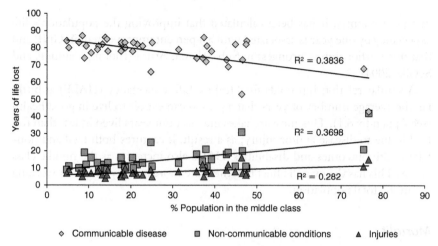

FIGURE 8.3 Broad causes of Years of Life Lost (YLL), 2008 (sources: WHO: Regional Office for Africa, 2011; middle-class data from AfDB (2011a))

younger ages, which are, a priori, preventable. It takes into account the age at which deaths occur by giving greater weight to deaths at a younger age and lower weight to deaths at an older age.

As the proportion of the population in the middle class increases, premature mortality resulting from communicable diseases decreases, while mortality due to non-communicable diseases (NCDs) increases (see Figure 8.3). The latter is not surprising, as NCDs are generally more prevalent among the elderly. As the middle class grows, life expectancy increases and more people reach old age.

Burden of diseases

It is important to take into account non-fatal conditions, as well as deaths, when assessing the causes of loss of health in populations. The Disability-Adjusted Life Year (DALY) is a summary measure used to give an indication of the burden of disease. One DALY represents the loss of the equivalent of one year of full health. Using DALYs, the burden of diseases that do not cause death but do cause disability (e.g. cataracts causing blindness) can be compared with that of diseases that cause early death but little disability (e.g. measles).

Both the YLL and the DALY charts illustrate that non-communicable conditions are increasing in relative importance versus communicable conditions as the proportion of the middle-class population increases (see Figures 8.3 and 8.4). The burden of NCDs now accounts for nearly half of the global burden of disease for all ages (WHO, 2008a). Even in low- and middle-income countries, almost 45 percent of the adult disease burden globally is attributable to NCDs. In many developing countries, population aging, lower fertility rates, and changes in the distribution of risk factors have accelerated the NCD share of the total disease burden.

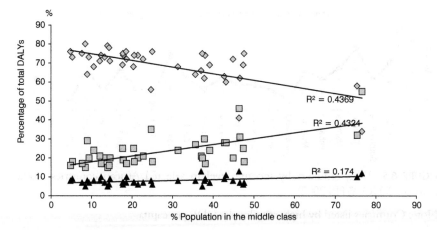

◇ Communicable diseases, maternal and perinatal conditions, and nutritional deficiencies
□ Non-communicable conditions
▲ Injuries

FIGURE 8.4 Distribution of disease burden as percentage of total DALYs, 2008 (sources: WHO: Regional Office for Africa, 2011; middle-class data from AfDB (2011a))

NCDs such as hypertension and other cardiovascular diseases (CVDs) are becoming important causes of mortality and morbidity in all developing countries. NCDs may soon challenge infectious diseases as a health priority when determining budgetary allocations. This is exemplified by the high prevalence (21 percent) of hypertension and related risk factors among Cameroonian urban dwellers (Kengne et al., 2007).

Key determinants of health

Tobacco smoking

Cigarette smoking is a major cause of the burden of NCDs. It can lead to lung cancer, respiratory disease, ischemic heart disease, and cerebrovascular disease (WHO, 2008b). Tobacco is the leading preventable cause of death in the world (WHO Regional Office for Africa, 2011b).

In the 46 countries of the WHO Africa region, NCDs are forecast to increase by 27 percent over the next decade and to account for more than 50 percent of all deaths by 2030 (WHO Regional Office for Africa, 2011b). The increasing use of tobacco is a significant driver in the epidemiological transition from communicable diseases to NCDs in the Africa region (Lopez and Mathers, 2006). Tobacco-related disease usually does not begin for years or decades after tobacco use starts. As many developing countries are still in the early stages of the tobacco epidemic, they have yet to experience its full impact.

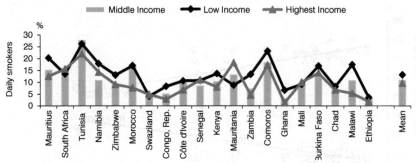

FIGURE 8.5   Daily smokers by income level in selected African countries, 2002 (source: WHO, WHS 2002)

Note: Countries listed by highest to lowest GDP per capita.

It is important to recognize the growing epidemic of tobacco use among adolescents in Africa (Muula and Mpabulungi, 2007). Because most women currently do not smoke, the tobacco industry aggressively targets them in their advertising campaigns to tap this potential market (WHO Regional Office for Africa, 2011b).

Regular tobacco users tend to be poor and male rather than female (Pampel, 2005; WHO, 2008b). Males have higher smoking rates than females and there is a slight and non-significant upward trend as the proportion of the middle class increases. There is much variation between classes in different countries but overall, the lower classes smoke more than those in the middle and upper classes (see Figure 8.5). Surprisingly, among countries with the highest GDP per capita, the middle-class populations in South Africa and Tunisia smoke more than the lower-income groups.

Alcohol consumption

Alcohol-related disorders are another important preventable contributor to the burden of disease in middle- and high-income countries. Alcohol is reported to be the main psychoactive substance responsible for treatment demand. In Africa, out-of-pocket payments are the main funding method for treating alcohol and drug-use disorders. The region is also characterized as having the fewest countries with substance abuse policies in place (WHO, 2010a).

Data from the WHS have shown a high level of variability in alcohol use across countries and income levels. In about seven African countries, the percentage of frequent heavy drinkers is greater among the highest-income category, while in other countries, this practice is more prevalent among the lower-income population. The middle-income population in almost all countries where data are available fall in-between.

Percentage reporting insufficient intake of fruits and vegetables

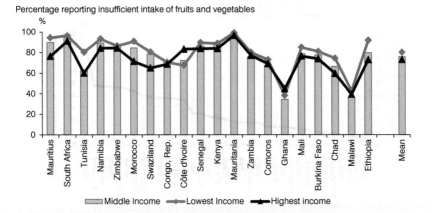

FIGURE 8.6   Percentage of population with insufficient fruit and vegetable intake by country and income level, 2002 (source: WHO, WHS 2002)

Note: Countries listed by highest to lowest GDP per capita.

Insufficient physical activity

Being physically active is very important for maintaining health. Data from WHS 2002 show wide variability across countries, ranging from 2 percent to over 50 percent of people reporting insufficient physical activity. Overall, there is not much difference between the economic classes. However, as the middle class increases, physical activity is expected to decline, as people move away from traditional farming and manual labor into sedentary jobs. As the population ages, this lack of sufficient physical activity will have detrimental impacts on health.

Food insufficiency

The Food and Agriculture Organization of the United Nations (FAO) estimates that 1.02 billion people were undernourished in 2009 – approximately 100 million more than in 2008 (FAO, 2009). Sub-Saharan Africa has the largest prevalence of undernourishment relative to its population size.

The WHS 2002 data show a gross insufficiency in the intake of fruit and vegetables in almost all the 20 African countries surveyed (see Figure 8.6). While the mean values for the middle- and higher-income classes are lower than for the lowest-income class, they are still above 70 percent. As the middle class increases and people move out of the countryside into cities, a traditional diet rich in fruit and vegetables is gradually being replaced by one high in calories from animal fats and low in complex carbohydrates.

Another indicator for monitoring the nutritional status and health of populations is child growth. Figure 8.7 gives the percentage of underweight

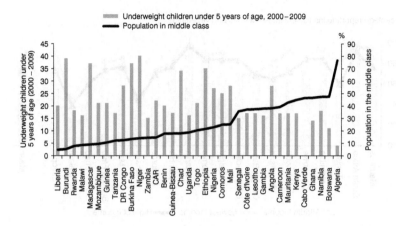

FIGURE 8.7   Percentage of underweight children under the age of five, 2000–2009 (source: WHO, WHS 2002)

Note: Countries listed by lowest (Liberia) to highest (Algeria) GDP per capita.

children under the age of five in the sampled African countries. As the percentage of the middle-class population increases, children are more likely to become better nourished (R^2 = 0.339, see Appendix 8.1). In addition to improving general health and wellbeing, from an economic viewpoint, better nutrition also contributes to a more productive workforce in the long term.

Solid fuel use for cooking

In the lowest quintiles of society, the use of solid fuel remains very high (usually 70 percent and above) across all but the highest level GDP per capita countries (see Figure 8.8). With a reduction in GDP per capita, solid fuel use increases, even in the middle- and highest-income households.

Household energy plays a fundamental role in improving child and maternal health. The use of solid fuels in households is associated with increased mortality from pneumonia and other acute lower respiratory diseases among children. It is also responsible for increased mortality from chronic obstructive pulmonary disease among adults, particularly women (Rehfuess, Mehta, and Prüss-Üstün, 2006).

The use of cleaner fuels can bring additional benefits. It can facilitate boiling of water and increase the number of hot meals per day, thus helping to reduce the incidence of waterborne diseases and leading to improved food and water hygiene.

Furthermore, switching to electricity or gas could significantly reduce the amount of time and effort that women and girls spend gathering solid fuels. This additional time could be more usefully spent on income-generating activities, including family subsistence, or on education (Modi et al., 2005).

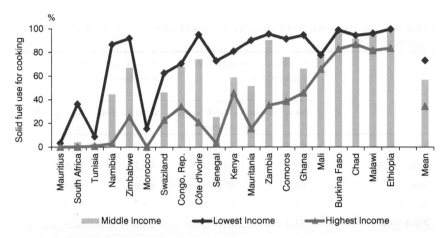

FIGURE 8.8 Solid fuel use by income level in selected African countries, 2002 (source: WHO, WHS 2002)

Note: Countries listed by highest to lowest GDP per capita.

Access to improved drinking water and sanitation

According to a 2010 report by the WHO, 884 million people worldwide lack access to improved drinking water sources and the majority of them live in Africa (WHO, 2010b). Improved water and improved sanitation go hand in hand. Access to drinking water and improved sanitation are fundamental needs and human rights vital for the health of all people. The health and economic benefits of improved water supply and sanitation to households and individuals (especially children) are well documented.

For the 20 African countries included in the WHS, it was shown that the middle- to highest-income classes had better access to improved drinking water and sanitation (see Table 8.1). Overall, as the percentage of the population in the middle class increases, so too does access to safe drinking water and improved sanitation (Figure 8.9, $R^2 = 0.2255$, see Appendix 8.1). On average, the rates ranged between 48 percent and 73 percent from lowest- to highest-income groups for improved drinking water and from 24 percent to 52 percent respectively for improved sanitation.

Furthermore, as the GDP per capita rises, those in the lowest-income class tend to benefit from a trickle-down effect. For example, in South Africa (GDP per capita = $2,376), the percentage of people with improved drinking water stood at 78 percent and 92 percent for the lower and middle/upper classes respectively in 2002, while for improved sanitation the proportions were 40 percent and 80 percent respectively. On the other hand, in Chad (GDP per capita = $213), the percentages were 24 percent and 51 percent for improved water sources, and 1 percent and 13 percent for improved sanitation respectively. Thus, the three top-performing GDP per capita countries in the sample demonstrate that as the proportion of the population entering the middle class increases, the benefits can

TABLE 8.1   Access to improved drinking water and sanitation by income level (% of population), 2002

	% with access to improved drinking water		% with access to improved sanitation	
	Lower income	Middle to high income	Lower income	Middle to high income
Mauritius	98.4	97.4	87.7	94.9
South Africa	78.1	91.7	40.2	79.6
Tunisia	64.9	95.4	61.8	95.4
Namibia	67.1	84.2	3.7	58.3
Zimbabwe	53.0	81.1	23.8	62.9
Morocco	42.0	93.9	41.6	85.2
Swaziland	35.3	54.4	27.4	46.5
Congo, Rep.	24.9	35.0	24.9	32.9
Côte d'Ivoire	75.2	85.3	14.0	50.5
Senegal	40.4	79.0	22.5	69.1
Kenya	37.4	74.3	25.6	43.2
Mauritania	40.1	59.2	6.1	51.9
Zambia	32.4	75.4	36.9	61.4
Comoros	46.3	80.3	6.9	44.0
Ghana	51.6	81.8	2.9	24.0
Mali	29.5	48.1	8.4	17.2
Burkina Faso	43.8	67.5	2.8	22.3
Chad	24.3	51.2	1.2	13.0
Malawi	51.2	73.8	42.7	66.4
Ethiopia	15.5	50.7	0.5	20.5
Mean	47.5	73.0	24.1	52.0

Source: WHO, WHS 2002.
Note: Countries listed by highest to lowest GDP per capita.

spread to the rest of society. This is because such countries have a stronger tax base and more resources, so governments are better placed financially to fund social services.

More recent data support this trend. In 2008, the proportion of the population with access to improved drinking water increased in line with the size of the middle class. At least 26 percent of the variation in access to drinking water across countries may be explained by the proportion of people in the middle class.

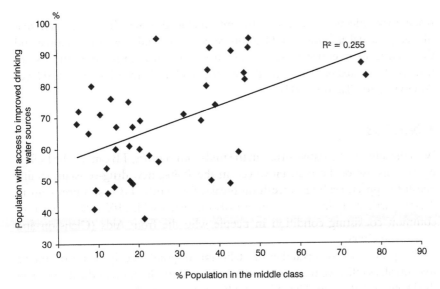

FIGURE 8.9 Population with access to improved drinking water sources (%) (sources: WHO: Regional Office for Africa, 2011; AfDB (2011a))

Health needs

In order to evaluate the effectiveness of programs in terms of better health outcomes, one needs to know disease rates and trends. Often, too little is known about disease incidence, prevalence, and severity to help policymakers in prioritizing policies and interventions that will contribute to the overall health of a population. While high-quality information does not in itself ensure good policy decisions or effective implementation, quality data availability is essential to help make the right choices. The continued improvement of regularly published health information consequently remains paramount for Africa's health systems (Jamison, Feachem, and Makgoba, 2006).

Communicable diseases

Infectious diseases have long been a major constraint on development in Africa. The slow rate of progress in the region is attributed in no small measure to the ravages of infectious diseases, many of which are preventable and curable. HIV/ Aids, tuberculosis (TB), and malaria alone are estimated to kill about 3 million people every year in the region (WHO Regional Office for Africa, 2006). The result is impoverishment and hardship as well as reduced productivity. The resources diverted into trying to manage these diseases place countries on a vicious cycle of poverty and ill health.

Six of the major contributors to short life expectancy in the region are infectious diseases, namely HIV/Aids, TB, malaria, diarrheal diseases, acute respiratory infections, and vaccine-preventable diseases. It is expected that higher personal incomes could improve access to and use of preventive and therapeutic interventions, such as antenatal care, immunizations, the use of insecticide-treated bed nets, and therapy for tackling diarrheal diseases and fever (Wagstaff and Claeson, 2004).

Tuberculosis[1]

With the advent of curative drugs in the mid-20th century, TB came to be looked on as a disease of the past. However, in the 1980s, new drug-resistant strains began to appear, leading to fresh outbreaks. Currently, TB is still prevalent in Africa, particularly for those who are also infected with HIV. TB is the most common coexisting condition in people who die from Aids (Chaisson and Martinson, 2008).

The prevalence[2] of TB and its mortality rate respond quickly to improvements in control, as effective treatment reduces the average duration of the disease and the likelihood of dying. The effect of TB control on incidence[3] is less immediate than the effect on prevalence or mortality, as TB can develop in people who became infected many years previously.

Neither the prevalence nor incidence of TB has shown any significant correlation with the size of the middle class (AfDB, 2011a; WHO, 2011). The lack of a strong relationship between TB and any specific economic class suggests that TB is still important among all classes.

Self-reported symptoms of TB were asked about in the WHS 2002. These were reported more often in the lower-income classes, with the overall country averages being 13 percent, 10 percent, and 8 percent in the lowest, middle, and highest-income classes respectively. In countries such as South Africa, Zimbabwe, and Swaziland, the prevalence of TB in the lower- and middle-income categories is almost identical (perhaps an indication of the high HIV/Aids rates in these same countries). However, in Tunisia similar TB rates among lower- and middle-income groups is a reflection of the high smoking rates in both groups. While the need for treatment is spread across all economic classes, TB screening in those respondents with self-reported symptoms was highest in the middle-income category, ranging between 4 percent and 28 percent.

HIV/Aids

The most significant impact on disease and mortality in Africa to date has been the HIV/Aids epidemic. It has infected more than 30 percent of adults in some countries and remains the leading cause of adult deaths (WHO Regional Office for Africa, 2006). The number of HIV-positive people on antiretroviral medicines increased eightfold from 2003 to 2005, from 100,000 to 810,000 (WHO Regional Office for Africa, 2006).

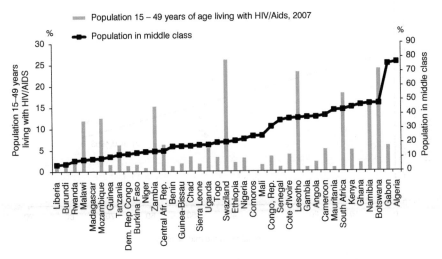

FIGURE 8.10 Population living with HIV/Aids in 2007 (%) (sources: WHO: Regional Office for Africa, 2011; middle class data from AfDB (2011a))

Figure 8.10 shows no relationship between the percentage of people living with HIV/Aids and the size of the middle class in the individual countries ($R^2 = 0.022$, see Appendix 8.1). Spikes of disease of ten percentage points or more occur across all levels of the middle class, particularly in Southern Africa (Botswana, Lesotho, Malawi, Mozambique, Namibia, South Africa, Swaziland, and Zambia). Moreover, there is no correlation between the percentage of people in the middle class and the percentage in need of treatment who have access to antiretroviral drugs.

The need for counseling and testing for HIV/Aids among respondents of reproductive age who are sexually active (i.e. who had intercourse within the last 12 months) is high (65–70 percent on average) across almost all economic classes and countries in the WHS 2002. However, although the percentage of sexually active respondents of reproductive age who had taken an HIV test and received the results of the test was low overall, it was higher in the richer countries and higher economic classes.

Consistent correct use of condoms within non-regular sexual partnerships substantially reduces the risk of sexual HIV transmission. Of those who have recently been engaged in 'risky' sex (defined as being with a non-cohabiting partner), those in the higher economic classes are more likely to use a condom. Thus, although HIV/Aids is an 'equal opportunity' disease, in that it is present across all economic classes, those in the middle and highest classes are more likely than lower economic classes to use medical tests and preventive measures to protect themselves.

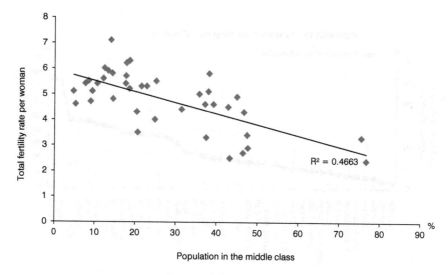

FIGURE 8.11 Total fertility rate per woman in Africa (sources: WHO: Regional Office for Africa, 2011; middle-class data from AfDB (2011a))

Women's health

Countries with a proportionately large middle class tend to have lower fertility rates (see Figure 8.11). As a society becomes wealthier, a woman is more likely to choose to have fewer children. In poorer countries, high levels of fertility lead to rapid population growth, which makes it far more difficult for families and countries to exit poverty. In fact, many of the Millennium Development Goals are difficult if not impossible to achieve with the current levels of population growth in the least developed countries and regions such as Africa (All Party Parliamentary Group on Population, Development and Reproductive Health, 2007). Emerging evidence shows that developing countries that have adopted national family-planning programs have seen a moderate to rapid decline in the birth rate and an improvement in the economy and the health of women and their families. The countries where the birth rate has not fallen have seen an explosive growth of urban slums and a failure of the state to keep pace with educational demands.

In middle-income countries that are making significant strides in reducing fertility rates, the health of women and their families is improving. In addition, more women are able to enter the labor force and to engage in formal employment.

Antenatal care

A woman's health and behavior during pregnancy can have implications for her baby. The baby's development can be held back if the mother suffers from severe illnesses (such as HIV/Aids), has a poor diet, or indulges in smoking, drinking alcohol, or takes certain drugs. Antenatal care is particularly important because many women have nutritional deficiencies (such as iron-deficiency anemia and deficiencies of vitamin A and iodine) when they begin their pregnancy (WHO, 2009). Furthermore, a woman's health can change during pregnancy. At this time, women should not only take good care of their health but also go for regular checkups with a professional health-care provider. These antenatal checkups can prevent most medical problems and, if there is a problem, early detection helps to better control it.

Data from the WHS 2002 show that middle-income countries (MICs) such as Mauritius, South Africa, Tunisia, and Namibia have a greater percentage of pregnancies covered by antenatal care. This is the case for lower-, middle- and high-income women alike in MICs. Once again, as the proportion of the population entering the middle class increases, there is a spreading of benefits to the rest of society, which supports the argument for a stronger and larger middle class. In the lower-income countries, we find that access to antenatal care is largely confined to those in higher-income categories and does not trickle down to lower-income groups.

Birth delivery care

According to the WHO, almost all maternal deaths could be prevented if women were assisted at delivery by a health-care professional with the necessary skills, equipment, and medicines to prevent and manage complications (WHO, 2009). In the WHS 2002, the overall country averages of female respondents of reproductive age who recorded a live birth in the last five years were 44 percent, 38 percent and 32 percent, for the lowest-, middle- and highest-income classes respectively. Thus, the need for birth delivery care is clearly greater in lower-income groups.

However, as with antenatal care, countries with a higher percentage of middle-class population also record a greater percentage of births attended by skilled health personnel ($R^2 = 0.285$, see Appendix 8.1). The percentages ranged from 14 percent to 95 percent in 2008. Poorer and less educated women and those living in rural areas are far less likely to give birth in the presence of a skilled health worker than better-educated women who live in urban areas. The reasons for this include physical inaccessibility and prohibitive costs, but may also reflect inappropriate sociocultural practices.

Maternal and infant mortality

Together with HIV/Aids, maternal conditions are a major contributor to the high burden of disease for women in Africa compared with other regions (WHO, 2008a). Complications during pregnancy and childbirth are leading causes of death and disability among women of reproductive age in developing countries, where 99 percent of maternal deaths occur (WHO, 2009). The causes of maternal deaths include hemorrhage, infections, obstructed labor, hypertensive

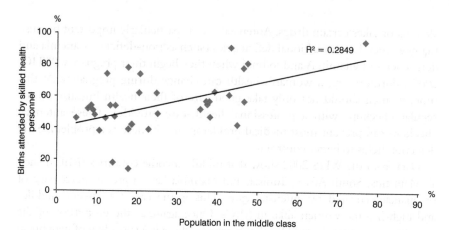

FIGURE 8.12   Births attended by skilled health personnel in Africa 2000-2008 (sources: WHO: Regional Office for Africa, 2011; middle-class data from AfDB (2011a))

disorders in pregnancy and complications of unsafe abortions. All these causes are treatable; moreover with improved hygiene, the availability of drugs and medicines and improved antenatal care, they are generally avoidable.

The maternal mortality ratio (MMR) represents the risk associated with each pregnancy. It is expressed as the number of maternal deaths occurring during pregnancy, delivery, or the postpartum period during a given time period per 100,000 live births during the same period. The MMR is an MDG indicator for monitoring Goal 5, relating to improving maternal health. All women should have access to skilled care during pregnancy and at delivery to ensure detection and management of complications.

As one would expect, lower maternal and infant mortality rates evince a positive relationship with better antenatal care and having skilled health personnel in attendance at births.[4] Moreover, maternal and infant mortality is lower in countries with a higher proportion of the population in the middle class (see Figure 8.12). It appears, therefore, that maternal mortality is one of the greatest divides, both between rich and poor countries and between different social classes within a country.

Non-communicable diseases (NCDs) and mental conditions

Communicable diseases are responsible for the largest disease burden in Africa, owing mainly to the rapid rise in HIV/Aids. However, chronic diseases or non-communicable diseases (NCDs) also represent a significant burden (WHO Regional Office for Africa, 2006). This leads to a double burden of disease. The widespread use of tobacco and increased consumption of fats, sugar, alcohol, salt, and animal products are critical risk factors for many NCDs. At the same time, the amount of physical exercise has been decreasing, leading to a sedentary lifestyle that is associated with obesity, diabetes, and hypertension, which are risk factors for heart disease. NCDs usually emerge in middle age after long exposure to this unhealthy lifestyle. Thus, the full burden of NCDs may not yet be realized in Africa, as they take time to develop and are usually found in older people.

Women's cancer screening

The top three cancers for women in Africa are cervical cancer, breast cancer and Kaposi's sarcoma (WHO Regional Office for Africa, 2006). Early detection leads to better treatment results, so screening for cervical and breast cancer in particular is very important. The average percentages of all female respondents aged 18 to 69 who self-reported in the WHS 2002 receiving a PAP smear test during a pelvic examination were 4 percent, 6 percent, and 12 percent for the poorest, middle, and highest classes respectively. The percentages reporting a mammography test or breast examination in the last three years were 3 percent, 5 percent, and 9 percent for the poorest, middle, and highest economic classes respectively. So, just as for TB and HIV/Aids, the middle and upper economic classes were more proactive with preventive and early treatment care than the lower-income class. Yet these percentages are still significantly lower than those reported in advanced countries.

Angina

Angina is a symptom of coronary heart disease, a progressive narrowing of the arteries that carry oxygen-rich blood to the heart muscle. Angina can be quickly relieved by rest and/or medication. It may be regarded as an 'early warning system' for cardiovascular disease (CVD).

In most African countries, CVD is the second most common cause of death after infectious disease, accounting for 11 percent of total deaths (WHO, 1999). Moreover, CVD is a major cause of chronic illness and disability. The Global Burden of Disease Project has projected that from 1990 to 2020, the burden of CVD faced by African countries will double (Murray and Lopez, 1997).

There appears to be a similar percentage of people who indicated having received a diagnosis of angina in the past 12 months across the economic classes, with a greater prevalence of angina in poorer countries (see Table 8.2). For 10 of the 20 African countries that participated in the WHS 2002, the averages of those who received a diagnosis of angina were 9 percent, 8.6 percent, and 6.7 percent in the lowest, middle, and highest economic classes respectively. However, the proportion of respondents with a self-reported condition who had received treatment or screening during the last two weeks were 30 percent, 35 percent, and 42 percent for the lowest, middle, and highest economic classes respectively. So, while a diagnosis of angina was slightly greater in the lowest economic class, the higher economic classes were more likely to have obtained treatment or screening.

TABLE 8.2   Prevalence and treatment of non-communicable diseases, 2002

	Angina	Cataracts (aged 60+ years)	Osteo- arthritis	Asthma	Diabetes	Depression
Need: Percentage of total respondents having received a diagnosis of the condition in the past 12 months (for cataracts, last five years)						
Q1–2	9.0	8.2	17.4	3.5	2.6	4.3
Q3–4	8.6	9.0	16.8	3.9	2.8	4.2
Q5	6.7	10.9	13.9	3.9	3.0	3.8
Overall	8.4	9.0	16.5	3.7	2.8	4.2
Coverage: Percentage of total respondents with a self-reported condition indicating that they have received treatment or screening for the condition in the last two weeks (for cataracts, last five years)						
Q1–2	30.0	43.1	28.0	38.7	47.6	21.0
Q3–4	34.9	48.4	33.0	34.8	50.6	21.4
Q5	41.9	39.2	39.1	38.2	60.8	28.6
Overall	34.3	44.4	32.2	37.0	51.4	22.7

Source: WHO, WHS 2002.
Note: Based on the average of ten countries: Chad, Côte d'Ivoire, Ethiopia, Kenya, Malawi, Mali, Mauritius, Namibia, South Africa, and Tunisia.

Asthma

Asthma is a chronic condition characterized by some degree of inflammation present in the air passages of the lungs. Inflammatory (allergic) triggers can cause inflammation of the airways or tightening of the airways' muscles. Symptomatic (non-allergic) triggers generally do not cause inflammation, but they can provoke 'twitchy' airways. Symptomatic triggers include smoke, exercise, cold air, chemical fumes, and air pollution.

Asthma is a global disease with rising prevalence rates, especially among children. Lack of agreed criteria in Africa for defining the condition has made comparisons difficult (Fawibe, 2008). The prevalence of asthma in SSA ranges from 2 percent in Ethiopia to 18 percent in Nigeria among children aged between 13 and 14 years. This may suggest an under-estimation of the prevalence of the condition in many countries, particularly among adolescents.

In the WHS 2002, there appears to be a similar percentage of people who had received a diagnosis of asthma in the past 12 months across the economic classes (see Table 8.2). The percentages of respondents who had received a diagnosis were 3.5 percent, 3.9 percent, and 3.9 percent in the lowest, middle, and highest economic classes respectively. However, for those with a self-reported condition who indicated receiving treatment or screening for the condition in the last two weeks, the percentages stood at 39 percent, 35 percent, and 38 percent in the lowest, middle, and highest economic classes respectively. So, only about one-third of those diagnosed with asthma were likely to have obtained treatment or screening across all economic classes.

Diabetes

Diabetes is a chronic disease that requires lifelong treatment and greatly increases the risk of serious long-term complications, including blindness, kidney disease, and neurovascular damage leading to foot ulcers and possible amputation, as well as predisposing to heart attack, stroke, and early death (Diabetes Leadership Forum, 2010; International Diabetes Federation, 2009). In addition, many of the lifestyle factors that favor the development of diabetes, such as reduced physical activity and obesity, are also implicated in the development of cardiovascular problems.

Diabetes was once considered a rare disease in Sub-Saharan Africa, but over the next 20 years it is predicted that SSA will have the highest growth rate for this disease in the world. The 2006 UN Resolution 61/225 recognized that 'diabetes is a chronic, debilitating and costly disease associated with severe complications' and, in the same year, the African Diabetes Declaration called on African governments and all stakeholders to prevent diabetes and related chronic diseases, to improve the quality of life and reduce morbidity and premature mortality from diabetes.

One of the consequences of a growth in the middle class is an increase in life expectancy, which will result in a greater number of older people. It is predicted that demographic changes alone will account for an increase of 9.5 million people with diabetes in SSA between 2010 and 2030 (Diabetes Leadership Forum, 2010). Age cohorts above 40 years will double in size. People aged 45–59 years are 8.5 times more likely to develop diabetes than those aged 15–29 years; while those above the age of 60 are 12.5 times more likely to develop diabetes (Lopez et al., 2006).

Urban residents have a 1.5 to 4 times higher prevalence of diabetes than rural residents (Jamison et al., 2006). Moreover with the rise of the middle class, more people will be living in urban areas. Relocation to towns leads to lifestyle changes, including reduced physical activity through increased reliance on motorized transportation and changes in dietary habits (Beaglehole and Tack, 2003).

Data from WHS 2002 show a similar percentage of people who indicated having received a diagnosis of diabetes in the past 12 months across all economic classes (see Table 8.2). The overall averages for people who had received a diabetes diagnosis were 2.6 percent, 2.8 percent, and 3 percent in the lowest, middle, and highest economic classes respectively. However, the percentages of respondents with a self-reported diabetes diagnosis who indicated that they had received treatment or screening for the condition in the last two weeks were 48 percent, 51 percent, and 61 percent for the lowest, middle, and highest economic classes respectively. Thus, the higher economic classes were more likely to have obtained treatment or screening.

Osteo-arthritis

Osteo-arthritis (OA) is the most common type of arthritis and typically affects multiple joints. The percentage of those affected by OA increases as the population ages. The overall averages from the WHS 2002 for those who had received a diagnosis of OA were 17.4 percent, 16.8 percent, and 13.9 percent in the lowest, middle, and highest economic classes respectively (see Table 8.2). The highest rates were recorded in Tunisia, where nearly 25 percent of people across all economic classes reported having been diagnosed with OA. Furthermore, there was a sharp rise in prevalence as early as age 45. However, the percentages for those with a self-reported condition who indicated that they had received treatment or screening for the condition in the last two weeks stood at 28 percent, 33 percent, and 39 percent in the lowest, middle, and highest economic classes. So, while OA was diagnosed slightly more in the lowest economic class, the higher economic classes were more likely to have obtained treatment or screening.

Cataracts

A cataract is a clouding of the crystalline lens of the eye, which causes a gradual progressive decrease in visual acuity, eventually leading to blindness. Age-related cataracts are by far the most common form. The condition occurs after the age of 50 with normal aging of the lens and has no other evident cause (Chitkara, 1999). Smoking, diabetes, and exposure to ultraviolet light (Abraham, Condon, and West-Gower, 2006) are the most consistent factors known to cause oxidative stress and degenerative lens changes.

Blindness leads not only to a loss of income and ill health for the individual, but also places an economic burden on the family and the community (Cataract Surgery in Africa, n.d.). There are both time costs and lost wages involved in caring for the blind. Children are often taken out of school to look after the elderly blind, losing the chance of an education and perpetuating the cycle of poverty within the community. In terms of the national impact, it is estimated that the burden of blindness on the African economy will be about 0.5 percent of the continent's GDP by 2020, if effective blindness prevention programs are not implemented (Frick and Foster, 2003).

The Vision 2020 recommendation is that a cataract surgical rate (CSR) of at least 2,000 should be achieved each year to eliminate unnecessary cataract blindness in Africa (Vision 2020, 2000). By 2005, only 9 of 46 countries in SSA had a CSR greater than 500 (WHO, 2005). Less than 20 percent of Africa's need for eye care services was addressed in 2004, and only 33 percent of countries had a national eye care plan ready by 2005 (WHO, 2005). The main reason for the lack of commitment to eye care is that it competes for funding with other services such as child health, HIV/Aids, and malaria programs (Etya'ale, 2004).

In the WHS 2002, the prevalence of cataracts was measured for the population aged 60 and above. The results indicate that there were more people in the upper-income classes who had received a diagnosis of cataracts in the last five years (see Table 8.2). The percentages of respondents who had received a cataract diagnosis were 8 percent, 9 percent, and 11 percent in the lowest, middle, and highest economic classes. However, the percentages of respondents with a self-reported cataract condition who indicated that they had received eye surgery for cataracts within the past five years were 43 percent, 48 percent, and 39 percent in the lowest, middle, and highest economic classes. Thus, while cataracts were diagnosed slightly more often in the higher economic class, the middle class was more likely to have obtained treatment or screening.

Depression

Mental disorders such as depression, alcohol use disorders, and psychoses (e.g. bipolar disorder and schizophrenia) are among the 20 leading causes of disability. The burden of depression is 50 percent higher for females than for males.

There are limited data available on depression in Africa. The most recent source is the WHO's *Mental Health Atlas 2011* (WHO, 2011). This indicates that a dedicated mental health policy is present in only 42 percent (19/45) of the African countries in the WHO region. There is a strong correlation ($r = 0.78$) between Gross National Income per capita and mental health expenditures per capita, suggesting that a country's financial resources are an important factor in mental health spending.

The proportion of total health expenditures directed toward mental health is an indication of the level of priority being accorded to this area by governments. The global median percentage of government health budget expenditure dedicated to mental health is 3 percent. In Africa, however, it is only 0.6 percent. Mental hospitals do not exist in ten of the African countries studied in this report. The median rate of psychiatrists ranges from 0.05 per 100,000 population in Africa to 8.59 per 100,000 population in Europe. Overall, the *Mental Health Atlas 2011* shows that Africa has a very low capacity for dealing with mental health problems. Given the range and magnitude of other health challenges facing the continent, this is perhaps understandable, although lamentable.

The *Mental Health Atlas 2011* found that wealthier countries devote a larger proportion of their health budget to mental health than do poorer nations. This supports the need for countries to grow their middle class. The same finding emanates from the WHS 2002. Data show (see Table 8.2) that the percentages of respondents with a self-reported depression who indicated that they had received treatment or screening for the condition in the last two weeks were 21 percent, 21 percent, and 29 percent in the lowest, middle, and highest economic classes. So, while depression was diagnosed slightly more in the lowest economic class, the highest economic class was more likely to have obtained treatment or screening.

Access to and use of health services

The Andersen health-care services utilization model is commonly used to explain behavioral patterns of health-care service use across countries. The model organizes determinants of use into three categories: predisposing factors, enabling factors, and need factors (Andersen, 1995). Predisposing factors constitute the propensity to use services and include age, sex, marital status, education, occupation, and health knowledge. Enabling factors are those that allow a person to access medical care and include income, insurance coverage, and having a regular source of care. Need characteristics are specific disabilities or diseases that cause a person to seek health care.

These latter characteristics were covered in the previous section. This indicated that, as the proportion of population in the middle class increases, so does the need for chronic disease care, while, at the same time, the need for communicable disease care does not disappear.

Utilization

Looking at a major predisposing factor, namely age, the proportion of population 65 years and older is growing in many countries across Africa (AfDB, 2011b). Aging is highly correlated with physical and mental disability and a number of

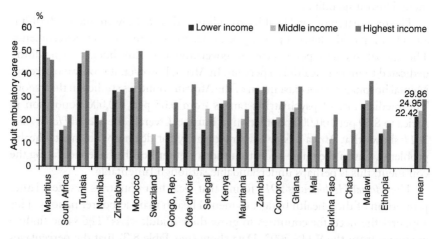

FIGURE 8.13   Self-reported use of ambulatory adult health services by income level, 2002 (source: WHO, WHS 2002)

Note: Countries listed by highest to lowest GDP per capita.

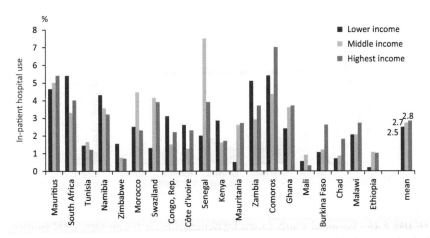

FIGURE 8.14 Self-reported use of hospital inpatient services by income level, 2002 (source: WHO, WHS 2002)

Note: Countries listed by highest to lowest GDP per capita.

long-term chronic conditions. Thus, ambulatory and in-hospital health service needs are likely to increase as well. As Figure 8.1 reveals, life expectancy and the associated effect of aging increase as a country's middle class grows. The question then arises: how does this translate into hospital and ambulatory care use?

Figure 8.13 shows that ambulatory care use increases as income levels rise. In Figure 8.14, hospital inpatient services are seen on average to be quite similar across all economic classes. However, people in the middle and upper economic classes use health care not just to treat major diseases, but also in a preventive fashion, to stay healthy. They use screening/prevention more often than those in the lower economic class to catch a condition at an earlier stage, when it is more likely to be successfully treated. Examples include HIV/Aids screening, antenatal care, and cancer screening among women such as PAP smears and mammography or breast examinations. Similarly, after a diagnosis with a chronic disease such as diabetes, angina, or depression, people in the middle and upper economic classes have greater enabling means to seek additional care, screening, and routine tests.

Unmet care needs

As noted earlier in this chapter, there are very low percentages of treatment and care for both communicable and chronic diseases in the region. Across all economic classes, about half of those with indications of diabetes reported having been treated, and one-third of those with symptoms of angina were under care (see Table 8.2). In the lower economic classes, on average only 44 percent of birth deliveries received assistance from a health-care professional.

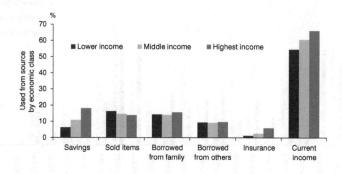

FIGURE 8.15 Financial sources used by households for health care, 2002 (source: WHO, WHS 2002)

Only 15 percent of those in the middle class with symptoms of TB reported having received a TB screening test.

In general, the poor (i.e. both low-income countries and people in the lower-income class) have more self-reported unmet care needs. We see greater satisfaction with health care as personal income rises, possibly because this provides the wherewithal to meet health care costs.

Patient costs for health care

Figure 8.15 shows the financial sources used by African households to pay for health services. The middle- and upper-income classes mainly use current income and savings to cover health-care costs. They are also better placed to take out health insurance, which is a noticeable benefit. Selling assets and borrowing from family and friends are methods used across all classes to raise funds, although selling assets is used more by the lower classes. Leive and Xu (2008) report that large proportions of the lower-income populations resort to borrowing and selling assets to cover high health-care expenditures. Having a large middle class means that more people are able to contribute financially to their personal health care.

The health system

Resources

Having a regular place of care is another enabling factor and an important component of health systems. To capture the availability and accessibility of health services, a range of indicators is needed. Currently, there are no such data for the majority of countries. In-patient bed density is one of the few available indicators for the level of health service delivery. Figure 8.16 shows a small but

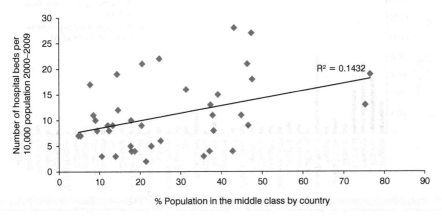

FIGURE 8.16 Hospital beds per 10,000 population, 2000–2009 (sources: WHO: Regional Office for Africa, 2011; middle-class data AfDB (2011a))

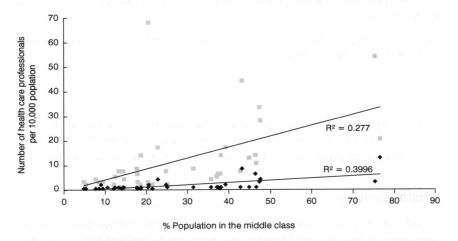

FIGURE 8.17 Health-care professionals to population ratios, 2009 (sources: WHO: Regional Office for Africa, 2011; middle-class data AfDB (2011a))

statistically significant association between the number of hospital beds per 10,000 population and the percentage of population in the middle class. Once again, having a sizable middle class helps provide the necessary infrastructure.

Figure 8.17 shows the association between health-care workers and the percentage of the population in the middle class across Africa. Even though there is no consensus about the optimal level of health workers for a given population, there is ample evidence that worker numbers and quality are positively associated with better immunization coverage, primary care, and infant, child and maternal survival rates.

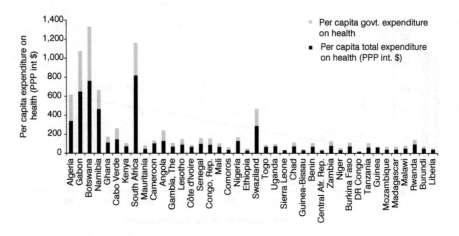

FIGURE 8.18 Per capita government expenditure on health in selected African countries (sources: WHO: Regional Office for Africa, 2011; middle-class data from AfDB (2011a))

Note: Countries listed by size of the middle class, Algeria having highest proportion (77%) and Liberia the smallest (5%).

There is a significant association also between the availability of health-care providers and the percentage of the population in the middle class. This is possibly due in part to the increased access to education in richer countries.

Health financing

Health care requires a considerable amount of resources from governments, communities, and families. However, governments in much of Africa spend far less per capita on health care than governments in developed countries (AfDB, 2011b). In fact, few African countries are on track to achieving the Abuja Target: namely to allocate at least 15 percent of public spending to the health sector (Fourth Session of the African Union Conference of Ministers of Health, 2009). To date, only three African countries have surpassed the 15 percent threshold, namely Liberia, Rwanda, and Tanzania, while Madagascar, Zambia, Burkina Faso, Chad, Botswana, and Gabon are close behind at 13 percent or above.

The data show that the larger the middle class, the greater the government expenditure per capita on health (see Figure 8.18 and Appendix 8.1). In other words, when the middle class expands, more funds become available to pay for public health care.

However, the same chart shows that 51 percent of health financing in Africa comes from outside government. The WHO's Commission on Macroeconomics and Health (CMH) estimated that a basic package of health services costs $34 per capita (the so-called CMH Target). Many countries in Africa achieve the CMH target only by including non-government funds. Nevertheless, in countries with a large middle class, governments are less likely to rely on external resources to finance health care.[5]

Conclusion

As the middle-class population grows, the mortality rate decreases and life expectancy increases. This leads to a higher proportion of the elderly in the population. Correlated with this is a sharp decline in fertility rates as well as a rise in physical and mental disability and an increase in the prevalence of a number of long-term chronic conditions.

Disability-adjusted life years (DALY) for chronic diseases increase as the middle class grows. Age-specific mortality rates from chronic diseases as a whole are higher in SSA than in virtually all other global regions, for both men and women (de-Graft Aikins, Unwin, and Agyemang, 2010). Over the next ten years, the continent is projected to experience the largest increase in death rates from cardiovascular disease, cancer, respiratory disease, and diabetes. In this study, we found that the need for the treatment of diabetes and cataracts was higher in the middle class than in the poorer economic classes. It is expected that the need for treatment will continue to rise for cancer and CVDs as the proportion of the population entering the middle class grows.

Communicable diseases are still overwhelming in their scale. Infectious diseases account for at least 69 percent of deaths on the continent (de-Graft Aikins, Unwin, and Agyemang, 2010). Thus, Africa faces a double burden of infectious and chronic diseases. Communicable disease is still a very important concern for the middle class, particularly in relation to HIV/Aids.

While access to improved water and sanitation improves as the middle class increases, there are also detrimental effects associated with a growing middle class. This concerns risk factors such as smoking, alcohol, lack of exercise, and poor diet, which cause chronic diseases in many African countries (WHO, Regional Office for Africa, 2011a). Chronic diseases and injuries are overtaking communicable diseases as the leading health problems in all but a few parts of the world. This rapidly changing global disease pattern is closely linked to changing lifestyles. The transition to the middle class is often linked to a diet rich in sugars and fats, to increased use of tobacco and alcohol, being overweight, and to physical inactivity. According to the WHO African Regional Health Report of 2011, these risk factors are on the rise and they are linked to urbanization and globalization. The development of a chronic disease in a person takes a long time, so it is important to address the risk factors now.

As the middle class increases, maternal health care improves. The number of children per woman decreases and the number of birth deliveries attended by skilled health workers goes up. Similarly, deaths of mothers and newborns decrease. This in turn leads to a growing percentage of working-age people in the population. To take full economic advantage of this demographic trend, disease prevention measures need to be put in place.

The middle class is more likely to seek better health care for themselves and their families than are the poor. Those in the middle class have higher treatment rates for communicable diseases, NCDs, and maternal health. They also make greater use of hospitals and ambulatory care facilities.

African health systems are generally weak. The number of hospital beds and health-care professionals is very low in most countries, while the cost of diagnosis and treatment is often prohibitive both for governments and individuals. Government expenditure on health is at a very low level, often just 2 percent of a country's GDP.[6] This equates to about $10 per person per year.[7] According to the WHO, a realistic estimate for the cost of providing minimum health care in Africa is about $34 per person per year. The results from WHS 2002 indicate that this level of spending may be feasible as the middle class grows and the tax base enlarges.

Unlike the poor, who for the most part meet their health-care needs through borrowing or the sale of assets, people with middle or higher incomes are more likely to use salaries and savings, i.e. personal resources; they are also more likely to have health/medical insurance cover. As such, there is a stronger incentive for governments to encourage and facilitate the growth of the middle class in order to ensure sustainable health care for all. An expanding middle class can provide an increased tax base to fund social programs.

The relationship between health and economic prosperity is highly complex. While economic growth can improve a population's health, disease has a major impact on economic development (Diabetes Leadership Forum, 2010). For the individual, disease leads to a loss of earnings plus an increase in expenditure on medication and treatment. For their families, there is greater economic loss through giving up work to provide nursing care, or loss of educational opportunities when children must work or care for an ill relative.

For employers and national economies, poor health reduces productivity due to lost working time and suboptimal performance; it also leads to the loss of skilled workers through early retirement and premature death. For the nation, poor health can lessen investment (including in infrastructure) and tourism, as well as eroding business confidence. Good health does the opposite.

The *Health of the People* report stresses that Africa can progress only by strengthening its fragile health systems (WHO Regional Office for Africa, 2006). Investing in health leads to greater productivity and economic advancement (Barro and Sala-I-Martin, 1995). Health alone cannot account for economic growth, but its impact is very significant. It has been said that 'over half of Africa's growth shortfall can be associated with its disease burden, demography and geography' (Bloom and Sachs, 1998). However, advances in health care are only possible if economies improve, and this depends on strengthening and increasing the middle class. Health is, therefore, both a product and an essential precursor of economic growth.

APPENDIX TABLE A8.1 Regression of various health indicators on the size of the middle class in Africa, 2008

Independent variable	Slope	Intercept	Standard error	p-value	R^2
Life expectancy	0.196	49.25	0.047	0.000	0.316
Healthy life expectancy, Male	1.810	−55.94	0.429	0.000	0.319
Healthy life expectancy, Female	1.708	−53.88	0.398	0.000	0.326
Adult mortality rate	−1.907	428.81	0.919	0.045	0.102
Under-5 mortality rate per 1,000 live births	−1.551	160.96	0.359	0.000	0.330
YLL: Communicable disease	−0.302	85.90	0.062	0.000	0.384
YLL: Non-communicable conditions	0.226	8.46	0.048	0.000	0.370
YLL: Injuries	0.077	5.71	0.020	0.000	0.282
DALY Communicable diseases, maternal and perinatal conditions, and nutritional deficiencies	−0.348	78.32	0.064	0.000	0.437
DALY Non-communicable conditions	0.305	14.90	0.057	0.000	0.432
DALY Injuries	0.046	6.64	0.016	0.007	0.174
Percentage of underweight children under 5 years of age	−0.325	29.65	0.079	0.000	0.339
Percentage of the population with access to improved drinking water sources	0.457	55.44	0.127	0.001	0.255
Percentage of people 15–49 years of age living with HIV	0.058	4.17	0.064	0.368	0.022
Total fertility rate per woman	−0.043	5.95	0.007	0.000	0.466
Percentage of births attended by skilled health personnel	0.577	39.84	0.159	0.001	0.285
MMR (per 100,000 live births)	−8.893	801.86	1.886	0.000	0.369
Infant mortality rate per 1,000 live births	−0.827	97.83	0.200	0.000	0.310
Hospital beds per 10,000 population	0.145	7.07	0.058	0.018	0.143
Physician-to-population ratio (per 10,000 population)	0.082	−0.46	0.016	0.000	0.400
Nursing and midwifery personnel-to-population ratio (per 10,000 population)	0.407	−0.17	0.107	0.000	0.277
Per capita government expenditure on health (PPP int. $)	4.434	−41.92	0.863	0.000	0.416
Per capita total expenditure on health (PPP int. $)	6.748	−42.72	1.421	0.000	0.373

Sources: WHO: Regional Office for Africa, 2011; Middle class data: AfDB, 'Middle of the Pyramid,' 2011.

Notes

1 *Mycobacterium tuberculosis* transmitted on airborne droplets causes a lung disease that will kill about half of all untreated patients.
2 Prevalence is defined as the number of cases of a specific disease present in a given population at a certain time.
3 Incidence is defined as the extent or rate of occurrence, especially the number of new cases of a disease in a population over a period of time.
4 Antenatal care coverage and medical professionals attending births are two indicators recognized as crucial in reducing the MMR (WHO, 2006).
5 External resources' health expenditure includes all grants and loans, whether passing through governments or private entities, for health goods and services, in cash or in kind.
6 For many countries, only 49% of health financing comes from government expenditure. The rest comes from external sources, which is a practice that is not sustainable.
7 By contrast, high-income countries spend $2,000 per person, or more (2011).

References

Abraham, A.G., N.G. Condon, and E. West-Gower (2006). 'The New Epidemiology of Cataract,' *Ophthalmology Clinics of North America*, vol. 19, no. 4, pp. 415–425.
AfDB (2011a). 'The Middle of the Pyramid: Dynamics of the Middle Class in Africa.' Report by the Chief Economist Complex. Tunis: African Development Bank.
AfDB (2011b). *Aging Population Challenges in Africa*. Vol. 1, Issue 1, November.
All-Party Parliamentary Group on Population, Development and Reproductive Health (2007). *Return of the Population Growth Factor: Its Impact upon the Millennium Development Goals*. London, UK: All-Party Parliamentary Group on Population, Development and Reproductive Health.
Alvarez, J.L., R. Gil, V. Hernández, and A. Gil (2009). 'Factors Associated with Maternal Mortality in Sub-Saharan Africa: an Ecological Study,' *BMC Public Health*, vol. 9, pp. 462 ff.
Andersen, R.M. (1995). 'Revisiting the Behavioral Model and Access to Medical Care: Does it Matter?,' *Journal of Health and Social Behaviour*, vol. 36, pp. 1–10.
Barro, R., and X. Sala-I-Martin (1995). *Economic Growth*. New York: McGraw-Hill.
Beaglehole, R., and D. Tack (2003). 'Globalisation and the Prevention and Control of Non-communicable Disease,' *The Lancet*, vol. 362, pp. 903–908.
Bloom, D., and J. Sachs (1998). 'Geography, Demography, and Economic Growth in Africa.' *Brookings Papers on Economic Activity*, vol. 2, pp. 207–295.
Bloom, D.E., D. Canning, and J. Sevilla (2004). 'The Effect of Health on Economic Growth: A Production Function Approach,' *World Development*, vol. 32, pp. 1–13.
Cataract Surgery in Africa (n.d.) www.ptolemy.ca/members/archives/2009/Cataract/index.html#R3#R3 (accessed 18 September 2014).
Chaisson, R.E., and N.A. Martinson (2008). 'Tuberculosis in Africa – Combating an HIV-Driven Crisis,' *New England Journal of Medicine*, vol. 358, pp. 1089–1092.
Chitkara, D. (1999). 'Cataract Formation Mechanisms,' in M. Yanoff (ed.), *Ophthalmology*. Philadelphia: Mosby.
de-Graft Aikins, A., N. Unwin, and C. Agyemang (2010). 'Tackling Africa's Chronic Disease Burden: From the Local to the Global,' *Globalization and Health*. vol. 6, p. 5.
Diabetes Leadership Forum (2010). 'Diabetes: the Hidden Pandemic and Its Impact on Sub-Saharan Africa.' Prepared for the Diabetes Leadership Forum, Africa,

Johannesburg, 30 September and 1 October, 2010. Edited by Professor Ayesha Motala and Dr Kaushik Ramaiya, and supported by Novo Nordisk.

Etya'ale, D. (2004). 'The Policy–Practice Gap: Supporting National Vision 2020 Action Plans,' *Community Eye Health Journal*, vol. 17, no. 51, pp. 35–36.

FAO Media Center (2009). '1.02 Billion People Hungry. One Sixth of Humanity Undernourished – More Than Ever Before.' Online at: www.fao.org/news/story/en/item/20568/icode/ (accessed 18 September 2014).

Fawibe, A.E. (2008). 'Management of Asthma in Sub-Saharan Africa: The Nigerian Perspective,' *African Journal of Respiratory Medicine*, vol. 3, no. 3, pp. 17–21.

Fourth Session of the African Union Conference of Ministers of Health (2009). *Health Financing in Africa: Challenges and Opportunities for Expanding Access to Quality Health Care*. Addis Ababa, Ethiopia. May 4–8, 2009.

Frick, K.D., and A. Foster (2003). 'The Magnitude and Cost of Global Blindness,' *American Journal of Ophthalmology*, vol. 135, no. 4, pp. 471–76.

International Diabetes Federation (2009). 'New International Diabetes Federation Study Reveals that People in Developing Countries Pay More for Diabetes Care and Have Poorer Health Results.' October 21, 2009. Online at: www.idf.org (accessed 18 September 2014).

Jamison, D.T., J.G. Breman, and A.R. Measham (eds) (2006). *Disease Control Priorities in Developing Countries*. Second Edition. Washington DC: International Bank for Reconstruction and Development / World Bank.

Jamison, D.T., R.G. Feachem, and M.W. Makgoba (eds) (2006). *Disease and Mortality in Sub-Saharan Africa*. Second Edition. Washington DC: International Bank for Reconstruction and Development / World Bank.

Jamison, D.T., L.J. Lau, and J. Wang (2005). 'Health's Contribution to Economic Growth in an Environment of Partially Endogenous Technical Progress,' in G. Lopez-Casasnovas, B. Rivera, and L. Currais (eds), *Health and Economic Growth: Findings and Policy Implications*. Cambridge, MA: MIT Press, pp. 67–91.

Kengne, A.P., P.K. Awah, L. Fezeu, and J.C. Mbanya (2007). 'The Burden of High Blood Pressure and Related Risk Factors in Urban Sub-Saharan Africa: Evidences from Douala in Cameroon,' *African Health Sciences*, vol. 7, no. 1, pp. 38–44.

Leive A., and Xu K (2008). 'Coping With Out of Pocket Payments: Empirical Evidence From 15 African Countries.' *Bulletin of the World Health Organization*, pp. 849–856.

Lopez, A.D., and C.D. Mathers (2006). 'Measuring the Global Burden of Disease and Epidemiological Transitions: 2002–2030.' *Annals of Tropical Medicine and Parasitology*, vol. 100, no. 5/6, pp. 481–499.

Lopez, A.D., C.D. Mathers, M. Ezzati, D.T. Jamison, and C.J.L. Murray (2006). *Global Burden of Disease and Risk Factors*. Washington DC: Oxford University Press and World Bank.

Modi, V., S. McDade, D. Lallement, and J. Saghir (2005). 'Energy Services for the Millennium Development Goals.' New York: Energy Sector Management Assistance Programme, UNDP, UN Millennium Project. Washington DC: World Bank.

Murray, C.J., and A. Lopez (1997). 'Mortality by Cause for Eight Regions of the World: Global Burden of Disease Study,' *Lancet*, vol. 349, pp. 1269–1276.

Muula, A.S., and L. Mpabulungi (2007). 'Cigarette Smoking Prevalence among School-going Adolescents in Two African Capital Cities: Kampala Uganda and Lilongwe Malawi,' *African Health Sciences*, vol. 7, no. 1, pp. 45–49.

Pampel, F.C. (2005). 'Patterns of Tobacco Use in the Early Epidemic Stages: Malawi and Zambia, 2000–2002,' *American Journal of Public Health*, vol. 95, pp. 1009–1015.

Rehfuess, E., S. Mehta, and A. Prüss-Üstün (2006). 'Assessing Household Solid Fuel Use: Multiple Implications for the Millennium Development Goals,' *Environmental Health Perspectives*, vol. 114, no. 3, pp. 373–378.

Vision 2020 (2000). 'The Cataract Challenge,' *Community Eye Health*, vol. 13, no. 34, pp. 17–19.

Wagstaff, A., and M. Claeson (2004). *The Millennium Development Goals for Health: Rising to the Challenges*. Washington DC: World Bank.

WHO (1999). *The World Health Report 1999 – Making a Difference*. Geneva: World Health Organisation.

WHO (2005). *The State of the World's Sight: Vision 2020: The Right to Sight 1999–2005*. Geneva: WHO.

WHO (2008a). *The Global Burden of Disease: 2004 update*. Geneva: WHO.

WHO (2008b). *Report on the Global Tobacco Epidemic, 2008: The MPOWER package*. Geneva: WHO.

WHO (2009). *Women and Health: Today's Evidence Tomorrow's Agenda*. Geneva: WHO.

WHO (2010a). *Atlas on Substance Use: Resources for the Prevention and Treatment of Substance Use Disorders*. Geneva: WHO.

WHO (2010b). *Progress on Sanitation and Drinking Water 2010 Update*. Geneva: WHO.

WHO (2011). *Mental Health Atlas*. Geneva: WHO.

WHO Regional Office for Africa (2006). *The Health of the People: The African Regional Health Report*. Brazzaville.

WHO Regional Office for Africa (2011). *Achieving Sustainable Health Development in the African Region: Strategic Directions for WHO 2010–2015*. Brazzaville.

WHO Regional Office for Africa (2011a). *WHO Atlas of Health Statistics: Health Situation Analysis in the African Region*. Brazzaville.

WHO Regional Office for Africa (2011b). *Tobacco – Overview*. Brazzaville.

WHO World Health Surveys (WHS). 'World Health Survey Results' www.who.int/ healthinfo/survey/whsresults/en/index1.html (accessed 18 September 2014).

CONCLUSION

Mthuli Ncube

This book has presented a picture of the emerging middle class in Africa. Statistics on consumption patterns, jobs, education, entrepreneurship, gender, and health all tell a story about the factors driving the growth of this important segment of the population, and its implications for African policymakers. The analysis has looked at how people become middle class – be it through education and access to the formal labor market, by relocating to areas where there are better-paid, steady jobs, or through their own entrepreneurship. We have also examined how behavior alters in the process, in terms of consumption patterns, including spending on health, education, housing, amenities, and material assets. Another crucial dimension is whether growth of the middle class affects gender relations. We have examined the evidence to assess whether men and women share equally in the benefits and status of increasing affluence and what policymakers might do to improve women's life chances.

Africa is a continent of such scale and diversity that experiences across countries vary widely. However, we hope to have captured some commonalities. In this concluding chapter we summarize our findings, drawing out the defining characteristics of what it means to be part of the emerging middle class in Africa. We have also seen how living in a city as opposed to rural areas can positively affect job and entrepreneurial opportunities and access to services, which support middle-class lifestyles.

Africa's middle class has grown rapidly in recent years thanks to improving governance and economic progress in many countries. About one-third of the population lives on $2 to $20 a day, nearly two-thirds (63 percent) of whom fall into the floating class, with consumption expenditure between $2 and $4 a day. Policymakers have to pay greater attention to the emerging middle class, but more importantly, to the 'floating middle class' that is vulnerable to falling back into poverty.

Continued growth in consumer spending by the middle class will provide a key source of domestic demand, stimulating private sector growth and foreign direct investment in Africa. As incomes rise, households shift their spending from purely subsistence needs such as basic foodstuffs, to more expensive luxury items, and to durable consumer goods such as motor cars, televisions, computers, and refrigerators. Middle-class households also spend more on education and health, on improved dwellings, and on entertainment and leisure activities.

A key to understanding the development of the African middle class is to examine how Africans earn their income. This book has looked at what distinguishes those who earn more than $2 a day (those officially above the second poverty line) from those earning less. Two major differences emerge. First, those in the middle class have moved away from agricultural subsistence employment toward salaried jobs in the non-agricultural sector. Second, those in the middle class typically hold salaried jobs with a predictable monthly wage and predictable hours. This differentiates them from poor employees, who are typically casual laborers paid on a daily basis, with unpredictable hours, no job security, and few benefits.

Education and geographic mobility are essential ingredients to obtaining middle-class employment, as they allow people to move into new sectors or industries that pay higher wages.

Strong growth in manufacturing and service industries such as telecommunications and finance is expected to translate into sustained growth in middle-class jobs in the future. Africa's cities will continue to expand at a rapid pace, creating environments conducive to innovation and higher labor productivity. Despite these positive trajectories, the informal sector will still dominate the African labor market in the coming decade, as growth of steady, well-paid employment is starting from a very low level.

School enrollment is rising rapidly in many parts of Africa. Enrollment in primary education increased more than fivefold from 1970 to 2010. Secondary school enrollment grew tenfold over the same period, and tertiary enrollment rates also grew significantly. The greatest progress, though, has been at the primary level, with many African countries having achieved the MDG of universal primary education.

In much of Africa, the number of private primary and secondary schools as well as tertiary institutions has grown, in response to the growing demands of the middle class. Middle-class families can afford to send their children to private schools to acquire quality education and to enhance their employment prospects. Although pre-primary school coverage remains low in Africa compared with other developing regions, it is growing and has reached 60 percent in Algeria, Angola, Cabo Verde, Ghana, Liberia, Mauritius, Morocco, São Tomé and Principe, Seychelles, and South Africa. Most of these countries also have relatively large middle-class populations.

The evidence on health shows that middle-class people spend more on their health and wellbeing than do their poorer counterparts. As the percentage of the population in the middle class increases and more resources to achieve positive health outcomes become more available, mortality, particularly due to communicable diseases, is expected to decline. Likewise, the focus will shift from disease burden to the social, economic, and environmental determinants of health. The broad and non-discriminatory nature of these determinants of health will require a new approach to achieve equity in health coverage for all citizens and ensure that people have access to health services they need, when they need it. Health equity will also place significant emphasis on closing the gender gap in access to and use of health services, promoting maternal and child health, supporting mental health, the elderly and the disabled – all groups that have been sidelined in part because of limited resources for health care at the country level.

The rise in the middle class brings a number of challenges including an aging population, and a concomitant rise in physical and mental disability and long-term non-communicable conditions such as cardiovascular diseases, diabetes, and cancer – all associated with a middle-class lifestyle. This means that there will be a need to alter the structural nature of health-care systems in Africa, to adopt a broader approach to health care. Education about healthy lifestyles and better management of chronic conditions will become critical inputs in the health care of the population. As in more advanced countries, health education campaigns will need to focus on behavioral issues such as nutrition, smoking, alcohol consumption, and physical activity, which would be of particular concern to the middle class. On environmental determinants of health, health education programs will need to include climate change adaptation initiatives and promote disaster risk reduction.

In light of the increased health-care needs as the middle class grows, the health sector will increasingly be viewed as a productive and job-creating sector, providing career opportunities for large numbers of people. It is estimated that the health-care sector will become a labor-intensive industry that can provide up to 3 million skilled jobs for young Africans and contribute to economic growth on the continent. As the pharmaceutical, medical technologies, and ICT segments develop, there will be opportunities in research and development, manufacturing, sales, and distribution. Within this industry, other opportunities will be driven by the hospital, health insurance, and medical education segments. In many countries, private health facilities that offer insurance coverage have emerged and are an alternative to often crowded and ill-equipped government hospitals.

On the political front, maintaining political stability will be critical to the sustainability of the middle class. Government policies that encourage private sector development and expansion, while limiting its influence in the entrepreneurial class, need to be implemented. Economic liberalization, resulting in removing the hegemony of state monopolies, has helped the entrepreneurial class to reassert itself. The private sector is expanding in areas that were traditionally the preserve of government. Many African countries have seen a sharp increase in the number of private telephone services, private educational institutions (including universities as well as primary and secondary schools), private airlines, and private medical clinics and hospitals. At the same time, the managerial, professional, technical, and clerical personnel in these firms have fueled Africa's real estate boom, from housing estates to shopping malls, and the spread of affluent neighborhoods and automobile ownership.

Yet as Africa's middle class grows, poverty levels have not declined proportionately. This is because, unlike other developing regions of the world, Africa has been slow to reduce population growth rates. Thus, even with rates of economic growth of 5 percent to 7 percent, growth in per capita income has either lagged several percentage points behind or remained more or less stagnant in countries with high population growth rates. This slow decline in poverty levels is even more evident in a widening gap between the middle class and the poor in many countries. It presents major challenges for governments, and unless tactfully addressed, could be a major source of discontent in a number of countries.

The rise of the middle class, which is a strong indicator of socio-economic progress, and which has the potential to provide enduring social peace and stable democratic societies, could become a source of political unrest. On the one hand, growth may foster a sense of well-being among those who have enjoyed upward mobility, but on the other, it may foster a sense of having been left behind among those who have not.

Policy implications

Over the next 20 years, with the appropriate policies focused on human capital development, improved delivery of essential services such as health, education, energy, water and sanitation, job creation, greater transparency and accountability in government operations, including impartiality in the judiciary, Africa can expect a transformation of its social fabric, as a much greater share of its population joins the ranks of the middle class. These will need to be coupled with a sense of inclusiveness for the majority of the population.

To ensure gender equality in upward mobility, governments will need to institute policies that focus on legal reforms, secure land tenure and other productive resources for women, enhance private sector opportunities, and provide a business climate that is open to women. In order to increase women's empowerment, governments and the private sector alike need to facilitate women's access to and control over financial resources and services, promote affirmative action in favor of women, particularly in fields and sectors where they are least represented, and increase their productivity both in agriculture and non-agricultural sectors.

In light of current and future global economic uncertainty, it is likely that governments would rely more on the middle class and the private sector to finance health care. Many African governments face increasing demand for health financing, despite having fewer resources available and dwindling donor financing. This disconnect compels governments to find innovative financing mechanisms to achieve the Millennium Development Goals. A public-private partnership has been found to be most suitable way to achieve this objective. Thus, African governments need to be more self-reliant to provide health care to all. Developing equitable and sustainable health financing systems will be the key for African governments in the next decades. National governments must raise and streamline domestic resources to achieve self-reliance and health system strengthening. New mechanisms aimed at generating additional resources through taxes and other innovative means need to be promoted in the future, as well as reallocations of governments' budgets in favor of the health sector (increasing the share of budgetary spending on health).

Africa's economies continued to demonstrate resilience in 2013, with average GDP growing by 4.8 percent. Although political and social upheavals affected some North African economies, and civil strife continues in a few Sub-Saharan African countries, the momentum in industrial production growth has strengthened in recent years, signaling an improvement in economic activity. Sub-Saharan Africa continues to reap the benefits of the natural resource boom, supported by vigorous domestic demand, notably, investment growth and large export volumes.

Average inflation in Africa, at 8.9 percent in 2012, was above that of comparable regions in the developing world, where inflation was about 6 percent, and the Eurozone, where it was only about 2 percent. In contrast to past decades, however, African inflation was mostly below 10 percent during the 2000s, a reflection of the strength of macroeconomic management in recent years. Inflation in Africa edged down to 6.7 percent in 2013 and has largely been contained in most countries.

Prudent fiscal and monetary policies are still required. Continent-wide, fiscal deficits declined to 2.4 percent of GDP in 2013 (from 3.1 percent in 2011), with noticeable differences between net oil importers (4.3 percent) and oil exporters (0.9 percent). Africa's foreign direct investment (FDI) inflows ($50 billion) – with much of the investment going to oil and gas, mining, finance, wholesale and retail commerce, transportation, telecommunications and manufacturing sectors – and remittances ($63 billion) remain high, while net aid inflows are tepid. Government spending continues to rise at a moderate pace, as governments scale up their efforts to reach the Millennium Development Goals. Equitable policies that support improved infrastructure, sustainable and shared growth, enhanced human resources, greater private sector engagement, and improved accountability and governance will also foster middle-class growth. The continued rise of Africa's middle class will require governments to introduce policies supportive of this trend, so that their economies can flourish. This means, on the one hand, bolstering the incomes of those already in the middle class, and on the other, helping those in the bottom quintile to exit poverty and transition to this growing and more affluent class. In addition, governments must pay more attention to the 'floating middle class' to ensure they do not fall back into poverty. For this to happen, there needs to be more spending on education and health, better access to basic amenities for households, and incentives for greater private sector participation in areas such as education, health, housing, infrastructure development, and for increasing entrepreneurial participation by all segments of society.

INDEX

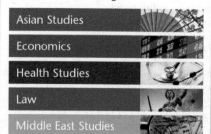